ESSAYS IN APPLIED CHRISTIANITY

ESSAYS IN

APPLIED CHRISTIANITY

by REINHOLD NIEBUHR

selected and edited by D. B. Robertson

LIVING AGE BOOKS

published by MERIDIAN BOOKS *New York*

REINHOLD NIEBUHR

Reinhold Niebuhr is vice-president of the faculty and professor of applied Christianity at Union Theological Seminary in New York City. He was born in 1892 in Wright City, Missouri, where his father was an Evangelical Church pastor. After preparing for the ministry at Eden Theological Seminary in St. Louis, he studied at Yale University, taking his B.D. degree in 1914 and his M.A. degree in the following year. He then became a pastor in Detroit, where he served until 1928, when he was called to teach philosophy of religion at Union Theological Seminary. Among his many books are LEAVES FROM THE NOTEBOOKS OF A TAMED CYNIC *and* AN INTERPRETATION OF CHRISTIAN ETHICS, *both of which are available in Living Age Books editions.*

A Living Age Books Original
Published by Meridian Books, Inc. April 1959
First Printing March 1959
Second Printing July 1960

CONTENTS

ESSAYS IN APPLIED CHRISTIANITY

INTRODUCTION *by* D. B. *Robertson*

Since the beginning of the ecumenical movement and the totalitarian attacks upon the church which have generally paralleled this movement, a great deal of thought has been given to the question of the nature of the church and of its peculiar function in society. More attention has been given to the "doctrine of the church" in this period, in fact, than in any time since the sixteenth century on the continent and the seventeenth century in England. There are those who would say that the question has been more thoroughly examined in our time than at any time before in the history of the church. While some of the outstanding Protestant theologians of our generation (including Barth, Brunner, Tillich, and Niebuhr) could not be said to have been preoccupied with questions of "faith and order," they have all, nevertheless, each in his own way, shared in the church's new awareness of itself and its place in the world.

It has been said by numerous people, speaking from a number of positions, that Reinhold Niebuhr has given little attention to the question of the church. John Bennett wrote over twenty years ago that Niebuhr gave "little attention to what an awakened church can do" and that some emphasis upon the "creative possibilities of a Christian group which has been brought to repentance" would be helpful (*Religion in Life*, Winter, 1937). Recently the question of the church has been referred to as an "undeveloped area in his thought" and a "critical omission in Niebuhr's social picture of redemption" (William J. Wolf, in Kegley & Bretall, *Reinhold Niebuhr, His Religious, Social, and Political Thought*, p. 249). In this same volume

Paul Scherer notes that the church is not one of the themes in Niebuhr's preaching, though it may "stand in the wings" (p. 331). It is significant too that in this symposium, devoted to Niebuhr's thought as a whole, no chapter on the church was included. Niebuhr himself says that he has "increasingly recognized the value of the Church as a community of grace" (p. 437). Actually he has given a rather large amount of attention to the church, as this collection of articles will show, and he also values the institution more highly and positively than his reputation would seem to allow.

The greater part of what Niebuhr has written on the church is to be found in his fugitive essays, scattered through a dozen magazines and journals. This volume brings together most of the writings which deal with the church and groups them in five major divisions. Part I contains articles on various aspects of common worship in America and its relationship to the weaknesses and strengths of sectarian Christianity. Part II relates the faith of the church more specifically to the whole range of moral-political problems. Part III presents Niebuhr's version of the "Anglo-Saxon" view of the church's social ethic which he states in opposition to the Barthian or "Continental" view. Part IV contains Niebuhr's analysis and criticism of the Catholic conception of the church and of the natural law ethic of the church. Part V brings together most of Niebuhr's writings about the ecumenical movement.•

• A statement of his view of the church is to be found in *Faith and History*, Chap. XIV. There are some references in *The Nature and Destiny of Man*, II, pp. 225-6, relating to the sacraments. A short definition of the church is given in *Beyond Tragedy*, p. 62, and there are many briefer references throughout his books and many of his articles. A few magazine articles which did not fit into this present volume are: "The Paradox of Institutions," *The World Tomorrow*, August, 1923; "Reverend Dr. Silke," *The Christian Century*, March 11, 1926; "Beauty as a Substitute for Righteousness," *The Christian Century*, September 29, 1927; "The Minister as an Expert," *Effective Preaching*, Boston University Conference on Preaching, 1929; "The Church and Political Action," *The Christian Century*, August 1, 1934; "The Radical Minister and His Church,"

First, a brief general statement about Niebuhr's view of the church may provide a context for this group of essays. His thought about the church developed in its first stages during the thirteen years which he spent as pastor of Bethel Evangelical Church in Detroit. The pastoral experience, as he said, tamed his "cynicism," and his published record of these years (*Leaves from the Notebook of a Tamed Cynic,* 1929) shows not only the polemical approach to the church and the ministry for which he is noted, but also a deep appreciation of the possibilities of grace and growth in a congregation. What he said about the ministry in this book (p. 18, Meridian Books edition) he might equally well have said about the whole church. "I make no apology for being critical of what I love." And critical of all the "fragments of the church" he has consistently been. For, says he, "When I see how new evil comes into life through the pretension of the religious community, through its conventional and graceless legalism and through religious fanaticism, I am concerned that my growing appreciation of the church should not betray me into . . . complacency" (Kegley & Bretall, p. 437).

While Niebuhr would not try to lay down too explicitly the characteristics of *the* "true church" in terms of a historic institution, he nevertheless belongs clearly in the Reformation, nonconformist tradition. His own church was the Evangelical (later the Evangelical and Reformed), the American version of the German Prussian Union, a union of Lutheran and Reformed groups. As it is made clear in the following articles, Niebuhr has some very definite ideas about the nature of the church and its functions—about polity, the ministry, the sacraments, liturgies and worship services, its theology, its witness to and against the world.

The church is founded upon the faith that "God, the Creator, is revealed as forgiving love in the drama of Christ's life, death, and resurrection" (*ibid.,* p. 432). In spite of the many historical corruptions which the church

---

Radical Religion, winter, 1936; "Does the Church Pray?" *Christianity and Crisis,* June 15, 1942; "Churches and Society," *New Statesman and Nation,* September 18, 1948; "The Heresy Trials," *Christianity and Crisis,* December 26, 1955.

has fallen into, it yet bears the "oracles of God," as Paul said of Israel. The church is variously referred to as "that place in human society where men are disturbed by the Word of God," as the place where "the word of mercy, reconciliation, and consolation is heard," and where "the kingdom of God impinges upon all human enterprises" (*Beyond Tragedy*, p. 62). It is sometimes called a "community of hopeful believers" or a "community of forgiven sinners" (*Faith and History*, p. 238) or a "curiously mixed body" of those who remain self-righteous and those who "live by a broken spirit and a contrite heart" (Kegley & Bretall, p. 7). Something of the Reformation conception of the invisible church continues to be a meaningful and essential instrument for keeping all particular churches under judgment. For, Niebuhr emphasizes, the "church is always in danger of becoming anti-Christ" because it is tempted to pray, "Lord, I thank Thee that I am not as other institutions." The church, as he sees it, not only shares the tendency of all institutions finally to choke the life out of every idea or impulse which they are created to foster; the church is especially vulnerable, for no fragment of the church "understands as well as the prophets of Israel understood how severely the judgment of God falls upon the community which is the bearer of the judgment" (*Faith and History*, p. 242). In fact, "every vehicle of God's grace, the preacher of the word, the prince of the Church, the teacher of theology, the historic institution, the written word, the sacred canon, all these are in danger of being revered as if they were themselves divine. The aura of the divine word, which is transmitted through them, falsely covers their human frailties" (*Christianity and Power Politics*, p. 219). But to be forever aware of the dangers of institutions, forms, and vehicles of grace is not, of course, to deny their relative importance.

The question of polity is not the all-important question to Niebuhr, but it has its importance. He refers to polity as "the skeleton of the common life of the church" as theology is also "the skeleton of the faith of the church," and "the full stature requires the support of the skeletal structure" (p. 273, this volume). But it might be said of Niebuhr's view that if the polity is the skeleton of the church's common life, the skeleton would seem to be worn on the outside of the body, and it is expendable like the skin of the snake. That is, polities come and go, are contingent, but God's church remains. "The 'order' of a church, its rites and its polity, belong clearly to the realm of the historically contingent" (*The Nature and Destiny of Man*, II, p. 225). The form of the polity of the church is not a part of the givenness of the church. "God gave the church its gospel and the Holy Spirit keeps faith alive in it. But human genius creates and human sin corrupts all the historical and relative forms of the church" (*Beyond Tragedy*, p. 122). To make polity the heart of the matter is to put one's trust in man, or man-made institutions.

Important values in all the various contingent types of church polity are recognized, but, of course, the less democratic churches have certain built-in dangers or tendencies to pride, vainglory, and the abuse of power. "My democratic soul rebels at the obsequious verger who bows him (the bishop) into the pulpit," he wrote after attending a service. But his democratic soul has not prevented his full appreciation of the liturgical strength of this church and even of its type of government, as many references in this collection of articles will show. He argues against sectarian "liberty" and independence of the congregation that "the congregation is not powerful enough and its resources not great enough to maintain the uniqueness of the Christian witness against the world," and that the sect in its celebration of liberty has not recognized the value of the bishop's authority in "maintaining the witness of the church against the world" (p. 274, this volume. Numbers hereafter refer to this volume unless otherwise indicated.). He recognized the strength of the more centrally organized churches in some social situations, such, for instance, as the Southern integration struggle. The minister and the local church may be less subject to the pressures of the local community than is the case with the sectarian congregation. The Reformation was not so much an attack on authority in favor of freedom as an attack upon the tendency to idolatry in the church.

In summary, Niebuhr's view of the church, reflecting his own denominational heritage, calls for more unity and authority than sectarianism allows and more flexibility and freedom than the more "catholic" churches have tolerated, and also for the constant witness of the divine word to bring judgment to bear upon all fragments of the church. Niebuhr suggests that the Reformation concept of the invisible church may be a valid source of judgment of particular churches (*The Nature and Destiny of Man,* II, p. 139), though he does not develop the use of this idea in his own thought. However, he seems to combine something of the two concepts in this statement: "The secure church is precisely that community of saints, known and unknown, among whom life is constantly transformed because it is always under the divine word" (*Faith and History,* p. 242).

PART I

Niebuhr has had much to say about worship in the American churches, and Part I reveals the many aspects of his concern in this area of church life. Twenty years ago he saw a "crying need for liturgical reform in American Protestantism (p. 48), a need which continues to our own day (p. 57). Our peculiar weaknesses and corruptions of common worship in America are traced to the dominance of the sect in our heritage. Sectarian protests against the church's preoccupation with liturgy, theology, and polity had a good measure of validity in their time, and Niebuhr notes how regrettable it is that the Reformers did not accept the seriousness and legitimacy of their protest. But "spirit without discipline, form and tradition is also vain. The trouble with American Protestantism is that its protest against the various forms and disciplines led to their destruction" (p. 62). Worship becomes formless, secularized, vulgarized, and the church, like the theater, more often presents a spectacle or a stunt rather than a worship service, from the exhibitionist choir director to the banal "chatty conversations with God" which the minister offers as prayers. The priestly function of the minister has an important place in the life of the church.

Episcopal liturgies have appealed to Niebuhr personally ("Though a nonconformist myself, I prefer a liturgical church with as little sermon as possible." p. 29), as a number of references in these pages suggest. Liturgical churches have much to teach those of the nonliturgical tradition. Attending a service in an American cathedral in 1933, he was prompted to observe that "the adequacy of the liturgy and the inadequacy of the sermon is roughly symbolic of the fact that the central message of the Christian religion still lives in the tradition of the church but that it is not being made applicable for the problems of our common life. When we sing our religion all the ages of Christian wisdom speak to us. But when we preach it the petty illusions of the nineteenth century . . . obscure the profundities of ancient insights" (p. 33). But for all the recognized adequacy of the liturgy, American churches are warned against merely copying liturgies or simply adopting them for aesthetic purposes. A better example for American churches, he points out, is the nonconformist tradition in Europe. It was during a visit to Europe in 1924 that Niebuhr first developed a great appreciation for "ritualistic services" of the type he observed in the nonconformist churches there (*Leaves from the Notebook of a Tamed Cynic*, p. 81), and he used adaptations of them in his church in Detroit. Later he was particularly attracted to what he observed in the Scottish Church and thought it to be a "better example in the art of worship than we could secure anywhere else," for "the Church of Scotland, since the reunion between the established and the free church, has blended the liturgical tradition of the former with the free tradition of the latter" (*Christianity and Crisis*, March 3, 1947). Part I contains numerous specific suggestions on how to improve worship services. He has been particularly concerned with the importance of adequate prayers (pp. 48ff.; 52ff.) and sung responses, and it has been noted that in his own prayers one finds expressed Niebuhr's deepest appreciation of the Christian community.

Niebuhr's view of the church is interestingly symbolized in his interpretation of the use of the sacraments (see especially *The Nature and Destiny of Man*, II, pp. 225-6; *Faith and History,* Chap. XIV). Early in his ministry he recorded that he was "losing some of the aversion to the sacraments cultivated in my seminary days" (*Leaves . . . ,* p. 24). By the time of the Gifford Lectures he believes that the "eschatological emphasis in the sacrament is a true expression of the eschatological character of the church." In *Faith and History* (p. 240) he says that "a community of grace, which lives by faith and hope, must be sacramental. It must have sacraments to symbolize the having and the not having of the final virtue and truth."

Niebuhr is strictly Protestant in his emphasis on the function of the preacher. The sermon is necessary for channeling religious emotion "into all the thirsty areas of life" (p. 31). He expressed no shame at "having the Bible rather than the altar as the center of nonconformist worship" (p. 42). Early in his ministry he determined not to be a "preacher of pretty sermons" (*Leaves . . .* p. 27) and noted that "pulpit eloquence" may cover a failure to make the Gospel relevant (*ibid.,* p. 85). Prophetic religion preaches the Word of God to specific time, place, and circumstance. It is Niebuhr's attacks upon the liberal church because of what he regarded as its confusions and failures in the realm of applied Christianity and his attacks upon the ecclesiastical pretensions of all groups which have left something of a negative impression of his views of the church.

PART II

Part II represents the area of interest to which Niebuhr has given the great portion of his attention in his ministry and his writings. His thinking about the life of the church is many-sided, but he never wanders far from his concern that the Kingdom of God, which is not of this world, be "made relevant to every problem of the world." These selections from his occasional writings (as well as those in Part III) should illustrate clearly and in a fairly brief form the depth and breadth of his thought about the church and moral-political questions. He never loses sight of what he calls the "first business of the Christian church," as orthodox critics suggest that he does. This first business is "to raise and answer religious questions within the framework of which these moral issues must be solved" (p. 88). While he emphasizes that neutrality between justice and injustice is "untrue to our gospel" (p. 101), he is equally insistent that a utilitarian attitude toward the faith debases it to "a mere instrument of the warring creeds" (p. 95) and that the introduction of religious absolutes into politics may easily produce self-righteous fury and intolerance. "If there is no power and grace in the Christian church 'to bring down every high thing which exalteth itself against the knowledge of God' (and this includes the church itself), the church becomes not merely useless but dangerous" (*Christianity and Society*, Spring, 1950).

PART III

The group of articles on Barth and Barthianism has a place in this collection of writings because of Barth's great influence in the church, particularly in Europe, and his conception of the ethical task of the church and the relationship of theology to culture with which Niebuhr disagrees. It is believed, too, that the points of difference between Barth and Niebuhr constitute an important and continuing question for the church. Charles West (in *Communism and the Theologians*, p. 14) speaks of "the Barthian he (Niebuhr) truly is." What Niebuhr has in common with Barth is perhaps well enough known, and their common ground has been important for the ecumenical church and will continue to be. Niebuhr's reservations about Barthian theology were first expressed in print thirty years ago. This group of articles rather underscores the Barthian which Niebuhr truly is not. This section includes all the articles Niebuhr has written about Barth, though there are brief references in various of his books.

There are broad areas of difference between Barth and Niebuhr. One area of difference which is particularly relevant to the subject of this volume is the relationship between the church and the world. Barth seems to Niebuhr really to insulate the church and theology from the world.

The way Barth conceives his "political watch," for instance, does not represent sufficient "care of the world" on the part of the church. Their differences, too, are expressed in varying conceptions of eschatology. These articles will indicate how Niebuhr argued on several occasions that Barth is "too consistently 'eschatological' for the 'nicely calculated less and more' which must go into political decisions" (p. 186). "The 'end' stands only above history and the Biblical idea of the 'end' is obscured" (*The Nature and Destiny of Man*, II, p. 309). Related to this "defect" in Barth's theological approach to social ethics is what Niebuhr calls "his extreme pragmatism, which disavows all moral principles" (p. 186). Here he is thinking of the sort of general statement Barth made in *Against the Stream* (p. 114): ". . . the Church never thinks, speaks or acts 'on principle.' Rather it judges spiritually and by individual cases." Niebuhr also taxes Barth in some of these pages and elsewhere with combining a "sophisticated knowledge of all the disciplines of modern culture with a frantic effort to isolate the Christian faith from the allegedly debilitating effects of philosophical and scientific speculations" (*The Self and the Dramas of History*, pp. 108-9).

The criticisms which Niebuhr has aimed at Barthian thought have not gone totally unchallenged. E. G. Homrighausen wrote an article ("Barthianism and the Kingdom," *The Christian Century*, July 15, 1931) in answer to Niebuhr's criticisms of Barthianism in "Let Liberal Churches Stop Fooling Themselves" (March 25, 1931, issue). Niebuhr's reply is reprinted here. Barth on one occasion answered Niebuhr's criticisms,• claiming that Niebuhr had

---

• The following exchange occurred in 1948-49: "We Are Men and Not God," *The Christian Century*, October 27, 1948, by Niebuhr, in answer to Barth's Amsterdam address. The essential parts of Barth's address were published in the December 8, 1948, issue under the title: "No Christian Marshall Plan." In the February 16, 1949, issue Barth replied to Niebuhr's article in "Continental vs. Anglo-Saxon Theology, a Preliminary Reply to Reinhold Niebuhr." Niebuhr concluded this exchange in "An Answer to Karl Barth," published in the February 23 issue of *The Christian Century*. The same exchange is discussed in Danielou, Jean, "Gespräche nach "missed the mark" in his understanding and criticism of "Continental theology," and that he (Barth) did not find himself "where the 'Continental' theology and I appear to him to be." Furthermore, he argued, Niebuhr had not found the heart of the difference between the "Continentals" and the "Anglo-Saxons." Barth thought the major difference to be in the "irresponsible attitude toward the Bible" among the Anglo-Saxons. In the case of the last article and exchange in this section, the article on Barth and Hungary, Barth has remained silent, but a group of his students engaged in an "exchange" with Niebuhr, and Niebuhr's statement is reprinted here.

PART IV

The selections in Part IV are intended to bring together Niebuhr's typical analyses and criticisms of what he has called "the Catholic heresy," as well as his estimate of the Catholic social ethic and its reliance on natural law.● The "Catholic heresy" is the error of "regarding the historic church as the unqualified representative of Christ on earth so that the enemies of the church become the enemies of God" (p. 296). Basically the error springs from the exaltation of the church as an extension of the Incarnation. A related error "changed the gospel of forgiveness to contrite souls into a great scheme for assuring men of their salvation if they would climb a 'ladder of merit'" (p. 336).

While particular attention is given in this section to the Roman church, it should be noted that Niebuhr, here and elsewhere, points out that this "heresy" is not confined to

Amsterdam," Evangelischer Verlag A. G. Zollikon, Zürich, 1949.

● Other articles and chapters not included in this collection are: "The Pope," *Radical Religion,* Autumn, 1936; "Catholicism and Communism," *Radical Religion,* Winter, 1936; "Catholicism and Anarchism in Spain," *Radical Religion,* Spring, 1937; *The Nature and Destiny of Man,* II, pp. 134-56; 220-5; *Christian Realism and Political Problems,* Chap. 10; "A Protestant Looks at Catholics," *The Commonweal,* May 8, 1953; see also Niebuhr's reply to Gustave Weigel in Kegley & Bretall, *op. cit.,* pp. 444-6.

the Roman church alone. Greek Orthodoxy exalts the "unbroken tradition of the church." Anglo-Catholicism, while not as consistently pretentious as the others, does present problems in their relationship to other churches in the deliberations of the ecumenical church. But even further, Niebuhr argues, no church, Protestant or Catholic, escapes the temptation to make itself a vehicle of sin and yet exempt itself from the necessity of repentance, though some Christian groups, because of their understanding of the nature of the church, are more given to the error than others.

Some of the articles in this group discuss the Catholic position on specific issues and deal with matters in the news a couple of decades ago. Some deal with pressing current issues. The fact that Dr. Niebuhr was wrong in his predictions about Cardinal Pacelli's chances of becoming Pope (pp. 201ff.) does not destroy the interest of his article as an analysis of Vatican politics from the outside.

Dr. Niebuhr was perhaps more sharply critical of the Roman church twenty years ago (largely because of the Fascist issue), though the basic points of his difference, as the later articles will indicate, continue essentially the same. More recently, however, he has been concerned with the "scandal" of deteriorating relations between Catholics and Protestants in this country. He emphasizes that while we should oppose any Catholic political actions which seem to us unjust and a danger to our democratic life, we should nevertheless strive to do this without malice. As long as "we meet each other only vituperatively in the public prints," he says, "the secularists may plausibly contend that a society can be saved from the fury of the theologians only by its secularization" (p. 237).

It is characteristic of Niebuhr's thought about the church, Catholic or Protestant, that he often points out that God's work in the world is many times done not by the church but by the "enemies" of the church. " 'The wind bloweth where it listeth' (John 3:8), said Jesus to Nicodemus; and that is a picturesque description of the freedom of divine grace in history, working miracles without any 'by your leave' of priest or church" (*The Nature and Destiny of Man*, II, p.

208). Secular idealism may speak "the word of God" on some issues (p. 94). Democracy may be in its own time God's instrument (p. 162). The church must humbly recognize that it was a "secular age" which granted women recognition as persons, and in many ways the church still lags behind our society in general in its treatment of women in the household of faith (pp. 93, 179). Sports groups and labor unions have preached the "gospel" to the church in the development of decent race relations.

PART V

The last part contains practically everything Dr. Niebuhr has written on the ecumenical movement, except the items which were published in connection with the ecumenical conferences.•

Already in the 1920's Niebuhr was active in the interdenominational work in the United States. He noted early in his ministry the desperate necessity for ecumenical relationships because of our religious pluralism, but he has understood profoundly our peculiar religious history in America and why so much of the discussion in the world church seems irrelevant to it (pp. 56, 265ff.).

Niebuhr has been active and influential in the world church since the period of preparation for the Oxford Conference. He participated in preparing for Oxford (1937), Amsterdam (1948), and Evanston (1954), and he attended the first two of these conferences. From Oxford to Amsterdam there came into existence in the world church an explicit outline of a common ecumenical philosophy of society, and none was more influential than Niebuhr in the development and formulation of this common philosophy.

• "The Christian Church in a Secular Age," address at Oxford Conference on Church and Community, published as Chap. 16 of *Christianity and Power Politics*, 1940; "Christian Faith and the Common Life," Oxford Conf. Series, Vol. 4, 1938; and "God's Design and the Present Disorder of Civilization," and "The Situation in the U. S.," in Vol. III, Amsterdam Studies, *The Church and the Disorder of Society*, 1949; substance of Amsterdam address published in *Christian Realism and Political Problems*, Chap. 8.

His most active participation in the ecumenical life of the church has paralleled the high points of the "Life and Work" aspect of ecumenicity, as the focus of these three great conferences suggests. His own focus of interest and emphasis has in fact been in "Life and Work" rather than in "Faith and Order." He sees the significance of the World Council of Churches essentially in the work in this area and notes that "Faith and Order" are consigned to a study commission "where they belong." And to those who see the union of the church in any absolute sense as possible and desirable, he warns that "the divisions can never be absolutely healed, unless all fragments of the church submit to the fragment which makes the most extravagant pretensions" (*Faith and History*, p. 241).

Like many leaders in the world church, Niebuhr has been critical of any tendency toward an uncritical centrism. As many passages in these articles show, his emphasis has contained the common note of emphasis upon renewal more than reunion, on an operating or working relationship more than on organization or agreement about a "doctrine of the church." These words, written by Niebuhr thirty-five years ago, suggest a persistent element in his thought about the ecumenical movement:

> Eager ecclesiasts think they can make the church the one agency of world salvation if they can only achieve a new catholicism . . . What we need is a supernatural conscience in the church rather than an international organization. "The Paradox of Institutions," *The World Tomorrow*, August, 1923.

While Niebuhr believes that there might very well be more unity among the churches than has yet developed (p. 279), he does not see this as the "genuine ecumenical task." This task is one of "appropriating each other's treasures for a fuller testimony of the many-faceted truth in Christ" (p. 280). There are two wrong reasons for promoting more unity in Protestantism. One wrong reason for promoting unity is to give Protestantism a united front in competition with Catholicism. Another wrong reason is the desire to give the Christian message more power, prestige, and authority in the world (pp. 280, 284). The authority of the church does not come from its unity. The authority of the church comes from Christ and his gospel.

A word of general appreciation is offered to my colleague, Professor W. Gordon Ross of Berea College and also to Professor John Bennett of Union Theological Seminary. Both have offered help and encouragement in numerous ways. A special word of thanks is due to Dean Walter Muelder of the Boston University School of Theology. His talks with me about the nature and function of the church and the contemporary discussions of it have enlightened the whole context of this volume.

I am grateful to the editors and staffs of the following periodicals for permission to use articles they have published: *The Christian Century, The Christian Herald, The Ecumenical Review, The Messenger, The Nation, Religion in Life, The Reporter, Theology Today, Union Seminary Quarterly Review;* and to Dr. Niebuhr for permitting the use of material from *Radical Religion, Christianity and Society,* and *Christianity and Crisis.*

PART I: *The Weakness of Common Worship in American Protestantism*

A CHRISTMAS SERVICE
IN RETROSPECT

I went to church in the cathedral on Christmas day. It is one of the few days of the year on which I am able to attend church without preaching myself. On that day, though a nonconformist myself, I prefer a liturgical church with as little sermon as possible. It is not that I don't like to hear anyone but myself preach. I merely dislike most Christmas and Easter sermons. Only poets can do justice to the Christmas and Easter stories and there are not many poets in the pulpit. It is better therefore to be satisfied with the symbolic presentation of the poetry in hymn, anthem, and liturgy. The sermons which interpret these stories usually make a rational defense of their historic validity or they qualify them rationally to make them acceptable to the intellect. I have preached many of the latter type in my own parish days, but I now feel sorry for the people who had to listen to them. I suppose it is necessary and inevitable that the poetry of religion should be expressed in rational terms but something is always lost in the rationalization. Dogma is rationally petrified poetry which destroys part of the truth "embodied in the tale" in the effort to put it into precise terms.

Belief in the Christmas Story

I believe the Christmas story. It expresses the idea that the great God of the universe has purposes which are relevant to man's purposes. That is very difficult to believe.

29

There is, as a matter of fact, a note of rational absurdity in the belief. Human values must achieve cosmic validity if any religion is to live. Yet there must be in this belief some suggestion of the mystery of life and of the majesty of the divine which transcends human life. True religion must therefore be conscious of the difficulty and the absurdity of the human claiming kinship with the divine, of the temporal trafficking with the eternal. If the divine is made relevant to the human it must transvalue our values and enter the human at the point where man is lowly rather than proud and where he is weak rather than strong. Therefore I believe that God came in the form of a little child born to humble parents in a manger "because there was no room for them in the inn."

But if I put all this in rational terms I lose something of the rich variety of the Christmas story. I prefer, therefore, to do what I did on Christmas day: I like to sing "Hark the herald angels sing" and "O come, all ye faithful." I like to hear the soprano of boys' voices rejoicing, "Glory to God in the highest." (Why is it that a boy's soprano gives a suggestion of the supernal not to be found in a woman's voice? Why should these urchins who have such a difficult time keeping quiet in their choir stalls suggest the song of angels to me?)

. . . Until the Sermon!

Even when we come to the Nicene creed I enjoy it. I should not like to commit myself to the Nicene creed in cold blood. Here poetry has been transmuted into dogma— "very God of very God, begotten not made." I want to raise some questions about that. But why bother? The choir is singing it to an E flat tune by Eyre. The curse has been taken from the dogma. The alchemy of the service has changed what was once poetry and has been made into dogma back into poetry again.

The priest reads the lesson from the altar. He intones, "The word was made flesh and dwelt among us." That is a very philosophical statement of the Christmas story and I believe it. But I don't like to have a little man in a frock coat reading it to me from behind a desk. I would rather hear that imposing and sonorous phrase coming from a priest who is hidden from me by the choir screen and who intones it with a suggestion that a mystery is involved in this simple statement. In short, I am inspired by everything in the cathedral service until it is time for the sermon.

Of course there must be a sermon. Religious emotion must be made relevant and applicable to the problems of everyday life. The church has a teaching function. Let it inspire religious emotion, but the religious emotion must be channeled into all of the thirsty areas of life. The bishop is preaching this morning. I don't like anything about his sermon. My democratic soul rebels at the obsequious verger who bows him into the pulpit. I don't like the bishop's kind of self-consciousness. He talks about the lowly Jesus with the accompaniment of imperious gestures calculated to suggest that he—the bishop—is a prince of the church. Perhaps I am prejudiced against this bishop because I happen to know many of his attitudes on public and theological questions and I don't agree with any of them.

Christ Our Judgment

Yet if I had never heard of or seen this bishop before I would not have liked his sermon. His text was "Jesus Christ, the same yesterday, today and forever." The bishop said that the spirit of Christ would solve all problems. If men only followed Him there would be no more war and the injustice of poverty and riches in industry would be abolished and all the churches would be united. If men only followed Him! I have heard all that so often. The bishop did not suggest that Christ is our judgment as well as our hope. He did not say that none of us, not even in the churches, live by the law of Christ. There was nothing in the sermon to suggest that at the foot of the cross men become conscious of the sin of self-will and the tragedy of unrealized ideals. He did not even suggest that the life in the manger ended upon the cross and that ours might end there if we really emulated it.

As usual, the mystery of Christ was reduced to the ideal of mutuality. We must all love one another and the world will be saved. But what are we to do since we are not good enough to love one another? What political and what religious conclusions are we to draw from the fact that we are selfish? The bishop was certain that the world would really follow the law of Christ if only all men believed that Christ was God. Many other preachers have held that the world would follow the law of Christ just as soon as men ceased believing that he was divine and regarded him as a human example. There was nothing in this sermon, as there is not in most sermons, to suggest that when the word was made flesh it not only revealed the relevance between the human and the divine but the distance between the human and divine.

We can touch the divine by our ideals. We know we ought to love. But we do not, as a matter of fact, love our neighbor as ourself. We can love enough to know that the highest human ideal must be stated in terms of love and that thus stated it becomes a symbol of the divine. But we do not love enough to have the word made flesh in us.

Thus I rebelled against the bishop's sermon. There was no note of humility in it. There was only the suggestion that the church had a message which the world had not yet heeded. I knew that the bishop is not celebrated for the spirit of humility and I may for that reason have been offended by the suggestion of unconscious arrogance in his message. But he might have been a much more humble man than he is personally, and his sermon would still have been inadequate. The world is in moral confusion partly because religion is not fulfilling its task of helping people to know themselves. How can we know ourselves if we do not scrutinize ourselves from the perspective of the absolute? That is how we learn how selfish we are.

If we estimated our selfishness accurately we would not be deceived so easily by the efforts to reform the world by persuading people to be a little less selfish than they are.

We would know that to the end of history selfishness will clash with selfishness. Knowing that, we might be more ready for political programs which place a social restraint upon human egoism and we might also be more ready for a religion which plumbed the depths of life, and ceased to move merely upon its surfaces.

Obscuring Ancient Insights

It would be foolish to suggest that, because the bishop's sermon failed to help while his cathedral did, we ought to have fewer sermons and more liturgy. The poetry of religion must, after all, be interpreted, if it is to become most effective. It would be truer to say that the adequacy of the liturgy and the inadequacy of the sermon is roughly symbolic of the fact that the central message of the Christian religion still lives in the tradition of the church but that it is not being made applicable for the problems of our common life. When we sing our religion all the ages of Christian wisdom speak to us. But when we preach it the petty illusions of the nineteenth century, the illusions that men are good and are becoming better, that the kingdom of God is around the corner, obscure the profundities of ancient insights.

In the bishop's liturgy the prayer of general confession acknowledged "that we have done those things which we ought not to have done and have left undone those things which we ought to have done and there is no health in us." But there was no such suggestion of contrition in the bishop's sermon. That is, roughly stated, the difference between the gospel and the gospel as we preach it. I say "we" because the reader will have discovered by this time that I hate the arrogance of the bishop so much because it is my own arrogance slightly accentuated.

SECTS AND CHURCHES

One of the basic difficulties of American Christianity lies in the fact that its predominant churches are sects which have become churches and do not know they have undergone such a change. The difference between church and sect, as understood in Europe, is not known in America. Sectarianism, among us, merely means the multiplication of denominations. But there is an important difference between the church and the sect. The sect is a voluntary and exclusive religious fellowship with standards of faith and conduct different from the general community and therefore conscious of a tension between the Christian ideal and the life of the community. The sect is usually either pietistic or apocalyptic—that is, it tries in terms of pietistic individualism to achieve the Christian ideal in personal conduct, or it is dominated by the hope of the establishment of the kingdom of God on earth. Thus the Baptist sect was originally apocalyptic, carrying the faith of the disinherited of reformation days, that the Kingdom of God would be established on earth. It set itself against the pessimism of Lutheran orthodoxy, in the creed of which the Kingdom of God lay beyond the possibilities of any earthly achievement. The Methodist sect is on the other hand pietistic. It is the child of the evangelical-pietistic movement and its spirituality is a fruit of the pietistic protest against the sacramental piety of the church, in which the doctrine of justification and forgiveness frequently leads to religious formalism. Against this formalism pietism emphasized both personal religious experience and a rigorous ethic.

One of the curious developments of American church history, for which I know no explanation, is that the Methodist church, with its pietistic, individualistic past, should be socially more radical than the Baptist church with its apocalyptic and therefore socially oriented past.

Baptism as a Symbol

In contrast to the sect, the church is inclusive in its membership, and expresses a more social concept of religion by assuming the Christian faith of its members without expecting a special religious decision. In a sense, child baptism is the symbol of this involuntary membership, while adult baptism is the most perfect symbol of the voluntary membership. The church is, at least in its European background, coextensive with the total community. It does not separate its membership from the community. It lives on the assumption that the entire community is Christian. It regards itself as the expression of the Christian conscience of the community. Yet at the same time the church knows that the state is not Christian. It knows in fact that no one lives by the law of Christ. Its emphasis is therefore upon the grace of God which redeems sinners. The sect challenges the world; the church accepts the world, knowing it to be challenged and standing under the judgment of the law of Christ. Broadly speaking, one could say therefore that the church has partially resolved the tension between Christ and the world, while the sect tries to maintain it.

What has brought confusion into the American religious scene is that the sects have become churches (without knowing it) and that the churches have become sects (without being willing to admit it). A church is fully a church only if it has an organic relationship to the total community. No American church has that. They are therefore forced into a system of voluntary membership, just as, on the other hand, the sect churches substitute rather secularized "decision days" for the religious experience which was once a prerequisite of membership. Denominationally, the most obvious instances of the church type in America are the Lutherans and Episcopalians. Both the Presbyterian and Congregational denominations are churches with sect features, which do not derive altogether from the American environment but are inherent in their European history.

Churches Have Learned from Sects

The Congregational church is probably more sectarian in its characteristics than the Presbyterian, largely because its congregational polity tends to depreciate the more organic conception of the church in favor of the more individualistic and voluntaristic concept. Denominations with an unqualified church tradition become slightly ludicrous when they make absolute church pretensions in America. The Episcopal church is probably more given to such pretensions than the Lutheran church. A church which has an organic relation to a total civilization, as the Anglican church to British life, needs to possess a higher degree of grace than is vouchsafed most church leaders, in order to find just the right adjustment between its tradition and the indubitable fact that, as in America, it is merely a small denomination side by side with many others.

The churches which have become sects in America have probably sacrificed less of what is valuable in their tradition than the sects which have become churches. The churches have learned more from the sects than the sects from the churches. They have borrowed from the sects the principle of lay leadership and the advantage of lay initiative. This is, of course, not a pure advantage, because it subjects the American parson to lay pressure to a much greater degree than the European parson. The churches have also learned to take a more robust attitude toward the state. The principle of a free church in a free state is really a principle of the Enlightenment which the real churches in Europe have never been willing to accept but which sectarian Christianity knew how to make the basis of a new religious vitality. The churches of America have learned some of the sect's self-reliance and independence in regard to the state, though it must be admitted that, since the sects have become churches, they sometimes capitulate as easily to the unofficial state (community opinion) as the European churches capitulated to the official state.

But since the most powerful American denominations have sect rather than church traditions, the spiritual problems of American Christianity are more implicated in the drift from sect to church than from church to sect. In general terms the problem could be put like this: The church knows that Christianity in an absolute sense cannot defeat the world. It knows that men will continue to live in a world of sin and that both as individuals and more particularly as social groups there is a law in their members which wars against the law that is in their mind. It knows that human lives can be transformed by the grace of God, but it also knows that the grace of God must express itself not only as a power unto righteousness but as forgiveness of sins. Hence the sacramental emphasis of the church. Frequently the church is betrayed into a premature compromise with the world. In American history, for instance, the Presbyterian and Episcopal churches were usually either indifferent toward social-political issues or they allowed their pessimism to become an instrument of political and social reaction.

Tension with the World

The sect, on the other hand, tries to defeat the world in the name of Christ, either in the lives of individuals (pietism) or in the hope of a Kingdom of God to be established upon earth (apocalypticism). The original sect maintains a stronger tension against the world than does the church. The American sect contributed more to the establishment of egalitarian democracy and to the elimination of slavery than did the church. The sect churches of the frontier, in fact, were wholehearted supporters of Jeffersonian and Jacksonian democracy against the opposition of Hamiltonian plutocracy, frequently supported by the churches. So far the advantage lies with the sects. They labored for the approximations of the Christian law of love in politics and economics, while the church mourned over a lost world.

Nevertheless, the sect churches of America are today religiously less vital and less capable of survival than the churches. They are more frequently secularized, and their religion vulgarized, than the churches. One of the reasons for this is that the peculiar circumstances of American history betrayed the sect into a relaxation of its tension with the world. It began to believe that the world would submit to the law of Christ. The expanding American frontier, the expansive nature of American economy, the success of American republican government, all these factors seemed to guarantee that the Sermon on the Mount could be applied to politics and be successful there.

The sentimentalities of American Christianity, its failure to grasp the tragic character of man's collective life, its easy confidence that a few more sermons on love would subdue the sin in the human heart, all these limitations are not simply borrowed from secular liberalism. They represent rather the consequence of the ease with which sectarian Christianity was able to put religious passion behind the social goals of secular liberalism and actually gain a victory over the enemy. It deluded itself into believing that its victory was final and that it was living in a Christian world. It had made the world Christian. Thus the sect lost its tension with the world and became at home in the world. And all this happened (tragedy of tragedies!) over the precise period when the world of Jeffersonian liberalism and agrarian democracy was being gradually transmuted into the sorry realities of industrial capitalism.

Two Alternatives

Facing the cruelties of this world in its period of expansion and the even greater cruelties of its period of contraction, liberalized sectarian Christianity could adopt only one of two alternatives. It could either preserve its faith, sometimes naively and sometimes frantically, that the sins of the world could be overcome by preaching the ideal of love (the old social gospel) or it could become politically realistic and seek for a political program which would implement its ideals of justice. Both of these things have been done. Stanley Jones's, "The Christian Alternative to Communism," is a belated example of the first method. Most of the younger social-gospel preachers have become politically more realistic. They know that justice in society can be established only by implementing religious-moral ideals with political techniques. In either case the approach represents a secularization of Christianity. Social techniques are used without religious reservations—that is, without recognition of the fact that political techniques of conflict and coercion are necessary but also dangerous, and that they stand under the judgment of the absolute command of love. In the case of Stanley Jones the old evangelical piety is vital enough to prevent secularization, and in that he is typical of many others in the sectarian tradition. But while this type preserves religious vitality and avoids secularization, it does not avoid sentimentality.

The historical basis of the whole of Protestant liberalism in America is really this defaulted sect. In genuine Christianity the law of love is always an impossible possibility. The world must be challenged by it and also changed by it, that is, through its approximations. But the world, particularly every political and economic order, must also be judged by it, judged and found wanting. In thousands of Christian pulpits the richness and breadth of the Christian gospel is lost in a moralistic radical-social preaching which belabors middle-class people for not acting politically like proletarians. If the preaching is liberal moralism, rather than radical, it may be even worse, inasmuch as it gives middle-class comfortable people the illusion that they are living by the law of Christ because they have never participated in violence.

Disintegration of Sectarianism

The disintegration of sectarian Christianity leaves our American Christianity in a sad state. It is theologically in confusion because in its vital period it lived by spontaneous religious emotion and held theology in contempt. But theology is a necessary means of preserving religious conviction. It is difficult to perpetuate undefined religious beliefs. Because of its lack of a theological tradition sectarian Christianity was split into two camps, those who fell into a dry orthodoxy and those who leaned on secular liberalism and redefined Christianity in terms which usually add only pious phrases to the concepts of secular liberalism. This division is most obvious in the Baptist and Disciples denominations. In both cases there is practically nothing in common between the two wings. They can exist together at all only because they do not live intimately with one another. Their congregational polity makes it impossible for one group to bring the other under its discipline.

The Methodist church has been able to escape the rigors of this theological controversy because it has continued to remain essentially untheological. The Methodist church does not, however, escape the general processes of disintegration. When the old evangelical piety is dissipated and there are not powerful theological and liturgical forces to preserve the Christian faith and feeling the tendency is to sink into vulgarity or into a pure moralism. In all sectarian churches there are today types of vulgarized Christianity in which both sermon and service seek to intrigue the interest of the religiously indifferent masses by vaudeville appeals of various sorts. This represents the worst form of disintegration. The best form is to be found in the championship of various moral and social causes.

Vulgarization of Christianity

The Prohibition movement may be regarded as a rather pathetic effort of sectarian Christianity to preserve its tension with the world. The degree to which this became a pure political movement is the measure of the secularization of the church. Some of the finer spirits among the secularized prophets in sectarianism today now place all their efforts into the cause of world peace and social justice. Their courage is admirable and their striving not without significance or success. But what they say upon these issues is the same gospel preached in every woman's club and every open forum. Little is to be discovered in this preaching of the fact that historic Christianity measures the dimensions of life in much more ultimate terms than secularism and that it distinguishes itself from modern interpretations of life by a much profounder pessimism and more ultimate optimism.

The vulgarization of sectarian Christianity is partly due to its difficulty in finding proper forms for the social expression of its faith. In the period of its vitality the sect may hold the church in contempt for its formal and stereotyped prayers and liturgy. Spontaneous prayer is more vital than stylized prayer. But prayer which has ceased to be spontaneous and simulates the appearance of spontaneity, that is, the pastoral prayer of the sectarian church, with its formlessness and lack of beauty, the monotony of its reiterations, destroys the religious ethos in the congregation. Formal liturgy does not necessarily preserve vital religion. But it is like well-cultivated garden beds into which seeds may be dropped and spring to life. The individual worshiper may find in it the occasion for, and prompting to, religious aspiration which may be all the more effective because the form of the liturgy is beautiful enough to carry religious emotion and not sufficiently specific to interfere with the particular moods and needs of the worshipers.

This criticism of the sect in America is not meant to imply that the churches in America are making a greater contribution than they to our religious and moral life. Churches which have become sects have just as difficult problems of adjustment as sects which have become churches. But the problems of the sects are more important because they represent the dominant force in American Protestantism. Perhaps they are also intrinsically more important. The church lives in conscious compromise with the world. The vitiated sect lives in unconscious compromise with the world. The first attitude may lead to premature defeatism. The second leads to sentimentality and self-deception. In our present state of spiritual life the second peril is greater than the first.

SUNDAY MORNING DEBATE

My wife and I were on our way to the Sunday morning service at the cathedral. To compensate her for the number of times she has to hear me preach I go with her on my two free Sundays of the year to the cathedral. This bargain is further weighted to my advantage by the graceful concession from my wife which permits such tardy arrival that we can miss the sermon and yet hear the litany. "We Anglicans," declared my wife, "do not need a sermon if we have the service. There is more genuine religion in a well-sung litany than in any sermon." I agreed to that. A good boys' choir covers a multitude of sermons, particularly if the sexless and austere beauty of its song echoes through the majestic vaults of a cathedral. It is too bad that there are so few places where you can hear both a vigorous sermon and a good choir.

My spouse countered this by enumerating the parsons in her denomination whom I like to hear preach. There are quite a number, I admit. "You may have more good preachers than we," she said, "but you need them more desperately and do not have them in proportion to your need. We do not need them."

The Numinous Not Enough

I suggested that every church needs them. The sense of the numinous is not enough. Let God impress man not only by the distance between God and man but by specific words of truth out of that distance. I am not ashamed to have the Bible rather than the altar as the center of the nonconformist worship. This is prophetic religion, God speaking to man and not simply man aspiring to the infinite God.

"The Bible is well enough," answered my wife, "but there is a little frock-coated man behind the Bible in your church who sometimes imagines himself God."

We were off on an old argument. The American Protestant church is too secularized, my wife insists, from the sermon on current topics to the nineteenth-century Moody and Sankey lilts. I am inclined to admit that and deplore it. Religion is the dimension of depth in life and the Protestant church does not suggest depth. "But," I ask, "is it possible to create the sense of depth merely by building the high vaults of a cathedral?"

I recalled the words of Solomon: "The Lord hath said that he would dwell in the thick darkness but I have built a house of habitation for thee and a place of thy dwelling forever." Is it really possible, I inquired, to symbolize the majesty of God and the distance between God and man? Isn't it better to let His throne be thick darkness than to build a house? The house will inevitably be for Solomon's glory as much as for the Lord's. It will be intended to glorify a particular church, or perhaps the bishop. (I have heard of a bishop who speaks of *my* cathedral.) It will symbolize pride rather than humility.

At this particular stage of the argument we approached the beautiful new and massive doors of the cathedral, recently dedicated. In one of the panels of the doors we saw engraved, "To the glory of God and in memory of . . ." The memorial was in honor of one of the great financial overlords of the past decade, recently deceased. You see, I observed, these things are never purely for the glory of God. Human pride is always mixed with them. Perhaps we ought not try to symbolize the truths of our religion in stone and steel. The result is usually some unhappy combination of the sense of divine majesty and human pride.

We entered the great unfinished nave of the cathedral. Or rather, it is finished but still empty. I could not deny that its very size and proportions were overawing, prompting a sense of religious awe. Was the emptiness, I wondered, an advantage, giving everyone the opportunity of expressing his specific religious ideas in terms of its great dimension? Or was this perhaps symbolic of the Christian church in our era? An empty gothic church fane of majestic proportions! Let the gothic symbolize what is archaic in the church's message, for surely this gothic does not express anything relevant to the thoughts and aspirations of our generation. Let the emptiness of the unfinished cathedral symbolize that the message of the church is vacuous when it is not archaic. It has nothing to say to this generation that would make the Christian gospel relevant to the problems which we face.

Protestantism's Advantage

I was inclined to insinuate a certain degree of denominational pride into these reveries, as we passed through the long nave. For I thought that a quasi-secular Protestant church with a relevant message might have its advantages over a more religious Catholic church which either had no message or only speaks with the voice of the past. Furthermore, a Protestantism that is not secularized has the possibilities of a greater religious tension than Catholicism. It does not glorify the visible but the invisible church and occasionally some of its prophets find the message in its Bible which reveals both the majesty of God and the relevance of his word to the human heart. In other words, Protestantism is either better or worse than Catholicism. Catholicism symbolizes the eternal in church, edifice, altar, priest, and liturgy. It expresses too exactly what cannot be expressed. That is its virtue and its vice.

It was too late to make these reflections the basis of an argument. We had entered the part of the cathedral where the service was being held. The bishop was still preaching. We arrived at the part of the sermon in which the bishop was telling the congregation how to fight modern paganism which, he said, abounded in modern civilization. "First of all," he declared, "the church must be sure of its own mes-

sage. It must not be afraid to state that it is both supernatural and miraculous."

I failed to understand just how the bold proclamation of
miracles would give modern paganism its *coup de grâce*.
Was the bishop perhaps thinking of the miracle of conversion? But he said nothing about conversion; and one would
hardly expect the miracle of conversion as a natural consequence of a mere faith in miracles. Not being a naturalist,
I didn't mind his emphasis upon supernaturalism, if he had
only said what he meant by it and in what way it was related to the spiritual life. But the bishop's only hint of a
definition implied that he thought there were two layers
of reality, one spiritual and another material.

The Morality of Jesus

The second point of the sermon was that the church must
develop fervent missionary zeal against modern paganism;
but no hint was given of the method in which the zeal
might express itself. I thought we might come to grips with
reality a little more on the third point, because the right
reverend preacher said that the third point of attack was
to uphold the morality of Jesus against the morality of con-
venience. "We must understand that morality is what God
reveals in Christ and not what we may want or desire," he
said. But he made no suggestion of the content of the morality which Christ revealed. He couldn't have meant the
injunction of Jesus, "Sell all thou hast and give it to the
poor." Nor could he have been thinking of the words,
"Resist not him that is evil." At least, I doubt whether that
could have been on his mind, considering the number of
sermons he has preached excoriating pacifists and extolling
the splendors of our navy.

I could make nothing of his idea of Christian morality
except that he seemed to make inconvenience a test of
goodness. Anything which conformed to our desires seemed
to be bad. But just what was it that he regarded as good?
At this point my mind wandered and I thought of the ages

of controversy in moral theology on the validity of the perfectionist principles of the sermon on the mount. Is it possible to make the "morality revealed in Christ" a guide in
specific problems of conduct? And if not, just what kind of
a morality does the church set against the pagan world?

As I summed up the bishop's points I was struck by the
remarkable similarity between the sermon and the cathedral. It was both empty and archaic; or rather it was archaic
when it was not empty. His conception of supernaturalism
was archaic, his idea of missionary zeal was empty and his
exposition of "Christian morality" was both.

Loyalty to the Prayer Book

But I must not forget the final point of the sermon. It
was that the church must resist the pagan world by loyalty
to the prayer book. That evidently limits the hosts of the
Lord to that part of the church which has a prayer book.
In fact the bishop became a little confused at this point
about the relation of his church to the church universal.
He praised the prayer book as "the greatest handbook of
religion of all the ages." As a good Protestant I wanted to
say a word in favor of the Bible, but in the next moment
the bishop became less inclusive and presented the prayer
book as the religious foundation of the Anglican church
and the Anglican church as the universal church of the
"English-speaking world."

But the church which holds such a pre-eminent position
in the English-speaking world, according to the bishop, was
also somehow or other in a special way the apostolic and
universal church. I think the bishop was a little uneasy
about this argument because he tried to bolster it by asserting that there were Anglican churches in every nation of
the world. The argument didn't seem quite fair, considering that some of these churches are little chapels, the chief
purpose of which is to make Englishmen feel at home in a
foreign land. I remembered the disgust with which that
great soul of the Anglican church, the late Studdert-
Kennedy, once reported after a world tour that some of the

churches of his communion seemed to serve the purpose of English clubs among the natives. He might, of course, have observed that the Lutheran church serves the same purpose for Germans in the Balkans and elsewhere.

The Bishop Confused

The bishop was clearly confused in the peroration of his sermon on one of the most fundamental problems of religion, the relation of the transcendent God to the partial, contingent, and relative forms of life and culture with which the worship of God becomes associated and which falsely appropriate the majesty of God for themselves. Even the Catholic church is "Roman" for all of its claims to universality, claims which are historically and geographically more plausible than those of the bishop's church. This is the point where even the best religion becomes evil, trying to domesticate God in some little world of time and place, and imagining that the thunder of His voice betrays some delightfully familiar accents of our particular nation, culture, time, and place. To make a prayer book the source of religious pretension, is that not akin to building a cathedral for the "glory of God" and the incidental aggrandizement of some bishop, donor, or denomination?

Of course, I must not blame the bishop for not solving these vexing problems since they have never been solved. What vexed me was that he didn't seem to be aware of them.

"I assume," said my wife as we left the cathedral, "from the diligent notes you took during the sermon, that you found it very profitable." I confessed that the notes represented a violent debate with the preacher rather than a reverent record of his words. My wife assured me that the confession was unnecessary. She knew very well that when I take notes during a sermon or address I am making ready for debate and not in appreciation.

"If you must debate," she said, "please don't regard everything you hear in my church as typical of my church. What you heard this morning is no more typical of my

church than a holy roller revival meeting is typical of nonconformist Protestantism." I conceded the point and generously remembered that the most saintly Christian I know
is a bishop in her church and that a beautiful service is
really a partial compensation for this kind of sermon. I
even agreed to her contention that some of the frock-
coated, bespatted, and boutonniered ushers in some of our
churches look like floorwalkers in a department store and
are symbols of the secularized church. We finally restored
marital felicity by the mutual agreement to regard what
seemed to be typical in the respective communions as perils
rather than typical realities.

WORSHIP AND THE SOCIAL
CONSCIENCE

What we have to say on the subject of worship and radical
preaching would apply with equal validity to most of the
services of our American Protestant churches. We say it to
radical ministers because they frequently accentuate the
natural weaknesses of the Protestant worship.

There is a crying need for liturgical reform in American
Protestantism. The prayers and the "opening exercises" of
our services are not calculated to arouse and to express religious thoughts and feelings. The minister is too much in the
center of the worship. The prayers are usually formless and
without beauty. The old spontaneity having departed from
the evangelical churches, the prayers which once expressed
a tumultuous religious passion have degenerated into chatty
conversations with God in which, moreover, the minister is
preaching indirectly to his congregation. The same clichés
appear again and again in every prayer. "Bless each and
every one of us." "We thank thee for the opportunity of
worshipping thee this morning." "Bless the speaker of the
morning and endow him with a message from on high" and

countless other stereotyped phrases are repeated *ad nauseam*. Scriptural language and liturgical form are completely absent from the prayers.

Liturgical language and Scriptural phrases are not valuable for their own sake, and we do not ask for more beauty in the worship service as an end in itself. There are, in fact, tendencies in the nonliturgical churches to copy the forms of the liturgical churches which are primarily prompted by aesthetic considerations, and we do not support them. What we need is more spiritual reality in the worship service. This is not possible if the minister does not take his task as priest seriously. The task of the priest is not to speak to God in a casual fashion, making a few desultory remarks which usually combine stereotyped phrases and ideas taken from the morning sermon. The priest must know how to express the basic religious aspirations and feelings of a whole congregation. This is a difficult task which requires a high measure of discipline. The discipline is necessary because the temptation is to forget and to neglect the basic and common and perennial religious needs of all men when the prayer is not carefully prepared.

From the standpoint of radical religion it is particularly important that concern for our social problems should be intimately related to the basic forms of our faith and the whole range of religious attitudes. To illustrate, let us consider the various aspects of prayer in turn.

1. *Praise and Thanksgiving*

The Christian prayer acknowledges God as the author and creator of life. Thanksgiving for the supply of life's necessities can therefore be made an acknowledgement of our sense of stewardship without a too obvious belaboring of the point. Our thanksgiving ought moreover to include gratitude for what we have, not only through the bounties of nature but by the working of an intricate system of service and production in modern society. Thus gratitude to God becomes also an expression of our awareness of our mutual dependence and our indebtedness to all who by their faithfulness in their several callings contribute to our necessities.

2. *Humility and Contrition*

The expression of contrition is a natural consequence of the soul's self-discovery in the sight of God. In worship we become conscious of our violation of the law and the will of God. We confess that we have done the things we ought not to have done and left undone the things which we ought to have done. Usually this confession of sin is too vague and general. It ought to include contrition for the dishonesties and deceits which we practice in our attitude toward social issues, in which we always mix idealism with self-interest. Naturally it will express our sense of responsibility for the collective sins which bring society into constant confusion, the violence of nations, the oppression of the weak, our indifference toward the needy, the pride of the powerful, and the envy and jealousy of the frustrated. Human sin expresses itself in every area of human existence, in secret thought as well as overt deeds, in family life and in the relation of the family toward society. The whole range of human sinfulness cannot be touched in each prayer. It is important therefore to deal with a particular area of human wrongdoing from time to time and search the heart in regard to it. But it is also important to express the relation of sins to each other, particularly their common root in the pride of man and the relation of so-called social sins to individual sins.

3. *Intercession*

Our prayers of intercession express our sense of unity and common responsibility in the sight of God. Sometimes we may limit them to those who are bound to us by the ties of our common faith. At other times we will think of the unity of mankind without regard to this particular bond. We will pray for all "sorts and conditions of men." But to discipline the imagination the sorts and conditions ought to be named and their special needs expressed: the unemployed, the victims of cruelty and oppression, those who live in economic insecurity, the racial minorities who suffer from the arrogance of our race. We might also include in our prayers men of business who stand under particular temptation

that they may regard the services they render as something more than a profit-taking device and the responsible
leaders of government that they may not forget their
sacred trust. At certain times we ought also to include the
various callings and professions, nurses, teachers, doctors,
writers, artisans, housewives, etc., in our intercessions,
remembering their particular duties, temptations, and op-
portunities. Such prayers give specific content to what may
otherwise become a meaningless "Lord bless each and
every one of us."

4. *Aspiration*

The prayer "Thy will be done on earth as it is in heaven"
must take many forms in the pastoral prayer. We will pray
for peace and for a just social order, for the elimination of
particular abuses in our common life, but above all we
will make it a rededication of our own wills to an obedient
love toward God. Sometimes it would be well to meditate
upon the will of God, using various classical Scripture
passages in which the character of His will is expressed.

In summary, our priestly function must be performed in
terms of greater relevance to all the specific problems, personal and social, in which our people stand and in terms
of greater contact with the whole Biblical and religious
tradition of our faith, including the liturgical history of all
the Christian churches. We ought, incidentally, not count
only upon our own resources but use material from all
prayer book sources. Even when we do not use prayers of
the past, just as they have been written, it is well to read
them for the sake of acquiring a decent style. If style may
seem an inconsequential matter to passionate prophets
of the gospel it may be well to remind them that without
it they will merely parade their own personalities and
prejudices in prayer. A good style is a cloak of anonymity.
That cloak is very much needed in our Protestant churches.
We preachers constantly border on the abyss of exhibitionism.

A PROBLEM OF EVANGELICAL CHRISTIANITY

The occasion which prompted these reflections on the state of Evangelical Christianity was an early morning Easter Service in a large movie auditorium. Easter is supremely the climax of the Christian church year. The incredible Easter story of the empty tomb gains credibility only as a part of, and against the background of, the whole Christian story. The Christian faith is, that if we die with Christ we will also be raised with Him. The idea has a double significance. St. Paul seems sometimes to be thinking primarily of the dying to sin and the rising to righteousness, and at other times primarily of the guarantee in Christ of the victory over death.

In any event Easter is a day in which men ought humbly to consider all the false and pretentious ways by which they have sought to live and to cover up the insecurity, frailty, and sinfulness of life; and joyfully to realize that there is forgiveness and resurrection for those who are of penitent heart. It is a question whether any sermon, even the best, can convey the Easter message and hope, if the whole atmosphere of the Gospel is not created and re-created in prayer and song.

Evangelical Christianity in all of its various varieties began as a protest against formal religion. It believed that the formal prayer and the theological subtleties of the traditional church did not sufficiently emphasize that we cannot live with Christ if we will not die with Him. It desires, so to confront the soul with Christ, that as Judge he would drive the old self to despair and that as Redeemer he would transmute despair into repentance; and repentance into new life. Evangelical Christianity desired, in other words, a more powerful impact upon the souls of men than the traditional offices and services of the church afforded.

One could not help but be struck by the sorrowful contrast between the desire and the reality as one worshipped on Easter morning in the movie palace. Nothing symbolizes the tawdriness of our modern culture more obviously than the moving picture palace. Not that any of the nice combinations of sentimentality and eroticism which is the daily fare of the movie audience obtruded this Sunday morning. The palace itself was chaste and free of the usual gimcracks which usually disfigure these places. One had the feeling that the directors of the palace were doing their level best to make the place fit for a Christian service. But such things cannot be done overnight. What was painfully evident was that the most non-Christian form of modern culture cannot provide the forms for a genuine Christian service of worship. The arrangements for the service were obviously left in the hands of the movie people. They did the best they could to transform a movie palace into the semblance of a church. There was a backdrop of a cathedral window. Between the choir and the window was a curious arrangement which might have been intended for an altar laden with Easter lilies. Yet it looked more like a huge coffin, smothered in flowers. Perhaps a cemetery scene was really intended; for before the altar-catafalque was a gilded fence with large gates. On each side stood figures which might have been angels or again they might have been props left over from some medieval décor.

The service began with the house in darkness and the gradual lighting of the stage, symbolizing the Easter dawn. The organist appeared with the spotlight upon him as his console emerged, trickily and automatically from its cubicle to full view. The choir was for some obscure reason gowned in a symphony of colors from deep blue on the outside to bright red at the center. I do not know what this symbolized and could not make up my mind whether it represented something left over from some spectacle or whether the red at the center was meant to be the rising sun. There was the usual rather exhibitionist choir director who spoiled by his antics what would otherwise have been quite acceptable Easter music. This exhibitionist director is one of the symbols of what the evangelical church has in common with the theater.

The whole trouble was that the movie people were quite obviously intent upon producing a "spectacle." This is what they are adept in. They wanted it to be subdued and solemn, but nevertheless a spectacle. They quite obviously wanted to make a real contribution to "religion." Here was a church service with so little of its own to go on that movie technic could dominate the spirit of it completely. The one adequate note of Christian faith and hope was expressed in a brief and simple but adequate and helpful sermon on the text "Thanks be to God who giveth us the victory through our Lord Jesus Christ."

Perhaps one ought not to be too critical. I am sure that the leaders of united Protestantism in our city were grateful that this great movie palace was filled with seven thousand worshippers at 7 A.M. on Easter morning. But the real trouble lies with the fact that we were not worshippers and could not be. There was nothing in the symbolism or in the service which might prompt us to behold the "beauty of the Lord" or His Majesty or the mystery of His Mercy. There was of course a "general" prayer which touched upon the themes of the Christian faith but no great act of adoration and praise, of penitence and contrition. Here there was no chance to confess that our life, as "carnally minded" leads to death, and to praise God for the grace by which death can be transformed into life, love, joy, and peace. One must not put too much emphasis upon a single service or upon a single symbol of the religious inadequacy of modern Evangelical Protestantism. The service had significance chiefly because it revealed the tragic problem of modern Protestantism. The formlessness of its worship sometimes achieves its own form in the simplicity of a village meeting house. But this formlessness is inadequate when confronted with the potent forms created by a modern secular culture. The forms of that culture suggest a content; and it is not the Christian content. The Evangelical Christianity of the frontier of yesterday cannot be transported into the highly competitive cultural currents of a modern metropolis and maintain itself without more adequate instruments. The old Evangelical spontaneity is lost in any event even in the village chapel. The Christian faith requires conduits of an adequate theology, an adequate liturgy and an adequate symbolism of worship. These forms are always in danger of becoming empty and require periodic protests against "devotion's every grace except the heart." But religious spontaneity without adequate forms degenerates into something even more graceless than a graceless formalism. It degenerates into a void which is filled by the potent symbols of a cinema secularism.

I left the "dawn" service and betook myself to a liturgical church and participated in Holy Communion with my family. The simple Communion service offered the possibility for the expression of every genuine Christian impulse of worship, and contained all the sublime affirmations of the Christian faith and hope.

The service held me completely enough so that it was only after it was over that I speculated ruefully upon the fact that I could not have received communion in this church except for the fact that the church was touched by the slightly heretical broadmindedness which the academic community had imparted to it. The liturgical churches, whether Lutheran or Episcopalian, fail to help the main body of Christianity in America because they set up barriers to fellowship, more formidable than is necessary to guard their peculiar treasures of faith and tradition. Thus they retain as a peculiar possession what should be flowing into the whole body of the church.

Our problem would not of course be solved by merely imitating their forms. Already that is producing in some nonliturgical churches theatrical versions of a liturgy and forms in which a sentimental aestheticism is more obvious than a Biblically inspired common worship.

The Christian faith in America faces many perplexing problems in expressing itself adequately amidst the confusions of modern culture and civilization. The problem which was illumined by this Easter service may not be the most primary. But it is certainly important. Ought there not be in America some real movement for the reconsideration of the relation of faith to worship and of worship to forms? Are not the experiences of our chaplains in the army proof of the same void which this Easter service revealed?

THE RELIGIOUS PLURALISM
OF AMERICA

The preceding article by Dr. Alec Vidler, editor of *Theology* and librarian at St. Deiniol's Library at Hardwarden, England, was written at our request.● Dr. Vidler is at present on a visit in this country and we were certain that his critical view of our religious life would be of great value to American Christians. We feel compelled to take issue with him on his criticism of our religious pluralism, all the more so because we are afraid that what will seem an unjustified indictment on this point may detract from the power of his general (and it seems to us justified) criticism of the "religiousness" of American churches.

The religious pluralism of America has its own special history, being partly the consequence of transplanting European "national" churches to a new nation into which they carry their old national ethos and partly the result of the protest of the sectarian and exclusive religious community against "national" and inclusive churches. Dr. Vidler seems to recognize no validity in this radical protest against churches which are too closely identified with the ethos of a nation. He seems to regard a "national" church as having some kind of special Scriptural warrant. Whatever the weaknesses of the "sectarian" church, which has set the pattern for American church life, one should think the prevailing secularism of modern culture, might give the

● "The Appalling Religiousness of America," pp. 4-5, same issue.

idea of an exclusive church a new validity. Is there any value in a "national" church pretending to be the whole nation at prayer when it is, as a matter of fact, a minority group within the nation, not only in a culture which is, like our own, officially secular, but also in European nations which are officially Christian but not actually so?

It would be wrong to be complacent about the anarchy of American religious pluralism. We are only slowly overcoming it, but perhaps not more slowly than European established churches are able to include dissenting churches into their fellowship. Dr. Vidler does not want to accept any present "established" church as the truly national church. But the higher degree of religious unity in European nations depends altogether upon the supremacy of such established churches; and their inability to find a common ground with dissenting bodies is derived precisely from the pretension that they are in some ultimate sense "the" national church.

One further question must be asked: If we are to insist with such emphasis as Dr. Vidler on "national" churches, what is to become of "Christ's Church"? Is not the national ethos which colors the church life of each nation a peril to the ecumenical movement, and do not all national churches assume that the contingent historical forces, which molded their history, have a universal validity?

THE WEAKNESS OF COMMON WORSHIP IN AMERICAN PROTESTANTISM

In almost every Christian movement of the world, concerned with the revitalization of the life of the church, liturgical reform, or at least liturgical concern, is one of its aspects. This is true everywhere except in America, where the concern should be greatest because the need is so urgent. Sometimes liturgical reform movements are interested in reclaiming some forgotten treasure of worship in the life of the church. Sometimes they seek to make the prayers of the church more relevant to the peculiar problems of our age; and sometimes, as in the more liturgical churches, they seek to relate the worship of the church more closely to its sacramental life.

In America there is no such movement. Perhaps this proves that it is possible for a church to lose a traditional treasure of grace so completely that it is not even conscious of a loss. The nonliturgical churches of America have felt inadequacy in their worship services at only one point. They have sensed a certain aesthetic inadequacy and have sought to overcome this by vested choirs, sung reponses to prayers, and rearrangement of the chancel to make the altar or communion table, rather than the pulpit, the focus of attention for the congregation. Sometimes silent prayers with soft organ music are added. The "free prayers," or the pastoral prayers of the minister, are not as formless as they once were. They do not as frequently begin with the phrase "We thank Thee Our Father that Thou hast permitted us to come together this morning." But they very frequently supplant the old banality and crude immediacy with a new sentimentality and rather too-purple poetry.

Since we rightly pride ourselves in America upon intimate ecumenical relations which permit the churches to borrow each other's treasures of grace, it is somewhat surprising that this mutual exchange has taken place so little in the field of common worship. Here nothing has happened but the appropriation of some of the "trappings" of liturgical worship.

The deficiencies in a large number of nonliturgical churches could be briefly enumerated as follows:

1. The pastoral prayer is both too long and too formless. The free worship gives too much freedom to the minister to speak to God without reference to the spiritual needs of the congregation. Instead of a long prayer, a series of short prayers, each devoted to a particular concern of the spiritual life is more likely to carry the con-

gregration with it. A bidding which announces the subject of the prayer is also very helpful. A rambling prayer in which various concerns are expressed without logical coherence is a kind of "performance" but not an act of "common worship."

2. Without the discipline of traditional and historic prayers there is a tendency to neglect some of the necessary and perennial themes of prayer: praise and thanksgiving, confession, dedication, intercession, etc. Sometimes when these various themes are in the prayer they are scattered about to such a degree that the thanksgiving fails to deal adequately with "all the blessings of this life" and the confession is not a significant expression of contrition for the worshipper's involvement in the evils of the world.

3. The language of the prayers of common worship is either too common, too sentimental, or too extravagant. The effort to make worship more "beautiful" has in recent decades tended to substitute rather extravagant poetic phrases for the original banality and commonness. What is still lacking is chastity. Chastity of phrase does not preclude poetic rhythm. The fact is that prayers should have something of the quality of good poetry; for worship must avail itself of the highest arts in the realm of speech as well as in music and in the graphic arts. The prayers should, furthermore, contain both Biblical material and Biblical phraseology. If this is done to excess the relevance of the Biblical faith to contemporary experience may be obscured. If it is not done at all the contemporary experience is not transfigured by the Biblical insight.

4. The use of Biblical ideas in prayer is necessary not merely to purify the expressions but to correct the thought. Most free prayers at funerals, for instance, tend to become heretical in their sentimentality; for they usually assure the eternal bliss of the dear departed on the basis of his good works on earth. A closer relation to Biblical truth would inevitably result in an expression of the Biblical faith that all of us, even the best, are in the final instance dependent upon God's mercy and forgiveness.

The lack of influence from either the Bible or the great

traditions of common prayer tend to betray the prayer to a consideration of the immediate situation to the exclusion of the total human situation. Thus, for instance, when pastors gather together in their monthly meeting to hear a visiting speaker, the prayers frequently consist of elaborate thanksgiving for the talents of the visiting speaker, and equally elaborate prayers for the inspiration of his message and expressions of the hope that his message may bear fruit in the hearts of his listeners. As one who is frequently made the subject of such prayers I must confess to an embarrassment not because I do not greatly need the inspiration which is the object of the intercession, but because a puny individual is made the center of concern. Obviously in such a situation the center of attention should be the "whole estate of Christ's church," thanksgiving for its unity, contrition for its divisions, and a meaningful relation of the church, as a community of grace to the whole range of problems in the communities of the world.

5. The free worship tends to be too personal in every respect. It centers too frequently in the personality of the leader of worship. Personalities are exchanged in the introduction of the preacher which are sometimes humorous, sometimes banal, and almost always quite unnecessary. The forms and traditions of the liturgical churches tend to hide the personal idiosyncrasies of the preacher and to guard against the temptations of exhibitionism. These temptations are much more considerable than is usually recognized.

6. The reading of the Scripture in Protestant worship leaves much to be desired. First of all, churches have almost completely dispensed with the reading of two lessons, taken either from the Epistles on the one hand and the Gospels on the other, or from the Old Testament on the one hand and the New Testament on the other. In consequence, the modern congregation, whose intimacy with Scripture is precarious in any event, is not instructed in Biblical thought; and the Old Testament becomes an almost completely unknown book. In the reading of the Scripture there is moreover a curious formality in contrast to the informality of the rest of the service. No word of

explanation of a Biblical phrase or paragraph is ever offered during the reading, though such a brief word would frequently make what seems irrelevant, relevant to the experience and the understanding of the congregation.

7. The participation of the congregation in the worship service is too minimal. When nonliturgical churches introduce responses to prayers, they usually limit them to sung responses by the choir but not by the congregation. There are nonliturgical churches that have books of common worship; but frequently they are not used. Some churches do not possess them. Without such forms it is very difficult to secure adequate participation of the congregation in the service. One of the most important problems confronting us in this whole realm is to help the congregation become a worshipping body, knit together as a community by its worship so that it will not be an audience, for which a kind of preacher-choir performance is being staged.

8. Choir music in the nonliturgical churches and in some liturgical ones is still affected by the sentimentality which began to corrupt religious music in the latter part of the last century. The soprano solo is still too frequently the main offering. Even the most modest church should have a choir; and the choir would do better to sing one of the great chorales than to present some insipid modern concoction. The paid quartet is usually no more integrated into the whole economy of worship than is the soprano with her solo. It is fortunate that choirs have increasingly achieved robes. A great deal of distraction has thus been avoided. But this remains a rather external advantage if the music of the choir is not more genuinely a part of the worship service than is usually the case.

All these detailed criticisms of banalities, sentimentalities, and lack of beauty, decorum, and religious breadth and depth in public worship, deal only with symptoms. Something more fundamental than a deterioration of aesthetic standards is responsible for the condition of public worship. The proof that this is so lies in the fact that a mere lifting of standards aesthetically still leaves much to be desired. The fact is that American Protestant-

ism is founded upon sectarian protests against preoccupation with theology, liturgy, and polity in the more orthodox
churches. These protests had their validity in their day;
for it is manifest again and again in the life of the church,
that the various disciplines of the church which are properly means of grace may also become corrupters of grace.
Liturgical worship may possess "devotions every grace
except the heart." Theology may destroy the vitality of
faith. Preoccupation with the polity and organization
of the church may express pride rather than the spirit of
fellowship. The protest against all these disciplines was
supported by the authority of the Pauline word "the letter
killeth but the spirit maketh alive." The letter does indeed
destroy spirit if it means a preoccupation with minutiae
of forms. But spirit without discipline, form, and tradition
is also vain. The trouble with American Protestantism is
that its protest against the various forms and disciplines led
to their destruction. It may be possible to have a brief
period of religious spontaneity in which the absence of
such disciplines does not matter. The evangelism of the
American frontier may have been such a period. But this
spontaneity does not last forever. When it is gone a church
without adequate conduits of traditional liturgy and theological learning and tradition is without the waters of
life.

In a sense the formless exuberance of American church
architecture in most of the churches built between 1870
and 1930 is a perfect expression of the formlessness inside
the church. Neither Gothic architecture nor the chaste
New England meeting house are the only possible archi-
tecturally-poetic frames to outwardly symbolize the spiritual reality of the church. A vital Christianity will express
itself in new architectural forms or in novel adaptations of
old forms to the new realities of a technical society. But
American church architecture in the period mentioned
revealed no discipline of any kind. It was merely the expression of free imagination and the fruit of some architect's conviction that a church should not look like a grain
elevator. Therefore it was distinguished from the latter by

as many turrets, arches, and other curious gingerbread as the architect could dream up.

It is neither necessary nor possible for the "free churches" to return to the traditional forms of the liturgical churches. There can well be more freedom and spontaneity than these forms allow. But the more vital liturgical churches have actually achieved a considerable freedom beyond their traditional forms, in the use of prayers, for instance, which are not in the prayer book, but which extend the spirit of the prayer book to contemporary occasions. It is necessary, however, that the free prayer become thoroughly informed by the whole Biblical faith and by the spirit and the form of the traditional disciplines. That such an end is possible is proved by the type of worship which we find in the Church of Scotland for instance. For there the pastoral prayers have achieved a Biblical form and comprehensiveness which our prayers lack; and the spirit of the service has a stateliness and dignity which we have not achieved.

It is rather suprising how little this matter of worship has been made an object of concern in the ecumenical church. This is a field in which churches of various traditions ought humbly to seek to learn of one another no less than in the field of religious thought, in which ecumenical exchange and mutuality is an established reality.

RELIGIOSITY AND THE
CHRISTIAN FAITH

A visitor to our shores would probably come to the same conclusion at which St. Paul arrived in regard to the Athenians, namely, that we are "very religious." But the judgment might not imply a compliment any more than Paul wanted to so imply when he called attention to the worship of many gods in Athens, including the "unknown god." Our religiosity seems to have as little to do with the Christian faith as the religiosity of the Athenians.

The "unknown god" in America seems to be faith itself. Our politicians are always admonishing the people to have "faith." Sometimes they seem to imply that faith is itself redemptive. Sometimes this faith implies faith in something. That something is usually an idol, rather than the "God and father of our Lord Jesus Christ," who both judges and has mercy upon sinful men and nations. Sometimes we are asked to have faith in ourselves, sometimes to have faith in humanity, sometimes to have faith in America. Sometimes, it is hope, rather than faith, which is really intended. We are to have hope that we will win the cold war or that the cold war will not break out into an atomic conflict.

These provisional hopes are no doubt rather better than despair, for desperate actions and policies are generated in despair. But the objects of faith are almost always idolatrous. For whether it is in ourselves, or in mankind, or in civilization, or in America, that we are asked to have faith, the admonition always points to an object of faith which is less than God and which certainly does not deserve unreserved commitment or adoration. The question is whether a generation which has lost its faith in all the gods of the nineteenth century, that is, in "history," or "progress," or "enlightenment," or the "perfectibility of man," is not expressing its desire to believe in something, to be committed somehow, even though it is not willing to be committed to a God who can be known only through repentance, and whose majesty judges all human pretensions. It is precisely faith in this God which is avoided in all this religiosity. A nation as powerful and fortunate as ours is not inclined to worship a God before whom "the nations are as a drop in the bucket," and "who bringeth princes to naught." Our modern religiosity, in short, expresses various forms of self-worship. It is a more specifically religious ethos than the so-called "secular" faiths which history in our tragic age has refuted. The strategy seems to be to bring the discredited pagan gods in Christian disguises, hoping that the traditional piety may be merged with the secular forms of self-confidence.

The cause of this procedure seems to be that we are so sure of ourselves, or our power and of our virtue, and yet we are not sure of our destiny at all. We live on the edge of an abyss, and at any moment our private securities may be swallowed in the world-wide insecurity. The religiosity which seems to correspond to this combination of self-esteem and anxiety would seem to be a secular faith clothed in traditional terms. The most disquieting aspect of such religiosity is that it is frequently advanced by popular leaders of the Christian church, and is not regarded as a substitute, but as an interpretation of that faith. The Gospel admonition, "Repent ye for the kingdom of heaven is at hand," this challenge to submit all our achievements and ambitions and hopes to a much higher judge than those judges who support our self-esteem, this admonition would seem to have little affinity with the "power of positive thinking."

It is significant that while this modern religiosity makes for self-esteem, particularly collective self-esteem, the nation is helped to find and to hold its rightful place in the perilous position of leadership in the alliance of free nations by many shrewd and critical "secular" thinkers who help us to weigh our responsibilities and judge the hazards of the task in which we are engaged. One must come to the conclusion that religion *per se* and faith *per se* are not virtuous, or a cause of virtue. The question is always what the object of worship is, and whether the worship tends to break the pride of the self so that a truer self may arise, either individually or collectively. If worship and faith do not serve this rebirth of men and of nations they are the source of confusion. We can, therefore, take no satisfaction in the pervading religiosity of our nation. Much of it is a perversion of the Christian gospel. It aggravates, rather than mitigates, the problems of a very successful people.

It will be remembered that the prophet Jeremiah was worried about the false prophets who did not speak "the word of the Lord" but spoke their own dreams and imaginations. He had a test for detecting false prophecy. The false prophet was one who accentuated complacency and promised those who despised God, "you shall have assured peace in this place." It is as difficult in our day as in the day of Jeremiah to preach "the word of the Lord," for that runs counter to the complacency of men and of nations. It is sharper than a "two-edged sword." It must hurt before it can heal.

PART II: *Can the Church Give a "Moral Lead"?*

THE WEAKNESS OF THE
MODERN CHURCH

Superficially considered the Protestant churches of America are the most vital churches of the Western world. Their public prestige may not approximate that of the English churches in quality, but they hold the allegiance of the masses to a larger degree. In Germany Protestantism has become a middle-class minority movement to a marked degree, and it has begun to take the disaffection of the great working classes for granted. Among us, where class consciousness is less marked, the church may be predominantly middle class, but it has not sacrificed the loyalty of the working classes completely. Whatever the weakness of the puritan tradition which informs the moral attitude of American Protestantism, it has considerable achievements to its credit. It has made for wholesomeness in family relations, for diligence and thrift in ecomonic life, and for rather generous philanthropic attitudes. The wealth of the nation may now be corroding some of the puritan virtues; yet there can be no question but that the puritan tradition made for robust self-discipline, without which the nation would have succumbed to the vices of sensuality more quickly than it did.

But in spite of these solid achievements the religious life of America is not in good health. One must suspect, in fact, that such vitality as the church evinces is partly analogous to the contortions of a feverish patient whose sickness drives him to fretful activity, though his strength is waning. The basic difficulty of the church is that it is not facing the central moral problems of our era. It maintains ethical attitudes in the interstices of our civilization, but does not build them into its structure. It embroiders life with its little amenities, but it does not change the pattern. The dominant pattern of social activity in our society is that of profit-seeking. The constitution of our civilization was written by Adam Smith, who gave himself to the illusion that each man could be selfish without any other restraint but that which the selfishness of others offered, so that a society of selfish individuals would nevertheless create a social harmony. This is the creed by which America lives, whatever its protestations. In Europe this individualism has long since been qualified to a large degree. In America our great wealth obscured the defects of an individualistic system until a very recent past.

The church has a gospel of love, which ought to have given it the insight to recognize the basic fallacy of the assumptions upon which our civilization organized its life. There is a word in the church's Scripture which it might have heeded more earnestly: "From whence come wars and fighting among you? Come they not hence, even from your lusts that war in your members? Ye lust and have not; ye kill and can not obtain; ye fight and war, and yet ye have not because ye ask not." Unrestrained economic selfishness, unchecked by adequate social control and increasingly free of the inner checks of a vital religion has piled up social injustice until America has become the enigma of the Western world. Strangers speak with amazement of a nation as rich as ours which permits millions of unemployed to beg the bitter bread of charity while thousands who gambled on the stock market live in luxury without disgorging their gain.

The gambling fever which possessed the country between 1925 and 1929 was not effectively checked by religion. Only a few voices in the church were raised against it, in spite of the fact that the desire to get something for nothing, which prompted it, is clearly contrary to any ethical view of life. Disaster followed upon this carnival of greed and riotous living, and today millions live in the misery of poverty and insecurity. The church is laudably busy in alleviating the sufferings of the unemployed. But any church that has gone into a thorough program of unemployment relief must know how absolutely unsatisfactory private charity is in such a crisis. What is needed is a sense of responsibility on the part of the whole of society for the needs of all its members. In regard to the needs of such a crisis as the present, that sense of responsibility must express itself in terms of social insurance, which happily some churches are beginning to advocate.

However, modern society can not be saved by this or that social reform, and selfish individuals are not brought to express themselves in Christlike terms by the advocacy in the pulpit of this or that radical measure. The church may well leave specific programs to other agencies provided, however, that it deal rigorously and honestly with the ethical problems of human nature and human society. It is at this point that the church fails most grievously. The orthodox church still convicts people of sin, but the sins of which it makes people conscious are usually not those which are most significant in our society; and the liberal church takes such a romantic view of human nature that it does not convict its members of sin at all. A religious institution which does not deal with kind and yet brutal frankness with human nature, and which does not make an astute analysis of the motives which drive men to action, may become very dangerous, because it may easily lead to hypocrisy.

To profess a gospel of love without letting that gospel convict each one of us of sinful selfishness means merely that we will suffer from the illusion that our actions have been brought into conformity with the ideal we profess, when in reality our ideal merely obscures the ethically indifferent character of our motives. The gospel of love and holiness has been at war with the immediate impulses of human nature from the very beginning. It is not maintained that a new malice has entered the human heart in our age which would make the preaching of repentance more needed than in other ages. But it is probably true that that selfishness expresses itself in greed and in the lust for power more unrestrainedly in our civilization than in any other.

We are living in a world in which the essential power is economic power. The men who hold this power either cynically or naively beat back every effort to restrict its force and to bring it under social control. They may reveal many amenities in their lives and may, in their intimate relationships, express themselves with charming grace. They may even be quite honest in their business dealings, though that may not mean too much, for a civilization which gives the profit motive rather unrestricted sway has curious standards of honesty. Now if a religious and ethical institution is unable to deal realistically and honestly with the human motives which express themselves in this power and in the insistence upon its maintenance, all of its claims to moral leadership must become hollow pretensions.

Let us make this very specific. Here is a good and pious member of a church who owns a factory. The factory makes such good profits that the directors decide to capitalize the income. They sell three million dollars worth of stock, the proceeds of which they pocket, except for one-third of it which is put into capital equipment. The workers in the factory are unorganized. Their wages average $25 per week. They have no protection against unemployment. They are, as a matter of fact, on a two-day week at the present time, and have nothing but a meager two-days' wage for their weekly sustenance. The majority stockholder has meanwhile made a handsome contribution to his church, which was received with uncritical and extravagant praise on the part of the leaders of the church, and there was in their gratitude the broad suggestion that he had really reached the last and perfect stage of Christian morality.

Meanwhile he lived in a gorgeous mansion, which must have cost him more than a quarter of a million dollars, and his yearly expenses could hardly be less than a hundred thousand dollars. His benevolences really represent the crumbs which fall from Dives table. He might have been much more generous than he was without making anything which could be called a sacrifice according to Christian standards. Having many friends in the bond business, it might be added that he took some fliers in stocks not connected with his business. Most of his profits have vanished since the stock-market crash in 1929, but that does not change his intention. He was perfectly willing to regard American industry as a Christmas tree which offered rich fruits to those who knew how to pluck them. He seemed perfectly oblivious to the social and moral implications of stock-market transactions, which loaded industry with a vast burden of ownership obligations, while the workers sought in vain for elemental security. In a recent drive for unemployment relief he gave $25,000, and honestly imagined himself very generous because he had counted his paper profits to his wealth, and pitied himself when he lost it.

The man I describe may be quite sincere within the limits of his social intelligence. He lives in a world in which privilege is taken for granted, and he does not think of himself as living luxuriously. Nor does he fully realize what the social consequences of his economic greed are. But if the Christian church to which he belongs does not help him to realize this, it is hardly true to its own highest insights. It has a gospel which proclaims that greatness must be measured in terms of service, and that self-realization comes through forgetting oneself.

This man finds greatness in the power he holds and realizes himself in the expression of his power. His benevolences are only incidental to this central passion of his life. Has the church ever helped him to analyze himself? Has it disclosed to him how sweet the lust of power is and how easily it is rationalized? Has it ever confronted him with himself? After all, that is one of the chief functions of vital religion. An honest religious experience makes the soul conscious of its own inadequacies and sins as it feels itself in the presence of God. That is why, when religion has achieved great vitality it has always produced a few ascetics who were so conscious of the demoniac power in the acquisitive instinct that they throttled it altogether.

The modern church turns its back upon this asceticism; but is it not blind to the moral sensitiveness which is at the root of asceticism, and does it produce anything commensurate with that kind of moral sensitivity? Our churches are filled with people who have never made an honest analysis of their own motives. They try to deceive their fellows with moral pretensions largely because they are themselves self-deceived. And sometimes their piety is one of the forces which is consciously or unconsciously appropriated for the purpose of maintaining this deception.

It is not only in helping people make an honest self-analysis that the modern church fails. It fails also to make a rigorous analysis of society for the benefit of those it claims to lead. Most men can not see very far. Their injustices are partly due to their blindness. They do not know what kind of a world they live in. They imagine that America is a thoroughly generous nation while the fact is that America, like all other nations, expresses itself in terms of economic greed in its relationship to other nations, the most significant aspect of its foreign policy at the present time being that it desires to sell other nations more goods than it is willing to buy from them. This policy is prompted to a degree by the fact that our workers do not get enough wages to buy the products of our own machines, and we must get rid of the surplus in foreign markets. Our present depression is partly caused by the fact that there is an increasing resentment in the outside world against this unmutual conduct. Does the church acquaint its members with the moral implication of this policy?

Or again the members of the church believe that every worker, if only he is diligent, will gain sufficient rewards, and that if workers are poor, that is because they are lazy. That creed is a part of the individualism which we have inherited from the past and which is thoroughly irrelevant to the facts of modern civilization. The fact is that the modern machine is displacing workers so rapidly that some two million of them could not find work even before this depression came upon us.

Does the church help its members to see this fact in modern life? Many of its members imagine that the workers have no right to organize because the owners know what is best for them, and are wise enough to pay them what they are worth. If the church is adequate to its task of moral leadership it will set present problems in the light of history. The average man does not know history. It would be well if the church helped him to see that history proves rather conclusively that benevolent despots have never been as benevolent as they imagined themselves to be. Such is the inevitable defect in the human imagination that we never quite see the interests of others as clearly as we see our own. The wise man will therefore conclude that he will never deal ethically with his fellowman, if his fellowman does not have the opportunity to match power with power.

A man of really great social intelligence would have to come to the conclusion that his workers must be organized so that they may help him to deal ethically with them. He will not trust himself. Only those who do not know history can stand in such naive confidence of their own virtue. They have a right to expect that the church will illumine their darkness by letting the light of history shine upon it.

Or again the members of the church live luxuriously and justify themselves to society and their own conscience with the excuse that their luxuries help to keep people at work. It is difficult to believe that they are honest in this conviction, but some of them are. It would be rather easy to prove to them that no amount of luxury will provide as much work as could be provided if families which now live on $1,500 per year could have at least $2,000. Both from an ethical and an economic standpoint the salvation of our society depends upon a more equitable distribution of income, and luxury expenditure as a substitute for this social end is a travesty. People of ordinary intelligence can be made to realize this with a little, or perhaps with constant, social education.

All this may seem to suggest that the church should engage too much in political education. But it need not become political at all if it will only interpret its gospel of love in terms relevant to the life of our day. Surely it is obvious enough that a high ethical ideal such as the church holds and which it can not escape, not only because the authority of its revered Lord is behind it but because the experience of history makes the logic of that gospel irrefutable, is a great peril. No institution can hold and proclaim such a gospel without sinking into hypocrisy if it does not subject itself to constant self-analysis.

Hypocrisy is so easy because subterfuges and substitutes for the real gospel are so ready to hand. A little philanthropy, a little honesty, a little decency in personal relations, a little kindliness in intimate contacts seems to put the mark of a Christian upon a character. But the illusion is transitory and those who suffer from economic greed cry with louder and ever more strident voices against the deception which these little amenities create. Either the church must take its gospel of love seriously in this world and apply it to the important relationships of life or it will die with our dying civilization.

What is needed to make this gospel effective is a combination of two qualities which are not always combined with ease: spiritual vigor and social intelligence. The spiritual vigor is needed to create in men the desire to check their expansive desires and to bring their clamant self-will under the will of God. So powerful are the forces of self that only a powerful religious devotion can bring them in check. But sometimes the religious fervor which creates the will to live the Christlike life is not accompanied with sufficient social intelligence to know what the Christlike ethic is. Therefore social education must accompany religious regeneration.

Some of the Christians of our day have no honest desire to live as God wants them to live with their fellows. They must be literally reborn. But there are others who are too ignorant to bring their life into a really social and ethical relationship with their brothers. They must be guided and instructed. The more intricate and complicated our modern life becomes the more necessary is education as a part of the redemptive process. The churches which frown upon education and continue to create moral sentiment in vacuum without channeling this moral sentiment into the areas where its application is needed are self-deceived. It is only in rare cases that moral good-will makes itself effective automatically. It must be directed. In the process of that direction the church will always be skirting the edges of pure politics and pure economics, which does not belong in its sphere.

There is some danger there; but there is greater danger in the policy of avoiding contentious issues. That policy leads inevitably to moral mediocrity. To advocate what everyone accepts means to advocate less than the best. To champion only conventional virtue means to play truant to a great task in a morally confused age. "Except your righteousness exceed the righteousness of the scribes and pharisees you can not enter the kingdom of heaven," Jesus declared, and that word is a perpetual challenge to the church in every age. The church of our age has not yet met that challenge.

If the church could attack the problems of our era with vigor and realism it might make greater progress in the important problem of church unity. Lacking organic relationship to our society, the churches are forced to preserve ancient traditions and maintain themselves by the perpetuation of loyalties which had significance only for the past. Denominationalism is becoming constantly less defensible because the loyalties and credos which divide the churches have less and less meaning. Our fathers could be denominationalists with honesty because they sincerely believed that they were defending righteous and important principles. We support our separate organizations without any great confidence that the various policies and principles which divide us are important, except, perhaps, as matters of taste.

But unity is not achieved as an end in itself. It is always the product of companionship in arms in a common cause. If the church could see the paganism of our civilization in sufficiently sharp outline and could sense the fundamental conflict between its gospel and the dominant moods of our civilization it would inevitably close its ranks for common action. In so far as it has actually done this it has been due to a recognition of this conflict. In so far as it has not closed ranks it proves that it is living on the heritage of the past without re-creating spiritual vitality in terms meaningful to our own generation.

MORALISTS AND POLITICS

The political discussion and controversy which the depression has prompted and the numerous pronouncements on politics made by moralists, lay and clerical, secular and religious, in the past months even before the political campaign is well under way, give overwhelming proof of the unrealistic approach of moralists to political problems. The metropolitan press has been filled for the last few weeks with commencement-day addresses made by college presidents and other savants who tried to justify the wisdom of the honorary degrees, just conferred upon them, by sage advice to the younger generation. The sentimentality and futility of most of these remarks fills the heart with dismay. The tenor of most of them was to the effect that the world was in a very evil plight, that greed and stupidity had brought it to its present pass, that the hope of the future lay in the younger generation whose college education guaranteed, or promised, at least, a more enlightened social attitude than that of their fathers, and whose youth would offer the dynamic necessary to build a new world order. Yet most of these same college graduates had voted only two weeks previously, in those inane elections which most senior classes conduct, that Mussolini was their favorite world figure and that Hoover was entitled to re-election.

Religious Idealism

The clerical words of wisdom have a slightly different note. The emphasis, in diagnosing the world's ills, is placed upon greed and "materialism" rather than stupidity, and the young men and women are advised that only a return to the religion of Jesus will solve our generation's problems.

In so far as genuine religious idealism and real social intelligence are absolute prerequisites of a social politic
adequate to the needs of our day, all this advice is sound
enough. It fails not in what is said but in what remains
unsaid. Hardly anywhere, from either academic or ecclesiastical political moralist does one hear a word about the
limits of morality in politics. The impression is imparted
that it is possible to secure sufficient social intelligence
and religious dynamic to change a social order without
any further difficulty. If only more people would attend
church or go to college, the rich who now have too much
of the world's goods would divest themselves of their
privileges and create justice within and between the nations. This easy solution for the world's ills is offered in
spite of the fact that the whole history of the human race
is a testimony to its error. It is not one bit advanced over
the romantic hopes of the eighteenth century which expected the Kingdom of God just as soon as the printed
word became ubiquitous and universal suffrage general.

There is no political realism in all this moralism. It does
not deal with the fact that human groups, classes, nations,
and races are selfish, whatever may be the moral idealism
of individual members within the groups; that this selfishness has something of the order of nature in it, predatory
man expressing himself in his collective capacity long after
he has been tamed in his individual capacity; that the
selfishness of human groups is not only "natural" but in a
sense diabolical, since human ingenuity arms the primitive
lusts of collective man and sharpens the teeth of the human beast of prey; that every human group which benefits
from a present order of society will use every ingenuity
and artifice to maintain its privileges and to sanctify them
in the name of public order; that political life is, in short,
a thinly veiled barbarism.

Thinly Veiled Barbarism

Overt violence is not necessary to reveal that fact. The
unwillingness of rich taxpayers to pay enough taxes to keep

the unemployed from starving is a proof of it. The stupidity of America and the pitiful combination of fear and hatred in France which is slowly strangling Germany under the reparations load and creating thereby the chaos and hatred which it fears, is proof of it. The willingness of barons of industry to use machine guns against striking workers, rather than permit their organization, is proof of it. The tendency of all efforts at interracial cooperation to accomplish little more than spin a thin veil of moral idealism under which the white man does not really hide his determination to maintain the Negro in a subordinate position in our civilization, is further proof of it. The fact that all projected solutions of our social problem emanating from the enlightened members of the privileged group, whether Gerard Swope, Owen Young, Howard Coffin, or any other, betray the philosophy of Fascism only thinly disguised, offering to meet the threat of social disorder not by social reorganization but by a more enlightened and more vigorous affirmation of the present social order, is additional proof of it.

Coercion and Persuasion

What the moralists, intellectual and religious, fail to understand, though it is written on every page of past and contemporary history, is that politics is an area in which the rational and the brutal, the moral and the predatory, the human and the subhuman are compounded in perplexing and infinite variety. That combination is present, in a measure, in all human activity. But it is particularly apparent in man's collective activity. Even the religious group is inherently imperialistic and merges its life with other groups only under the threat of a common foe, secularism, Catholicism, or what not.

Political strategy, therefore, always involves a combination of coercive and persuasive factors. Sentimental moralism which underestimates the necessity of coercion, and cynical realism which is oblivious to the possibilities of moral suasion are equally dangerous to the welfare of mankind. The former spends its energies in vain efforts to achieve a purely voluntary reorganization of society; the latter resorts to violent conflict and makes confusion worse confounded. The welfare of society demands that enough social intelligence and moral idealism be created to prevent social antagonism from issuing in pure conflict and that enough social pressure be applied to force reluctant beneficiaries of social privilege to yield their privileges before injustice prompts to vehemence and violence.

Practically, this means that the Negro will never win his full rights in society merely by trusting the fairness and sense of justice of the white man. Whatever increase in the sense of justice can be achieved will mitigate the struggle between the white man and the Negro, but it will not abolish it. Neither will the Negro gain justice merely by turning to violence to gain his rights. To do so means that he will accentuate the vices of the white man. If he is well advised he will use such forms of economic and political pressure as will be least likely to destroy the moral forces, never completely absent even in intergroup relations, but which will nevertheless exert coercion upon the white man's life. It means, to choose another illustration, that labor will never come to its full economic rights by trusting the intelligence and sense of justice of employers. They are circumscribed in their standards of justice by the prejudices of their class and the economic interests which bind them. If any of them should achieve a sense of justice which transcends these prejudices and interests—always a possibility—it will be just so much gain, but it will not abolish the fact of a class struggle.

How Dominant Groups Dominate

The laborer must develop both economic and political power to meet the combination of political and economic power which confronts him. His economic power consists in his capacity to interfere with the economic process controlled by the dominant economic group. His political power consists in the possibility of influencing or determining the policy of the political state, which always yields to group pressure though it affects to regard itself as the total society, impartially adjudicating conflicting group interests. The group which is able to wield the most economic and political power really determines its policies. If democracy were really pure, it alone could guarantee the resolution of all social conflict to nonviolent social tension in which a progressively higher and higher degree of justice would be assured by the increased ability of the underprivileged to use the weight of their numbers in the state in the interest of distributing the privileges of society more evenly.

Unfortunately, the dominant groups which control not only the state apparatus but the whole system of propaganda and education are able to frustrate a good deal of the potential political power of the disinherited by prejudicing the judgment of all but the politically most sophisticated. That is why proletarian groups tend to lose confidence in democratic institutions and to put their trust in violence. Their counsels will prevail, unless enough social intelligence can be created, not to prompt a voluntary equalization of privilege (which is a counsel of perfection) but to allow a measure of fairness in the state's adjudication of social controversy.

Social Pressure Necessary

If this analysis is correct it means that pure pacifism is an impossible goal for political life, if by pure pacifism we mean the use of nothing but moral suasion to resist injustice. Gandhi, who began his political efforts in India with the ideal of using nothing but soul-force against British imperialism, ended by initiating a vast strategy of nonviolent coercion. Sentimental pacifists still hail him as an apostle of pure love while pacifist perfectionists berate him for having abandoned his moral ideals. What he did was as inevitable as the tide when religious idealism really comes to grips with the political problem. He eschewed violence and disavowed hatred and reduced the social struggle to proportions in which the moral factor in inter-group relations could have the largest possible sway without trusting it to soften imperialistic minds and hearts alone. Nothing less realistic than Gandhi's policy can ever hope to be politically effective. All the fair-minded Britishers—and they are rather more numerous than in nations less consciously but not less really imperialistic—cannot overcome the force of self-interest and stupidity which determines the policy of every nation. The best they can do is to mitigate the severity of the struggle between India and England.

Religious idealists find it extremely difficult to accept the conclusions which any realistic analysis of political life forces upon the unbiased student. The Christian religion has an ideal of self-sacrifice which demands that men shall sacrifice themselves for others, thus obviating the necessity of conflict. This is really the ultimate moral ideal. Anything less than loving self-sacrifice is not really justice. Justice without love is merely the balance of power. But this ideal, too logical and inevitable to be disavowed, is achieved only rarely in individual life and is not achieved in group life at all. No nation, race, or class sacrifices itself. Human groups make a virtue of the assertion of self-interest and will probably do so until the end of history. The best that can be expected of human groups is a wise rather than stupid self-interest.

Since most human groups have not yet achieved this minimum ideal and the world is in danger of sinking into chaos because every modern nation is pursuing the interest of the moment in defiance of a more ultimate common interest with its foe and neighbor, the energies of intellectual and religious idealism must be bent to the purpose of achieving a sufficient measure of social idealism and intelligence to guarantee a minimum justice and fairness. Social pressure of various types will have to do the rest. The issue in our day is not between voluntary and coerced justice but between coerced justice and chaos.

Moralists find this lesson in politics an extremely unpalatable one and it is not entirely to their discredit that this is so. A high morality demands trust in human nature and a realistic political strategy presupposes a measure of cynicism. To maintain confidence in human nature and yet deal realistically with human evil is a task which requires a rather impossible combination of realism and idealism. If it is not achieved, sentimentalists and cynics will continue to guide our generation to disaster.

Practically every pronouncement on political issues by church bodies and by academic liberals and radicals is futile because it lacks political implementation for the social goals projected. It is declared that we need a better distribution of wealth, that we need social planning rather than anarchic individualism, but it is always assumed that these laudable social goals will be achieved with the cultivation of a little more social intelligence and idealism. If the religious and intellectual moralists and social idealists had the slightest idea of the kind of political and social conflict which would have to be waged before their ideals can be realized, their pronouncements would never be uttered. They want a more ideal social order, but the comforts of middle-class life and the illusions of detached intellectuals prevent them from realizing with what stubborn inertia the old order hangs on and with what poignant pangs of birth the new order comes into being.

CHURCH AND STATE IN AMERICA

There have been several episodes in recent weeks which have raised the question of the independence of the church from state control and give a welcome occasion to re-examine the character and the value of the historic American conception of the separation of church and state.

The first of these episodes was a letter by Mayor La-Guardia to the clergymen of the nation, asking them to observe Civilian Defense Week. His letter enclosed the outline of a sermon on the relation of religion to democracy which, he declared, "exemplifies the kind of message we are thinking of and which might be used effectively." Though no one denies that the sermon outline was a good one, it was undoubtedly a foolish blunder to send it, and it is unfortunate that the Office of Civilian Defense did not consult with responsible church leaders, who could have informed it of the inevitable reaction of parsons to "canned" sermons put out under government auspices.

The mistake which LaGuardia made was, of course, not as great as the absurd hysteria with which his mistake was greeted by the spokesmen of Christian isolationism. To declare that "Hitler and Goebbels never went further" in their control of the religious life of Germany than LaGuardia went in his predigested sermon is a charge so ludicrous as to require no refutation. Nevertheless, we hope we shall have no more such sermons.

Another episode which has aroused churchmen is the alleged action of a commander of an army camp near Denver in declaring certain churches in Denver "out of bounds" for his soldiers because isolationist meetings were held in these churches. The commander denies that religious services were affected by his order, but the incident has aroused apprehensions in the minds of church people.

The third and more serious episode centers about a young man, the son of a Methodist minister, who has been sentenced to two years imprisonment for draft evasion, after his local draft board and appeal board had rejected his plea that he is a conscientious objector. The Methodist Conference of Southern California and Arizona felt that this case represented a serious miscarriage of justice and the young man has the support of many Methodist clergymen who are not pacifists. Nevertheless, the local U. S. District Attorney threatened the entire conference with an F.B.I. investigation.

This particular incident calls attention to a serious defect in our conscription act in that its provisions for making appeals from the decisions of local draft boards are too administrative and not sufficiently judicial. The appeal is made to the President through the administrator of the conscription act. In Great Britain civilian tribunals have been set up to hear such appeals and they are manned by well-known leaders in the cultural life of the nation. They are able to separate the wheat from the chaff and their decisions, arrived at after sober public probing, carry a moral authority which no purely administrative decision made by overworked administrators of a draft act can have.

It would be well if nonpacifist Christian leaders could support pacifists in securing a better appeal system. For it is important that the part of the church which is not pacifist should nevertheless impress upon the general community that it understands the religious source of conscientious scruples against arms-bearing and that it appreciates this religious perfectionism, as the general community cannot, as a valid part of the Christian tradition.

It might be well to emphasize that the American tradition of the separation of church and state represents a delicate balance and cannot be maintained merely by the fiat of law. An absolute separation would require, as Roger Williams believed it did, that religion be regarded purely a private matter. This would mean that the church would not speak on public and social issues in return for the state's abstention from any control over the purely private religious convictions of its citizens. We have never had that kind of separation of church and state in this country and we certainly do not desire it. Any conception of Christianity which gives social content to its message makes a certain overlapping between church and state authority inevitable. The church does speak upon social and political issues. But if the state is to appreciate the function of religion and understand, in a measure, the profound religious sources of moral convictions, it is also necessary that religious teachers have a proper sense of responsibility toward the true function of political society.

It has been common among certain critics of our government in recent years to cry to high heaven at any real or imagined infringement of their liberty but to betray by their very criticisms that they are informed by essentially anarchistic conceptions of society. They have spoken of both legislative and executive acts of government as "Fascist" and as "tyrannical" when these epithets could have meaning only upon the assumption that the coercive acts of government are of themselves evil, which is to say that government is evil. For governments do coerce. The idea that we could move by progressive steps to a society of purely voluntary co-operation is an anarchistic and utopian illusion.

A religious criticism of policies of governments is important and necessary. For there is finally no vantage point, other than the religious one, from which to judge the self-deification of nations. But such criticisms can be effective only if the critic recognizes government as a divine ordinance and has a decent sense of reverence toward the majesty of the law which coordinates the vitalities of a nation.

Some of the hysterical criticisms made of our government in recent years have been either completely irresponsible, or they have been informed by implicit or explicit social philosophies which the historical experience of man has invalidated. These critics might do well to read Romans 13. They will not find the whole of the Christian attitude toward the state expressed in these Pauline words. But they will find a half of the Christian truth there, which they have neglected.

WHICH QUESTION COMES FIRST FOR THE CHURCH?

In both the religious and the secular world the question "What shall we do?" is raised with an urgency which sometimes rises to the pitch of hysteria. Its immediate forms are two: What shall we do about our relations with Russia? and What shall we do about the atomic bomb? These are important questions and must be answered. The fate of our civilization depends upon them. If relations with Russia continue to deteriorate, the mutual mistrust between the great centers of power may vitiate the hope for efficacy of the United Nations Charter and make that instrument irrelevant. If a solution for the problem of the atomic bomb is not found, the war which we will have failed to avert will most certainly destroy the last remnants of civilization. The moral-political issues which we face are, in other words, of unparalleled urgency.

Despite that fact, the first business of the Christian church is not to find an answer to those questions. Its first business is to raise and answer religious questions within the framework of which these moral issues must be solved. Our generation is in a religious, as well as moral and political, confusion because the ultimate religious question: What does life mean? has been falsely solved. We thought that life's meaning was guaranteed by the historical process. We believed in progress. Now we find that an atomic bomb stands at the end of the technical development. And at the end of the hoped for rational-moral progress we find little statesmen, representing little nations, drawing pretensions of omniscience from their military omnipotence, and playing with the powder which might blow up the world.

If we ask the question about the meaning of our existence, we must include in it the datum that we are unable to give a clear and decisive answer to the moral question: What shall we do? Not even the church, and perhaps least of all the church, can give a definitive answer to that question. Already sentiment in the church is divided between those who think we must first of all defend a "Christian civilization," and those who think we ought to make every possible sacrifice, even of Christian values, for the sake of an accord with Russia. A conference of international idealists recently met in Dublin, New Hampshire, and immediately divided into two groups. One group called for a world government, but did not suggest how we are to achieve it from the present position of international mistrust. The other group called for an alliance of democratic states, which means, for an anti-Russian alliance. The conference thus presented the nation with the alternative of an impossible solution on the one hand, and an irresponsible one on the other. We can do better than this conference. But a part of the tragedy of our situation consists in the fact that there is no clear way out of the present impasse.

We can also do better on the problem of the atomic bomb than the present May Bill before Congress. That bill practically guarantees that we will enter an armament race on the atomic bomb issue. We had better do what we can to kill that bill. But there is still no clear and obvious method of solving the problem of the bomb; and certainly not an unmistakable "Christian answer" for this issue.

There is meanwhile a very great task for the church to help people to live sanely in a very insecure world. A religious faith which trusts no historic securities too much, but understands the ultimate security of the assurance that "neither life nor death are able to separate us from the love of God," can become a resource of sanity in an insecure world. A religious faith which understands the perpetual disappointments in human history and knows that no historical achievement can be identified with the Kingdom of God, can prevent the disillusionment, bordering upon despair, which those feel who had expected the postwar world to be at least the vestibule of the Kingdom of God.

A religious faith which prompts us to live our life in obedience to God, and to recognize the self-justifying character of the sacrifice which such obedience may require, will not become involved in the hysterical conclusion that the sacrifices of the men who died upon the fields of battle have been in vain, if we fail now to achieve a world government. "Sufficient unto the day are the evils thereof." These men made their sacrifices, facing a horrible evil of their day. They destroyed that evil. New evils and new possibilities of world anarchy are arising, which may mean that, in terms of history, their sacrifices have only negative, and therefore only tragic, justification. But in God's sight these sacrifices have a more absolute justification.

It is, in other words, not possible to work sanely upon historical tasks, with a religion which confines the meaning of human existence to the limits of historic achievements and frustrations. From such religions spring the alternate evils of "sleep and drunkenness," which is to say, of complacency and hysteria. "Those that sleep, sleep in the night and they that are drunken are drunken in the night" declares St. Paul, but "let us who are of the day watch and be sober."

CAN THE CHURCH GIVE A "MORAL LEAD"?

If only it were as easy for the Christian church to define the "moral issues" confronting the world as many of the correspondents who write to a Christian journal seem to believe! "I believe," writes one correspondent, "that the church ought to give a clear moral lead for peace in this crisis. We ought to demand that we withdraw our troops from Berlin before it leads to war." While the editor perused this letter a telephone call requested that he sign his name to a petition, calling upon the President to make a solemn declaration that we will not under any circumstances "abandon our democratic allies in Berlin, who have been so heroically resisting the Communists." The almost hysterical voice on the phone expressed the conviction that we ought to treble the transport service into Berlin in order to serve notice on both the Russians and the Germans that we will not yield to Russian pressure and chicane. Here are two "clear" moral leads which cancel each other out. The Berlin situation represents a delicate strategic problem. If one were to hazard a guess it would be that the risk of remaining in Berlin is worth taking. But no one can deny that a tremendous risk is involved in the undertaking. We yielded to Hitler point by point because a decade ago we refused to take such risks.

Here is another letter. The author wants to know why the churches do not recognize that our government's abandonment of partition in Palestine was a "death-blow to the United Nations"? The missive rather corresponds to the editor's own prejudices or convictions. But another correspondent thinks that "The support of political Zionism by Christians represents an ignoble indifference toward the interest of Arab peoples, who are asked to pay the price for the unsolved problem of anti-Semitism in the Western World." On this particular question, the editor knows that the editorial board of the journal, which reaches agreement upon most issues, would find it difficult to arrive at a common conviction.

While meditating upon these evidences of the fragmentary and contradictory nature of moral convictions, inside, as well as outside of the church, another letter arrives to raise the question whether the American delegation to the Assembly of the World Council of Churches will make it quite clear to the Christians of Europe that we believe that democracy and the "free enterprise system" are wedded in an indissoluble union, and that we regard it as the mission of American Christianity to dissuade European Christians from their flirtation with "socialistic schemes which lead down the slippery slope of Communism." Here is a new facet of the "clear moral lead." A political ideology is identified, not with the Christian faith as such, but with an "American" version of that faith. But obviously the American version is regarded as the true and ultimate one. Otherwise there would not be so much concern that it be propagated at Amsterdam. One wishes one might take this correspondent along to Amsterdam so he might be confronted by certain European Christians who look askance at every American Christian because they believe him to be guilty of using the Christian faith as a façade for the power interests of the "only unreconstructed capitalistic nation of the modern world." When one recalls previous debates with some of these European Christians, particularly of the younger generation, one rather hopes that they will never learn about the story of the Boston clergyman who challenged the men of his congregation to grow mustaches "in order to prove our loyalty to the leader of the political party to which most of us belong."

There are undoubtedly some basic moral convictions, transcending political and strategic problems, to which all

Christians are committed. There are others to which they ought to be committed, though they are not. The church cannot afford to deal merely in vague generalities because it lacks unanimous convictions on the level of political strategy. It remains a fact, nevertheless, that the church is divided by every partisan interest of geographic or racial, economic or political origin. That fact alone is a proof that the sanctity of the church does not consist in the goodness of its members but in the holiness of its Lord.

Perhaps the church ought to be more concerned to bring the goodness of Christ as a judgment upon every fragmentary form of human goodness than to find the particular cause which might be identified with Christ. There are many good causes and just claims which turn into evil at the precise point where absolute validity is ascribed to them. Is not religion, including the Christian religion, a fruitful source of fanaticism and bigotry precisely because men pretend that their good is the ultimate good in the name of religion; and because Christians so easily claim Christ as an ally without ever having experienced his love as a judgment upon the shoddy character of their so-called "values" and upon the fragmentary character of even their best causes?

We must, as Christians, constantly make significant moral and political decisions amidst and upon perplexing issues and hazardous ventures. We must even make them "with might" and not halfheartedly. But the Christian faith gives us no warrant to lift ourselves above the world's perplexities and to seek or to claim absolute validity for the stand we take. It does, however, encourage us to the charity, which is born of humility and contrition. This is not a "clear moral lead" but a clear religious insight into the fragmentary character of all human morality, including the virtue of the saints and the political pronouncement of churches. "Our life is his in Christ with God." If we claim to possess overtly what remains hidden, we turn the mercy of Christ into an inhuman fanaticism.

THE CHURCH AND EQUAL RIGHTS FOR WOMEN

The refusal of the convention of the Episcopal church to seat women delegates who had been duly elected by their dioceses to their position raises some interesting questions about the reasons for the tardiness of religious communities in meeting the standards of secular society in the matter of equal rights for women. The church may sometimes have higher moral and social standards than the general community, and it may sometimes fall below them. But it is most consistently below the general standards of modern bourgois society in its refusal to grant women equal rights as persons, this refusal involving it in disobedience to the Apostolic injunction: "In Christ there is—neither male nor female." This tardiness is rather ironic in view of the fact that women bear more than their share of the burdens of the church and exceed their male relatives in devotion to the religious community. The action of the Episcopal convention was the more remarkable because it did not involve the question of ordination. The women were not knocking at the gates of the holy of holies. They were refused admission to the outer court.

This incident may serve to remind the church that the emancipation of women from the restraints to which they were subject in all traditional societies is one of the real achievements of modern secular idealism to which even the most advanced Christian thought made only ancillary contributions. It may be that there is some deep undertone in a religious community, having nothing to do with Christianity but profoundly related to the impulses of "natural religion," which accounts for the difference in standards between the religious and the general community. It would be well for the Christian church to recognize that however

"Christian" its conscious standards are, every church is something of a "religious" community as well as a Christian community. Therefore its life is informed to some degree by these general impulses of "pagan" or natural religion. One of the motives of this pagan religion, reaching far back into primitive life, is the "enmity between the priest and the woman." This enmity may have sexual origin or it may be the contest between the woman as protagonist of the family and the priest as the exponent of the larger community, contrived by priest and warrior. In India, for instance, women had comparative equality in the Vedic period but became completely disinherited when the triumph of the priests was codified in the "Code of Manu." It is worth noting that even in modern life churches have difficulty in dealing with the problem of women in proportion to the degree of sacramentalism in their piety. This does not imply an indictment of sacramentalism in general, but does suggest that the animus against women does arise where there is a very explicit area of the sacred. Yet it must be confessed that women have difficulties of some kind in almost every religious community. If a priest is not seeking to prove that a woman cannot be the representative of Christ because Christ was a man, some fundamentalist theologian will seek to disinherit her by quoting texts.

Perhaps the church could overcome these sub-Christian standards more readily if it ceased arguing about them on Christian grounds and recognized more frankly that there are primitive depths as well as sublime heights in religion, not known in secular idealism. That need not persuade us to become secularists. But it might make us willing to let secular idealism speak the "word of God" on occasion.

UTILITARIAN CHRISTIANITY
AND THE WORLD CRISIS

I

An ironic aspect of the present world situation is that the more Christians seek to commend their faith as the source of the qualities and disciplines required to save the world from disaster, the less does that kind of faith prove itself to have the necessary resources. It is significant that a purely utilitarian justification of Christianity tends actually to produce a type of religious idealism which is more likely to become a source of confusion to the conscience of the nation than a spiritual resource. Christ admonished us "to seek first the Kingdom of God and its righteousness" and assured us "that all these things would be added." But if we place our main interest upon the things that will be added—if we seek to justify Christianity because it preserves democracy, or inspires hatred of dictatorship, or makes a "free enterprise system" possible, or helps us to change such a system into something better, or creates a "third force"—our utilitarian attitude debases the Christian faith to the status of a mere instrument of the warring creeds from which the world suffers.

This utilitarian attitude destroys the real power of the Christian faith because it creates a type of piety in which there are no longer any genuine engagements between the soul and God, or between the nation and God, but merely a religious accentuation of various forms of ethical and political idealism. Even now many contradictory testimonies of various types of Christians in our nation tend to be either so irrelevant or so dangerous that a wise statesman will do well to ignore most of them; and he may well thank God that they cancel each other out sufficiently to make this indifference politically expedient.

Consider our situation: We are involved in a "cold war" with a great power which is more than a mere political power. It is the "fatherland" of a political religion which has transmuted the prophets of a utopian faith into tyrannical priest-kings of a vast system of exploitation. The fact that the original Marxist utopian dream has turned into a nightmare has not, however, disillusioned millions of impoverished people in Europe or in Asia, who look to Russia as a kind of messianic nation. Most recently China has capitulated to this illusion.

Opposed to this great power, which is able to add to its military might, the weapons of political chicane and moral illusions, stands a vast alliance of "free nations." These free nations have an imperfect unity, compared to the monolythic unity which tyranny can create. They are also filled with various forms of injustice, economic and racial. The former are responsible for inciting the rebellion of the so-called "industrial" classes against bourgeois democracy, out of which the Russian power grew. The racial injustices in the free world have done much to incline the peoples of Asia and Africa to Communism. At the "head" of this vast alliance stands our own nation. We are in this position of leadership not because of our superior wisdom or virtue. We hold this position because of our great economic power. Yet the stability and moral health of the free world will depend to a large degree upon the wisdom with which our very wealthy nation can relate itself to an impoverished world.

We believe that our free society is worth preserving, whatever its moral and political weaknesses. It is locked in mortal combat with a tyrannically organized world. It is not certain either whether we can prevent further encroachments of Communism in our world or whether we can avert a world conflict between the two centers of power. Such a conflict would mean the end of civilization even if we had the strength to gain a victory for "our" civilization. It is fairly obvious that in the event of such a conflict atomic weapons would be used, including the new type of hydrogen bomb. Mankind has never faced moral dilemmas of such staggering proportions.

How are the Christian churches guiding the conscience of the nation in this situation? It is not quite fair, yet it is not unfair, to suggest that they are all too frequently involved either in adding religious fury to the hysteria or the self-righteousness to which an embattled nation is naturally prone; or in finding religious grounds for evading our duties in a hard situation. Catholicism is more prone to the former error and Protestantism to the latter.

One form which hysteria takes in a tense situation is the curious desire to invite the catastrophe which we ought to avoid. The political form of this hysteria is the doctrine of an inevitable war; from which the proposition of a preventive war is quickly derived. The Catholic church does not believe in an inevitable war or a preventive one. But there are too many Catholic voices which hint at it; and there have been no official disavowals of the idea. The hints arise understandably enough from the teriffic conflict between Catholicism and Communism in the nations behind the Iron Curtain and the fear that Communism will do mortal damage to the church in those countries. The concept of a "just war" in defense of "Christian civilization" can easily lead to a moral justification of a final conflict with Communism. If such a conflict is inevitable there is no good reason for not choosing the moment most propitious to our cause for initiating it.

No one can guarantee that this conflict will not eventuate. But since Communism is not primarily a military but a moral-political force, one should have thought that the primary Christian emphasis ought to lie upon the moral resources by which alone we can overcome Communism, without of course relaxing our military defenses against the military threats of the Communist world.

Catholicism tends to accentuate the self-righteousness of the advocates of our cause, thus contributing to the moral complacency which may be our undoing. When it wars against "secularism" the Catholic church makes some pointed criticisms of the moral illusions of our bourgeois world. But when it wars against Communism it forgets these criticisms and speaks of our world, as a noted Catholic radio preacher did recently, as "the fellowship of Christ" at war with the "fellowship of anti-Christ." Meanwhile Communism still spreads among the agrarian, rather than the industrial, poor of Italy, because there has been no genuine land reform in this Catholic nation.

Finally, Catholicism has failed to check the hysteria in this country which expressed itself in the fantastic search for traitors in high places, when it is obvious to soberminded people that this nation is freer of an internal Communist threat than any other democratic country. It would be wrong to hold the church responsible for the antics of an irresponsible Catholic senator any more than Protestantism should be held responsible for the demagogues who have corrupted our heritage. But the seriousness with which Holy Name societies treat the hysterical warnings of an ex-Communist Catholic is not reassuring. Wrote a wise American from France recently: "The antics of Senator McCarthy have done us great damage in France. The more astute French people feel that it proves that we do not take Communism seriously enough, that we do not understand its threat as a world-wide force. They find in these investigations a frivolous effort to reduce a tragic drama to the proportions of a cheap melodrama." The church has not spoken a single unequivocal word to quiet the hysteria expressed in recent senatorial investigations.

II

The weaknesses of the Protestant testimony in the present situation are on the whole of a different order. The only Protestant words which are similar to the Catholic failings are those which aggravate the tendency toward self-righteousness on the part of a fortunate and powerful nation, by making it appear that the libertarian form of democracy which we enjoy is the final norm for a free world. This form of self-righteousness complicates our mutual relations with the impoverished nations of a free world, all of which have had to place greater checks upon the economic life than we, though many have given greater proof of their devotion to liberty and justice than we have been able to give.

Most of the Protestant mistakes arise from the tendency of the modern Protestant church to equate Christianity with a system of rigorous moral idealism, without regard for the endless moral ambiguities in the political realm. Thus we confront the awful possibilities of a new level of atomic destructiveness and a nation in anguish of conscience asks: What shall we do? Many Protestant idealists simply answer: "Let us be Christians and not make the bomb at all." Very simple, except that a good Christian in Europe writes: "We hope that America's qualms of conscience will not prompt policies of defencelessness which will expose us to a Russian occupation."

We are involved in a "cold war" with Russia. What shall we do about that? The Protestant answer frequently is: We must come to terms with the Russians. As if that were a simple thing. We are asked to reach an agreement with Russia on German unity in the name of Christian idealism. But suppose the Russians will accept no agreement which does not permit them to dominate a united Germany? We are asked to reach an agreement upon atomic weapons. But suppose the Russians ask as the price of such an agreement a total disarmament which will leave them free to do in Europe what they will? Or we are asked to achieve the even more impossible goal of a world government in the name of Christian idealism? But we are not told how a world constitutional system would be able to beguile either side from the fear and mistrust which would wreck any constitutional system.

The simple fact is that Christianity as merely a system of rigorous idealism can be discounted by any statesman, even if he is only moderately shrewd. For his responsibilities teach him that there may be tragic conflicts in history which are not easily resolved either by moral suasion or by constitutional devices. (Do we remember our Civil War?) They also teach him that a statesman can never follow merely one set of moral values but must usually seek to realize partially incompatible goals. In the present instance this means both the preservation of a free world and the prevention of war.

If Catholicism were not so sure of the virtue of its "Christian civilization" and Protestantism not so certain of the efficacy of its moral idealism, if in fact both were less concerned to validate their faith as relevant to the present situation, that faith might be more relevant.

A less relevant faith would, as did the prophets of Israel, give our nation a sense that its primary engagement is with God and not with its foes. That kind of religious engagement, in which the distinction between the righteous and unrighteous nations (or in the words of the prophet Jeremiah, the distinction between the "circumcised and the uncircumcised") is obscured, is the only source of humility for a nation so tempted as our own to regard its fortune as proof of its virtue. We could have less friction with our allies and be a better moral match for our foes if our engagement with a divine judge helped us to recognize the fragmentary character of all human virtues and the ambiguous nature of all human achievements. We might also be helped to see that what we regard as great generosity toward our poorer allies (as embodied in the European Recovery Program) is prompted not so much by Christian charity as prudent consideration of national interest.

A less relevant faith would have less to say about overcoming race prejudice in order to commend our cause to the peoples of Asia and Africa. It would be more concerned to bring race pride, as every other form of human pride, under divine scrutiny. Racial bigots will not be converted by the warning that lynching may hurt our cause in Africa. They face a more serious problem in their own souls. They must literally be "born again." There are intellectual as well as religious resources against racial bigotry. But the church is primarily concerned with the religious encounter between an ethnic group and the divine justice and mercy.

The encounter between nations and the divine justice always wipes out a part of the distinction between good and evil men, and between just and unjust nations. But the Christian faith also helps us to understand the necessity of preserving whatever standards of justice or virtue we have achieved against tyrannical power. It does not persuade us that we must not stand resolutely against tyranny, because we happen ourselves not to be just in God's sight. It helps us to appreciate the responsibilities which even sinful men and nations have to preserve what is relatively good against explicit evil. Neutrality between justice and injustice, whether derived from a too-simple moral idealism or a too-sophisticated Barthian theology, is untrue to our gospel.

The most important relevance of a Christian faith, which is not too immediately relevant to the political situation, is a sense of serenity and a freedom from hysteria in an insecure world full of moral frustrations. We have to do our duty for a long time in a world in which there will be no guarantees of security and in which no duty can be assured the reward of success. The hysteria of our day is partly derived from the disillusion of a humanistic idealism which thought that every virtue could be historically rewarded and encouraged men to sow by the promise of a certain harvest. Now we must sow without promising whether we can reap. We must come to terms with the fragmentary character of all human achievements and the uncertain character of historic destinies.

There is nothing new in all this. Our present vicissitudes merely remind us of the words of Scripture: "If in this life only we had hoped in Christ we are of all men most miserable." That is an expression of what a humanistic age calls "Christian otherworldliness." It is the Biblical illumination of a dimension of existence which makes sense out of life, when it ceases to make sense as simply upon the plane of history as it was once believed. We are, as Christians, rightly concerned about the probabilities of disaster to our civilization and about our various immediate duties to avert it. But we will perform our duties with the greater steadiness if we have something of the faith expressed by St. Paul in the words: "Whether we live, we live unto the Lord; and whether we die, we die unto the Lord: whether we live therefore, or die, we are the Lord's." In this final nonchalance about life and death, which includes some sense of serenity about the life and death of civilizations, there is a resource for doing what we ought to do, though we know not what the day or the hour may bring forth. The best statesmen of the world may, or may not, have such a faith. But a statesmanlike common sense is a closer approach to it than many forms of religious hysteria or religious idealism.

SOCIAL CHRISTIANITY

A serious development is taking place in American Protestantism. The alliance between Protestant pietism and political reaction which characterized Protestant thought in America through most of the nineteenth century, and which the Social Gospel effectively challenged, has achieved a new triumph. The old alliance was based upon three propositions: (1) The physiocratic theory which assured men that a "pre-established harmony of nature" guaranteed justice in economic affairs if only governments did not interfere with the automatic processes of a market economy was given a Christian baptism. The pre-established harmony of nature became the providence of God. (2) Poverty was attributed to sin; and the economic rewards of an expanding economy were interpreted as just deserts of virtue, particularly the virtues of diligence and thrift. Thus the Christian conscience was absolved of any concern for establishing justice in the intricacies of an ever-growing technical society. (3) Pietistic individualism was identified with bourgeois individualism, and the Christian emphasis upon individual responsibility to God was transformed into an assertion of the "rights" of the individual as against the claims of the community. Henry May's *Protestant Churches and Industrial America* is a fairly accurate description of this amalgam of Christian thought and the presuppositions of what is now known as the "American way of life."

The rise of the Social Gospel offered a welcome release from this moral and spiritual complacency. The Social Gospel insisted on the Christian's responsibility for justice in the community and challenged the doctrine that laissez-faire would make for justice, citing the unjust consequences of the ever-growing concentration of power in industry. Unfortunately the Social Gospel was not a fully sophisticated approach to social issues. On the right wing it was subject to the general moralistic illusions of Christian liberalism. It seemed to believe that the only reason men had not followed the love commandment in the vast collective relations of mankind was because no one had called their attention to the necessity. This it proceeded to do. But it had little understanding of the relation of love to justice and no understanding of the contest of power and the balance of interests which were required for the achievement of justice. On the left wing the Social Gospel degenerated into Marxism. Christian phrases and ideas were diluted with basically Marxist concepts in various degrees of consistency.

Right-wing Social-Gospel thought has suffered the fate which has befallen Christian liberalism generally. Its social convictions as well as its theological presuppositions were tender plants, unable to survive the wintry blasts of twentieth-century history. The left-wing Social Gospel, in its few remnants, is caught in the tawdry politics of Stalinism.

But whatever the defects of the Social Gospel, one must be grateful for its insights compared to the new menace of a degenerated pietism which is seeking to enslave the conscience of the Christian church and force it to speak in the accents of the National Association of Manufacturers. Thus Daniel Poling, once the international leader of the Christian Endeavour (perhaps still so if there is still a Christian Endeavour), challenges the World Council of Churches because it is too "confused" to understand the merits of American capitalism. James Fifield has long conducted his "Spiritual Mobilization" campaign in which the hosts of Christ are summoned to do battle against "statism" and the liberty of the gospel is identified with "free enterprise."

More recently a weekly newspaper entitled *Christian Economics,* with some very respectable names on its masthead, has developed the same theme, adding a venomous reactionary note on foreign policy which seems to come out of the mouths of George Sokolsky and Fulton Lewis, Jr. Norman Vincent Peale, who long ago reduced the Christian gospel to the dimension of a soporific for tired businessmen and a promise of success for aspiring ones, recently challenged the Christian church to "come out for capitalism." His *Reader's Digest* article, in the hands of many members of the business world, has been used as an instrument of pressure upon ministers in local communities. Why, ministers have been asked by local leaders, do they not follow Dr. Peale's example and assure their flocks that capitalism is the truly Christian answer to the world's problems?

In this situation it has become important to gather, organize, and inform that portion of the Christian church in America which has a real concern for the integrity of the church and for the truth of the gospel and is anxious to prevent the always dangerous mixture of religious sanctity with the moral complacency of a culture. The peril of this complacency has grown immeasurably in America in recent years. For a nation as powerful and as fortunate as America, is tempted to believe that the peculiar conditions of American life are the final standards of justice for the Kingdom of God. It is ironically tempted to this form of pride at the precise moment in history in which libertarian economic theory exists nowhere else but in America, and in which American practice is in sharp contrast to the theory. For we do have the beginnings of a "welfare state" which our religious and economic reactionaries describe as the first slip on the treacherous slope which ends in Communism, and which is in reality our bridge between the conscience of the free world and the American conscience.

The Frontier Fellowship, which issues this journal, recognized some years ago that the issue of socialism versus capitalism was not the real issue on which the conscience of the church and of America is to be challenged. Socialism in its pure form is not a live issue in America. For that matter, orthodox socialist doctrine is almost as irrelevant in European political life as in America, even though socialist parties have a power in Europe which they never achieved in America. The issue in America is the right and the duty of democratic society to achieve economic justice under the conditions of a technical society. That task cannot be performed if the conscience of a nation is confused by either of the contrasting dogmas which have brought a civil war into Western civilization. The one dogma is that the free play of economic forces will automatically make for justice. The other is that the socialization of property inevitably will lay the foundations for both justice and freedom.

In Europe Christian thought must resist both dogmas in the interest of a Christian realism which understands the perils to justice in all forms of power, whether economic or political, and which knows of the corruption of self-interest in all dreams of justice whether bourgeois or proletarian. But in America our business is to challenge the bourgeois rather than the proletarian illusions. The latter do not exist. America is a bourgeois paradise which has been spared a class conflict of European proportions, not by its wisdom but by the fortunate circumstances of a constantly expanding economy on a vast and virgin continent. But there is danger that the bourgeois illusions about life and justice, which have long since been punctured by hard realities in European history, should reach monstrous proportions in our own land. There is danger too that religious piety should give these illusions a final dimension of absurdity.

That is why it has become necessary to build and organize a movement of resistance of much wider and stronger proportions than the present Fellowship. This movement must not deal merely with the social and political problems of our day. It must be deeply grounded in the Christian faith and deal as rigorously with the religious and theological presuppositions of social policy as with the details of political and economic theory. The problem of achieving a more adequate organization of the forces within the church which believe in bringing the force of the gospel to bear upon the idolatries and injustices of our civilization and of finding a better expression of our common beliefs is so urgent that we invite any reader of these lines to write the editor, if he has suggestions of what may be done. Either the Frontier Fellowship should be enlarged and its instruments for reaching its members with significant material should be perfected, or a larger and better organization should be formed.

THE PROTESTANT CLERGY
AND U. S. POLITICS

There are indications that a long period of "creative tension" between the clerical leaders of American Protestantism and the American business community is coming to a close with the triumph of the business community over the churches. The creative tension (for it was creative on the whole) was due to the fact that the American business community is rather uncritically devoted to the principles of a laissez-faire economics, regarding "free enterprise" as a final and absolute norm of social organization, whereas the clerical leadership of the Protestant churches has been deeply influenced by the traditions of the "Social Gospel."

The Social Gospel movement was in fact a revulsion of the religious conscience against an alliance between Protestant individualism and pietism and classical economic liberalism. This alliance was very potent from the middle to the end of the nineteenth century. The social theories of Protestantism were little more than religious versions of the economic principles of Adam Smith. A Protestant journal in 1874 declared: "Labor is a commodity [that] . . . is governed by the imperishable laws of demand and supply."

It was characteristic of this Protestant individualism that it insisted upon purely individual explanations of social injustice. Thus even Henry Ward Beecher, the famous anti-slavery preacher, could insist: "Looking comprehensively at the matter . . . the general truth will stand, that no man in this land suffers from poverty unless it be more than his fault—unless it be his *sin.*"

One of the inevitable marks of this kind of individualism

was the fear that economic justice might eliminate the necessity of Christian charity. "The poor we have with us always," declared a Protestant journal in the 1870's, "and this is not the greatest of our hardships, but choicest of our blessings. If there is anything a Christian may feel thankful for, it is the privilege of lifting a little of the load of some of his heavily-burdened neighbors." The thoughtful reader may remember that in the early days of the depression President Herbert Hoover opposed unemployment insurance on the ground that it would leave no room for Christian charity. The echoes of this early creed can be detected in Mr. Hoover's economic theories.

Protestant Individualism

Before presenting the evidence for the recrudescence of this type of pious individualism in recent years, it is necessary to give a brief account of the effect of the Social Gospel upon American Protestantism. This movement was a revolt against the Protestant individualism, which refused to accept any Christian responsibility for the justice of social and political structures and which pretended to believe that personal virtue, plus the beneficent effects of a self-regulating economy, was all that was needed.

The Social Gospel movement had its rise at the end of the nineteenth century and extended to the first decades of this century. Its greatest exponents were Washington Gladden, a Congregational preacher in Columbus, Ohio, and Walter Rauschenbusch, a Baptist theologian. But there were many other influential figures in the movement, such as Francis Peabody of Harvard, the Wisconsin economist Richard Ely, George Herron of the Rand School, and Shailer Mathews of the University of Chicago. The most important document of the movement is undoubtedly Rauschenbusch's *Christianity and the Social Crisis,* first published in 1907.

The concern for social justice expressed in this movement was the product of the confluence of several different streams of thought. It was partly the fruit of a Christian radicalism that had developed on the American frontier,

where the old sectarian pietism had lost its pure individualism and had become related to Jacksonian radicalism. It
was partly the consequence of "theocratic" impulses in the
heart of Calvinism—impulses intent on bringing "the whole
of life under the dominion of Christ." Some of the thought
of the Social Gospel movement was derived from the
radical ideas of the sectarians in Cromwell's army.

All of these streams of thought united to define Christianity's purpose, in the words of Rauschenbusch, "to transform
human society into the Kingdom of God by regenerating all
human relations and reconstituting them in accordance
with the will of God."

It may be pertinent to observe that while a certain
amount of Marxist thought entered into this amalgam of
religious forces, the movement was, from beginning to end,
highly moralistic and liberal, almost pathetically anxious to
disassociate itself from every idea of a class struggle. A left
wing did indeed espouse pure Marxism. This left wing,
which was active primarily in the Methodist and (strangely
enough) in the Episcopal churches, also became enmeshed
in the toils of Stalinism. It has served the purpose of giving
American conservatives the pretext for insisting that the
churches are becoming "socialistic."

The Federal Council

Actually the Social Gospel movement, despite its great
virtue of insisting that social justice is a proper and necessary concern of the Christian faith, was always rather too
moralistic to understand fully the operations of economic
and political life with their inevitable contests of power and
interest. But these defects now appear to be minor when its
achievement is recognized: It delivered American Protestantism from meeting complex ethical problems of a technical civilization with an almost completely irrelevant
individualistic pietism and moralism.

Perhaps the most significant organizational achievement
of the Social Gospel movement was that, combined with
the growing church-unity movement, it created the Federal

Council of the Churches of Christ in America. This Council, which brought all major U. S. Protestant churches into a single co-operative organization, was born in 1908. In its very first meeting it adopted a "social creed" which, though subsequently amended and enlarged, has remained a guide to its social thought. In that creed it insisted upon "the right of workers to protection from the hardships often resulting from crises and industrial change; for the protection of workers from dangerous machinery and occupational disease; for the regulation of the conditions of toil for women; for the gradual and reasonable reduction of hours of labor; for a living wage as a minimum in every industry; for suitable provision for the old age of workers;" and so on. The right of collective bargaining was not asserted in this original creed, though it was implied. That right was added in a later revision; and it may be regarded as significant that the Protestant churches insisted upon this right long before the American business community was ready to grant it.

The social theories of the Federal Council, while originally inspired by the Social Gospel movement, achieved a maturity beyond the earlier sentimentality. The council was as active in the field of international relations as in the field of social theory. In international relations it consistently stood for the principle of America's responsibility to the world community against the isolationist tendencies of part of the American business community. Its educational program in international affairs reached its climax after the Second World War, when John Foster Dulles directed the work of its Commission of a Just and Durable Peace.

World Protestantism

The activity of laymen like Dulles in the affairs of the council refutes the charge of radicalism so frequently brought against it by men like John T. Flynn. The co-operation of leading laymen in its economic and social program also disproves the idea that the council represented merely clerical, as distinguished from lay, opinion. In recent years its National Study Committee on the Church and Economic

Life held a series of conferences in which some of the most enlightened leaders in business, government, and labor participated.

The last conference of the old Federal Council on economic problems was held in Detroit in February, 1950. It was attended by a genuinely representative group of laymen and clerical leaders and issued a report entitled "The Responsibilities of Christians in an Interdependent Economic World." This report contained no dogmas or isms of the right or the left; but it proved that decades of social idealism wedded to organizational responsibility had produced a high degree of ethical and political maturity.

The success of the Federal Council undoubtedly contributed in a very considerable degree to the formation of similar international organizations in which world Protestantism has become united. In turn, the contacts of American Protestant leaders with the leaders of Europe served to modify what Europeans always felt to be an undue optimism and sentimentality in American social thought. The world movement on Christian Life and Work began in Stockholm in 1925, developed through a conference at Oxford in 1937, and culminated in the organization of the World Council of Churches in Amsterdam in 1948. The Amsterdam conference, incidentally, gave the American business community a great deal of concern. For though it condemned Communism unequivocally, it also faithfully reflected Europe's and Asia's rejection of the American free-enterprise doctrine. It declared that the promise of laissez-faire capitalism, that justice would flow inevitably from economic freedom, had no more been fulfilled than the Communist promise that freedom would flow inevitably from equality.

Thus the old Federal Council of Churches was an instrument for achieving not only a viable pragmatic creed of justice for America but for relating American Protestantism to a world movement of Protestant churches. If in that world union American Protestantism lost some of its sentimentality in the field of political affairs, it also helped some of the churches of Continental Europe to overcome their undue social and political defeatism.

End of an Era?

The question now is whether this whole period of creative tension between the Protestant churches of America
and our dominant culture has come to an end. Recently a
whole spate of "organizations" has arisen to re-establish
the old alliance between Protestant pietism and economic
individualism. The word "organizations" is put in quotation
marks because these movements, though heavily financed
and able to send their literature gratis to practically every
Protestant parson, are not membership organizations.

One of them, called Spiritual Mobilization, is directed
by the Reverend James Fifield, Jr., of the First Congregational Church of Los Angeles. Its theory is that any government control of economic life is a form of "statism" and
that statism is a horrible form of idolatry that gives government the authority and reverence that are due only to God.
Even the mildest deviations from laissez-faire doctrine are
defined as the first step down the slippery slope that leads
to Communism. This organization, like similar ones, has a
political program identical with that of the National Association of Manufacturers, to which it adds merely a prayer
and religious unction.

More recently a biweekly journal entitled *Christian Economics* has made its appearance. It is also so well subsidized that it can be sent free to practically every clergyman in America. This journal is convinced that a sharp
distinction must be made between "man-made laws" and
"God's laws." "God's laws" are nothing else but "the laws
of nature" as the eighteenth-century physiocrats conceived
them. They are presumably unalterable norms of social
life, which prohibit every contrivance of statesmanship for
the regulation of human affairs.

According to this remarkable exposition of Christian
doctrine, even the Federal postal system is a mistake. We
would be much better off if the government made postal
service subject to competitive bidding. The combination of
economic and religious naivete exhibited in this journal is

a reminder of the fact that uncritical religion is frequently a plausible, and therefore dangerous, ally of uncritical ideological positions in the political debate. It is difficult to assess the influence of these movements. They are undoubtedly intended to make American Protestantism the devoted ally of the most uncritical and nostalgic form of American liberal-conservatism. For it is clear that American conservatism in its most unviable form is a kind of decadent liberalism that thinks a return to pure classical economic liberalism is a live option for America.

Financial Support

The financial support of Spiritual Mobilization and *Christian Economics* is something of a mystery. Both display boards of directors composed of clerical leaders. The businessmen behind them do not show their hands. Fifield's journal, *Faith and Freedom*, has a distribution of over 100,000. In an appeal letter some years ago, Fifield acknowledged a budget of $270,000, and referred his prospective donors to E. T. Weir (National Steel) and J. Howard Pew (Sun Oil and Sun Shipbuilding) as references. The same J. Howard Pew gave *Christian Economics* a check for $50,000 to start it on its way. But nothing is known of the subsequent financing. While these movements are religious versions of such organizations as Merwin K. Hart's National Economic Council and Leonard Reed's Foundation of Economic Education, they usually avoid the virulence that characterizes the polemics of Hart.

Many Protestant leaders who have labored for decades in the social and ethical program of the old Federal Council of Churches have naturally become apprehensive upon the discovery that the chairman of the finance committee of the new National Council of Churches is the same J. Howard Pew who has been one of the angels of the subsidized movements designed to bring American Protestantism back to the uncritical individualism from which it extricated itself over a period of half a century. They wonder how it is possible for a man who has insisted upon social theories which stand in absolute contradiction to the work of the Federal Council so suddenly to occupy a seat of power in an organization that is supposed to continue the traditions of the council. If Mr. Pew agrees with *Christian Economics* that unemployment insurance is wrong because "individuals with sensitive Christian consciences will organize private charity to take care of the needy," he certainly cannot agree with the social creed of the council.

The National Council

It must be explained that the new National Council of Churches has brought the old Federal Council, the International Council of Religious Education, The Home and Foreign Mission Councils, and other Protestant interdenominational agencies into one great superorganization. Two problems arise in such a new movement. The one is whether the sheer weight of organizational mechanism will not stifle some of the freedom that the several movements once had. This question is, to use the words of Santayana, whether "the harmony of the whole may not destroy the vitality of the parts." There has been some frustration on this score, which may, however, be overcome as the new council learns how to decentralize as well as to centralize authority.

The other problem is that of providing fuel for this vast machinery. The council has a budget of $4.5 million. That is considerably larger than the combined budgets of all the agencies that entered it. Mr. Pew, as chairman of the finance committee, is making valiant efforts to balance the budget. Recently he made an appeal to corporations for support of the council, in which he declared that over a thousand of them had placed the council on their contribution lists. He appealed for corporation gifts on two counts: the nondenominational character of the work, and the argument "that enterprises such as ours exist as long as there is a measure of freedom in the market place and freedom in the market place is only one of freedom's many parts." The logic is not altogether clear. But if anything is meant, it must be the idea that there must be an alliance between business and religion to overcome the threat of "statism."

It is not suggested that Mr. Pew and his business friends can annul in a single stroke the history of fifty years. The clerical leadership of the National Council is highly respected in all circles. The Presiding Bishop of the Episcopal Church, Henry Knox Sherrill, is president of the council. Dr. Samuel M. Cavert, who, as it were, grew up with the Federal Council, is now general secretary of the National Council. Such men as Bishop G. Bromley Oxnam are in positions of leadership in it. It is impossible to believe that they would easily yield to any effort to turn the National Council into a kind of big brother of Spiritual Mobilization. Behind them are thousands of Christian leaders in the churches who fervently believe that the churches must have their own voice on questions of social justice and cannot simply sponsor the moral complacency of a segment of our business world.

But it is also difficult to believe that Mr. Pew has moved into this great organization without intending a basic alteration of its social orientation. It is therefore likely that some interesting history will be made during the coming months in American Protestantism's central sources of authority.

PRAYER AND POLITICS

Why is it that our prayers and devotions, which we fondly believe to be the source of spiritual strength and humility for our people should, when they are transferred from the walls of our several houses of prayer to a big public gathering, be an offense alike to the devout and the scornful? In a memorable editorial this summer the *Christian Century* protested against the "exploitation" of religion by the political conventions. It spoke for many of us; but the word "exploitation" defines only a part but not the whole of the offense. Religion is exploited when it is used for ulterior purposes; there is a strong suspicion that it is so used at large political meetings. It is interesting that there would be a temptation to exploit it; for prayer is a discipline of humility and consecration which naturally creates the temptation to be used not for its original purpose but for pretending a humility and consecration which we do not have. One is reminded of Jesus' warning against praying in the market place "to be seen of men," and His admonition to pray in secret "that the Father who seeth you in secret will reward you openly." There is, incidentally, a strong inclination to use religious observances at conventions in order to seek the favor of the three denominational groups—Protestant, Jewish, and Catholic—who are invariably represented in the official prayers. Europeans find these religious observances at our political occasions quite as baffling as they find the political convention itself. Perhaps they illustrate an intimate and uncritical relationship between religion and public life in our nation which marks us at one and the same time as one of the most religious and the most secular of nations.

But the offense is given not only by conscious or unconscious "exploitation" of religion. It is also given by an accommodation of religion to the political purposes of the gathering. In detecting accommodation we make no criticism of the eminent clergymen who led the prayers at the conventions. Most of them did as well as any of the rest of us would do. Nevertheless the total effect of their labors was accommodation. The *Century* thought the prayers were "too long and too eloquent." The criticism is correct, but one must observe that they were only a little longer and a little more eloquent than the ordinary long prayer of our churches. (This may point to a distinctive Protestant failing, but it is worth observing that when Catholic priests or prelates conduct prayers outside their church and free from their liturgical disciplines, their prayers sound more like political harangue than the prayers of most Protestant ministers.) A prayer which is too long and too eloquent betrays that it is delivered for the ears of man and not God. Prayers must be eloquent only with the eloquence of brevity and chastity. Length and eloquence do not of themselves accommodate the prayer to ulterior purpose but they contribute to the effect. One remembers Jesus' warning against long prayers being coupled with His warning against prayers in public. In any event, how quickly the prayer loses its virtue in the new surroundings! Thus prayers of gratitude for God's blessings upon this nation easily turn into exercises in self-congratulation about the virtues of our national history. Prayers of contrition are easily bent to partisan purposes. Contrition for national corruption sounds like a political document in a Republican convention and repentance for national irresponsibility has the same effect in a Democratic convention.

We were most impressed by the quick degeneration of prayers of aspiration in which the ideal goals of the nation were held up as ends of consecration. How quickly these aspirations degenerate into sentimentality when the ideal goal is not held in proper balance with the forces of inertia and sin in life which prevent an easy realization of the goal. Some of these corruptions are not so much in the defects of the priest's prayer as in the pressures of the public gathering.

It would be defeatist to suggest that the way to keep religion pure is to preserve it from contact with these public occasions. Yet the public reaction to the prayers was a wholesome one. We know that public men who ostentatiously display their religious faith are treated with cynicism by the public, which expresses by its reaction its understanding of the fact that religion, which is usually a source of humility, may also be a "source of pride to those who are proud," and may on occasion be the instrument of insincerity, precisely because it is ideally a discipline of sincerity.

We religious people will have to accustom ourselves to the thought that religion may be a source of corruption as well as of wisdom and light; and that the corruption may come not from some flagrant distortion of malice, but from weakness in the heart of the devout. The same prayer which lifts the heart of men to God could also be used by the Pharisee to thank God that he was not as other men. And the same devotion which has a usual fruit of love "joy and peace" may also produce the fruits of fanaticism and cruelty. This is the fruit if men arise from their devotions with the conviction that their purposes are identical with the will of God.

The radical nature of human freedom makes it inevitable that in the final encounter between man and God the proper response of contrite recognition of the vanity of human pretensions should become among some the final vehicle of pretension. That is why it is difficult to isolate the true church of genuine believers for any one who does not look into the heart. Only God can look into the heart. That is also why we are taught that "by their fruits ye shall know them." The contrasting fruits of humble and vain prayer are obvious to us all.

COMMUNISM AND THE CLERGY

Many of us rejoiced over Bishop G. Bromley Oxnam's vigorous defense before the House committee on un-American activities and over his insistence that the committee clean up its files and eliminate the lies and slander contained in them. These files are evidently none other than those of the F.B.I., and they contain every kind of unsupported charge which malicious gossip could devise. There is some evidence that Mrs. Dilling's notorious *Red Network* of a few decades ago, filled with fantastic charges of alleged membership not only in Communist but in every type of left-wing organization, is still in the files. These charges are indiscriminate, and they are designed to hit every "liberal" even if he has valiantly fought Communism, as is the case with Bishop Oxnam. No one who knows the bishop and has knowledge of his activities would accuse him of Communist sympathies. But he is undoubtedly a social "liberal" and has been active in many social causes, some of which had Communists enlisted in them.

I

The bishop called attention to the fact that membership in the American-Soviet friendship organization, which was held against him, was recommended by General Dwight D. Eisenhower. This illustrates how many of the charges of the vigilantes gain plausibility by obscuring chronology and superimposing the temper of an age which finds itself in fateful conflict with Communism upon the realities of a period in which all men of good will tried desperately to build bridges between ourselves and Russia. The files of many of us who are targets of the vigilantes, although we have resisted the Communist illusion for two decades, contain evidence that we were once members of organizations which were subsequently dominated by the Communists. But they contain no record of our struggle to prevent this development, or of our withdrawal when it took place.

In many cases, honored and definitely not subversive organizations are listed as Communist. Membership in pacifist organizations is consistently recorded as evidence of communist sympathies. J. B. Matthews makes the ridiculous charge that 7,000 clergymen are members of Communist-front organizations. He does not bother to document as many as 700. Of these hundreds most are pacifists, many of whom (foolishly in my opinion) signed the "Stockholm Peace Appeal." Many were convicted of Communist sympathies because of their opposition to the McCarran immigration act, which shows how far the current hysteria has gone. Bishop Oxnam cited, as evidence of the kind of malice which prompts the gathering of evidence, the inclusion of sentences, taken out of context, from a sermon he preached years ago at the Indiana state prison. The sermon was a completely respectable exposition of the Christian idea of patriotism. It naturally did not satisfy the modern chauvinism.

There are thus good reasons for rejoicing in Bishop Oxnam's courageous challenge of modern vigilantism and for hoping that others will follow his example. Yet despite my admiration for the bishop and my general approval of his stand, I was left uneasy by his exposition of the relation of Christianity to Communism in his introductory statement. This was partly due to the fact that the statement was designed to prove that Christianity and Communism were so antithetical that no Christian could possibly be a Communist sympathizer. Such a statement causes difficulties because there are in fact Communist sympathizers and fellow travelers in the church. I wonder whether Bishop Oxnam ought not to have admitted this more freely, even before a committee not anxious to get at the truth.

Life never follows logic consistently, and the fellow travelers could presumably defy the antithesis which he stated. But I have a suspicion that they were able to defy it precisely because the antithesis is not as simple as the bishop made it appear. He stated the contradiction between Communism and Christianity as follows: "When I affirm: I believe in God the Father Almighty, I strike at the fundamental error of Communism, which is atheism." He went on to say that the Christian idea of the dignity and the responsibility of the individual prompts him to "reject the materialism which assumes that institutions and even morality are determined by modes of production." The difficulty with this statement is that the idolatry of Communism is more dangerous than its atheism; and the voluntarism by which it claims the right of a small group of elite to "master history," and incidentally their fellow men, is more dangerous than its materialism and determinism. Furthermore, it is precisely these emphases of Communism which make it so attractive to the fellow travelers who have been taken in by it.

II

It must be affirmed that there have never been many explicit Stalinists in the churches, and today their number is so insignificant that the hysterical labors of the vigilantes are completely irrelevant. Nevertheless there are a few and we ought to admit it. The fellow travelers range all the way from those who have no sympathy with Communism as a creed but (at least in Europe) prefer Russia to America, to those who were betrayed by an original Christian Marxist conviction to give their allegiance to the Stalinist cause. As the Stalinist policy followed its tortuous path through history and across the moral sensibilities of mankind, most of the sensitive spirits, in the church and out of it, who were originally attracted to the Communist utopia, saw the errors of their way. But a few maintained their allegiance and became ever more pathetic in trying to make the worse appear the better reason.

Strangely enough Mr. Matthews, despite the farrago of nonsense in his article "Reds and Our Churches," has named all the real Stalinists in the church. They are a handful. The only significant thing to be said about them is that they were long protected by anti-Stalinist "liberals" in the church who foolishly thought that the "prophetic" spirits in the church were bound to be accused of disloyalty and therefore that the charge of Communist sympathy was a validation of the "prophetic spirit." They did not stop to examine the curious logic which failed to make a distinction between the false charge of disloyalty and actual disloyalty, not to the nation but to the principles of democratic civilization and to the tenets of the Christian faith.

III

The European fellow travelers are of a different stripe. Ironically, some of the most eminent were heroic opponents of Hitlerism. Few are touched with Marxist ideology. Karl Barth indeed, despite an explicit disavowal of all secular ideologies, is influenced by a Marxist estimate of America as a "capitalist" country and a confidence in the "socialist" economy of Russia which obscures the nature of her totalitarian political regime. Niemöller, who is no ordinary fellow traveler, is influenced by Barth. He perversely interprets every phenomenon of Russian tyranny as evidence of "Russian primitivism." Hromadka, the eminent Czech fellow traveler, is influenced by Barth. He was originally motivated by a romantic idealization of Russia as the "big brother" of the Slav nations and by a hatred of "bourgeois" culture, acquired incidentally in his wartime residence among us. The Hungarian Bishop Bereczky is influenced by Barth and by an uneasy conscience about the connivance of the church of the past with Hungarian feudalism. He is not the only one who cannot conceive that a "progressive" movement may turn out to be worse than the civilization which it has destroyed. The notorious "Red Dean" of Canterbury has no obvious ideological ties with Marxism. He has a soft heart, a softer head, and an invincible vanity which only the big crowds, delivered by the Communists, can satisfy.

There is an interesting letter extant in which Barth lectures the Hungarian bishop on the error of taking the Red Dean seriously. On the whole, European fellow-traveling theologians adopt the slogan of the neutralist intellectuals: "A plague on both their houses!" Their traditional contempt for capitalism allows them to equate the errors of American pride with the cruelties of the most vexatious tyranny in history.

IV

While the matter is beyond the competence or interest of a congressional investigation committee it is proper, while we deal with these issues among ourselves, to admit that the pathetic clerical Stalinism could not have developed except against the background of a very considerable Marxist dogmatism in the "liberal" wing of the Protestant churches. On the whole the sympathy was for democratic socialism. It is scandalous that our conservatives try to obscure the difference between Communism and Socialism and to deny the rigorous anti-Communism of European Socialism as well as its great contributions to the extension of justice. But it would be idle to deny that these contributions depend partly upon the ability of democracy to draw the fangs from the Marxist error.

Those of us who used Marxist collectivism to counter liberal individualism, Marxist catastrophism to counter liberal optimism, and Marxist determinism to challenge liberalism, moralism, and idealism, must admit that the "truths" which we used to challenge "error" turned out to be no more true (though also no less true) than the liberal ones. But they were much more dangerous precisely because Marxism, in its orthodox variety, makes for a monopoly of political and economic power which is dangerous to justice; while a liberal society preserves a balance of power in the community, which makes for justice, though there are and were some flagrant injustices as the result of a monopoly of economic power. Those of us who were critical of capitalism were in short too uncritical of the Marxist alternative, even when we rejected the Communist version of Marxism and espoused the democratic Marxism.

The present writer is ready to confess to his complicity in these errors, though he is quick to affirm that the Marxist errors do not make more true the ridiculous dogma of laissez-faire, which our conservatives have used to prevent the political and moral criticism of the workings of power monopolies in the economic sphere. I must, however, exempt from this confession one illusion, generally held by the Christian left. I never spoke of socialism as bringing in a society in which "motives of service" would supplant the "profit motive." This was a complete confusion between systems and motives, unfortunately popular in Christian circles. It invested a collectivist system with a moral sanction it did not deserve. It furthermore obscured the fact that the so-called "profit motive" can hardly be eliminated under any system, particularly since it is usually none other than concern for the family, as contrasted with the total community. This concern may be excessive; but it is in any event "natural." Every parson who speaks grandly about supplanting the profit motive exemplifies it when he moves to a new charge because the old one did not give him a big enough parsonage or a salary adequate for his growing family.

Such confessions do not belong, as has been said, to investigating committees. But they are proper among ourselves, not for the purpose of reaching a greater conformity with our already too complacent nation and culture but for the purpose of making our "prophetic witness" against its complacencies more telling by eliminating political errors from its essentially religious judgments.

LITERALISM, INDIVIDUALISM, AND BILLY GRAHAM

Mankind, in its intellectual, including its theological, history, must frequently rethink itself and ask whether it has not discarded some truth with the error which it was intent on discarding. The development of theological thought from "liberalism" to "neo-orthodoxy" is a case in point.

The end of the First World War represented the effective end of the "liberal" world view, particularly the conceptions of human nature and human history, which were directly or indirectly inherited from the Enlightenment's view of the perfectibility of man and of historical progress. Christian theology had accommodated itself too much to this secular world view and tried to fit the Christian truth into the modes of thought generated by the Enlightenment.

This theological dependence upon the Enlightenment produced a "Christian liberalism" which seriously misinterpreted the human situation. It substituted the idea of historical inertia for the concept of original sin, and therefore obscured the fact that the sin of man was a corruption of his freedom and would be the constant concomitant of man's growing historical freedom. It tended to place the seat of virtue in the mind of man, and therefore could not come to terms with the integral human self in both its majesty and its misery—that is, in both its indeterminate freedom and its perennial corruption of that freedom for egoistic ends. Having made reason and history the means of redemption, it had no real place for the Biblical doctrine of redemption. And having interpreted history in Hegelian terms, it had no real place for revelation—that is, for the invasion of the historical by an absolute word of God.

Biblical Christ Not Needed

Consequently, the Christology of liberal Christianity departed from the classical and Biblical Christology. The Christ of the Bible was not needed in the modern schemes of redemption. It was the more convenient to rid theology of this Christology, since the "preaching of the cross" had been a perpetual scandal long before the modern day. It had challenged classical rationalism as much as modern historical rationalism. It had insisted that a character, event, and drama in history were more than an event in history, were the revelation of the divine judgment and forgiveness toward man and mankind. It had demanded faith and commitment of the whole person, beyond the necessary deductions of pure reason. It had also demanded the recognition of sin, repentance being the precondition and concomitant of faith. It was, in short, offensive to every type of "immanental" thought and moral consciousness.

Unfortunately, the elimination of this scandal from Christian preaching sacrificed the very heart of the gospel and led to misinterpretations of both human nature and human history—in fact, to misinterpretations of everything which had to do with human freedom, its responsibilities, its decisions and commitments, its corruptions and the concomitant guilt. It must not be obscured, of course, that there were many forms of "evangelical liberalism," which preserved much of the essential gospel. But on the whole "liberal Christianity" was a capitulation to the spirit of the Enlightenment, whether that spirit expressed itself in Hegelian or in Kantian rationalism.

The "neo-orthodox" revolution against this theological capitulation was undoubtedly initiated by Kierkegaard's polemic against Hegel and his justification of the Christian revelation as a necessary source of man's self-understanding. Man could not understand himself as a person without knowing himself to be a sinner in need of forgiveness. There were, of course, many types of "neo-orthodoxy." The most forceful and creative influence in theology was that of Karl Barth.

Barth's Attitude toward Scripture

Barth influenced all of us who stood in the neo-orthodox tradition, though many of us were embarrassed by the tendency toward literalistic orthodoxy which he did not so much promulgate as encourage among his disciples by a kind of irresponsibility toward the problems of interpreting the Scriptures honestly in terms of the knowledge which historical sciences had brought to the analysis of the books of the Old and New Testaments. Karl Barth was essentially irresponsible toward this problem, for he insisted that it was necessary to accept the Scripture *en bloc,* even though he allowed himself the freedom of suggesting that the story of the empty tomb was in the category of "saga" and that the Genesis stories were *Urgeschichte.* His disciples were usually not so sophisticated or so disingenuous.

This brings us to the first point of our complaint: that we are in danger of sacrificing one of the great achievements of "liberal" theology—namely, the absolute honesty with which it encouraged the church to examine the Scriptural foundations of its faith. This honesty involved not only loyalty to the truth but also fidelity to the standards of the whole modern world of culture, which rightly insisted that no facts of history could be exempted from historical scrutiny in the name of faith. Christianity was a historical religion. It rested upon the facts of history as interpreted by faith. But the faith would have to be profound enough to remain secure, even though peripheral myths with which former ages surrounded the truth of faith in the hope of validating it were disproved. In short, this honesty toward the Scriptural foundations of the faith was not only an act of loyalty to the whole enterprise of modern culture; it was also a method of purifying the Christian faith. For this honesty made it imperative for the believer to accept Jesus as the Christ because the revelation of God in Christ validated itself to him existentially and did not require the confirmation of "signs and wonders."

It is this distinct gain of liberal Christianity which is now imperiled, with the general loss of the prestige of liberalism and the general enhancement of orthodoxy. Perhaps the gradual ascendancy of "ecumenical" concern has contributed to this development.

Religious Purity and Honesty

The ecumenical movement is not explicitly orthodox; but the general presuppositions of the world-wide church certainly give stronger support to a traditional orthodoxy than to any formulation of the Christian faith which is partially determined by the disciplines of modern culture— which therefore takes Bultmann's questions about the nature of the kerygma seriously, even though it may not agree with his answers. At any rate, the general influence of ecumenical relations is to subordinate those questions about history and the history of "God's mighty acts" in Christian revelation which embarrass the more uncritical believers.

The net result of this tendency must be to widen the chasm between the Christian faith and the modern mind at the precise moment when the modern man is shaken in the alternatives to the Christian faith which he once took for granted. But he presumably remains a modern cultured man, who has scruples about believing incredible "facts"; and he probably finds those very facts, which some desire as validation of the gospel, hazards to true belief. But he is not deaf to the essential kerygma, which is that "God was in Christ reconciling the world unto himself." Religious purity is, in short, related to historical honesty. Surely this is a treasure of "liberalism" which we cannot discard and which, if discarded, we must restore.

Social Concern in Peril

But another treasure of "Christian liberalism" deserves the same consideration and prompts the same questions about a too hasty rejection. That is the social concern of liberalism, which in America usually was called the "Social Gospel." The Social Gospel made the mistake of assuming that the Christian could express his social responsibility merely by applying the love-commandment to the larger, rather than to the more personal and intimate, relations of life. Its defective analysis of human nature made it oblivious to the relation of love to justice and to the factors of interest and power which must be reckoned with in any system of justice. In modern parlance, it lacked "realism."

But it was infinitely more realistic than the pietistic individualism which it replaced. This pietism was completely irrelevant in the social life of Europe except, of course, that it was superb in prompting attitudes and acts of personal charity. In America pietistic individualism grew to great strength through frontier evangelism and was ambitious to become socially relevant. In so far as it generated disciplined and responsible individuals it did become indirectly relevant. But it was a source of illusion wherever it interpreted the problems of justice in America's growing industrialism as merely the fruits of a lack of individual discipline. It became particularly dangerous when it interpreted the differences between wealth and poverty as due to diligence on the one hand and sloth on the other hand.

Many of us, in our strictures against the Social Gospel, have forgotten the religious irrelevancies from which it saved us. This pietism, invariably coupled with perfectionist illusions, knowing nothing about the Reformation's restoration of that part of the gospel which revealed the moral ambiguity in the life of the redeemed, is still powerful in the evangelistic traditions of the American churches. It has come to our notice in our own day because it has a personable and honorable exponent in the person of Billy Graham. Graham has proved himself an able ambassador of American good will in the Orient and a good ambassador of Christ to Europeans, who are not inclined to accept anyone from America with sympathy. He has incorporated many of the Social Gospel's concerns for social justice into his pietism. And, though a Southerner, he has been rigorous on the race issue.

Graham's Pietistic Moralism

Nevertheless, Graham still thinks within the framework of pietistic moralism. He thinks the problem of the atom bomb could be solved by converting the people to Christ, which means that he does not recognize the serious perplexities of guilt and responsibility, and of guilt associated with responsibility, which Christians must face. No human goodness can heal the predicament of man, for which the gospel of divine forgiveness is the only final answer. There are no perfectionist solutions for the problems of an atomic age—or indeed of any age in which men have accepted responsibility for the justice and stability of their communities and civilizations, and yet have had the grace to measure the distance between the divine holiness and all fragmentary human righteousness.

Something of the same individualism associated with social awareness is revealed in Graham's discussion of the "seven deadly sins." He comes to the last sin, "avarice," and points out truly that this is the particular sin of Americans, living in their "economy of abundance" and tending to forget that "life consisteth not in the abundance of things a man possesses." But having dealt with this sin of a whole culture he irrelevantly presents Christian salvation as a kind of magic panacea, with the assurance that the "blood of Jesus Christ" can save us from this sin too. There is nothing here about the temptations to which even the most devoted Christians are subject in a very wealthy nation.

Something of the same weakness of individualism and pietism is revealed in Graham's attitude toward our large cities. He is inclined to castigate them for their sins, as if the evils of inevitable sexual vice were their only defects; and he does not give due regard to the achievements of community, despite technical mass culture. Certainly our cities, as well as our whole technical civilization, can be "redeemed" by no simple perfectionist devotion of a few or many saints. They and it are redeemed by the devoted services to the community of many people of different and indifferent religious persuasion.

The common services which the pious and the secular make and must make toward a tolerable community and for the preservation of a civilization must be recognized. There is a danger of obscuring this fact in all evangelistic efforts. The ultimate religious commitment is a personal and individual one, and it can therefore be most effectively made by a pietist who narrows the vision of religious awareness to highly personal dilemmas and needs. Hence the pietistic evangelist is probably most effective among individuals who have pressing personal, moral, and religious perplexities.

"Other Sheep" Must Be Respected

Meanwhile, however, there are many Christians and non-Christians who are committed to tasks and responsibilities and are involved in common human dilemmas which are not to be comprehended in any neat formulas of salvation. We assert as Christians that the message of Christ is a source of grace and truth to all men either in their individual dimension or in the social dimension of their existence. But we must also have a decent modesty and humility about the righteousness of those whose common decencies contribute to our security, whether or not they have solved the ultimate mystery through faith or have made an ultimate commitment to Christ. The mystery of the human and the divine is greater than is surmised in our philosophies. It cannot be measured by the neat formulas to which Christian orthodoxy is frequently reduced, any more than it can be exhausted in even the most elaborate theological systems. If the evangelistic effort tempts us to draw pharisaic lines between the righteous and the unrighteous, that is perhaps not so much the fault of the evangelist— particularly if he be as modest as Graham—as it is the dilemma of the Christian faith itself, which is bound ultimately to ask for a personal commitment but must always be aware that the grace of God is not bound by any of our formulas of salvation, that the Lord has "other sheep which are not of this fold."

The personal achievements of Graham as a Christian and as evangelist should be duly appreciated. But they do not materially alter the fact that an individualistic approach to faith and commitment, inevitable as it may be, is in danger both of obscuring the highly complex tasks of justice in the community and of making too sharp distinctions between the "saved" and the "unsaved." The latter may not have signed a decision card but may have accepted racial equality with greater grace than the saved. We must, in short, bring Christian evangelism into correspondence with the breadth and complexity of our social obligations as apprehended by any form of classical Christian faith, and at the same time into conformity with the Reformation insights, or better still the Biblical truths about the precariousness of the virtues of the redeemed. That will make us fit fellow workers with decent secularists in the common tasks of our civilization.

No Simplifying of the Gospel

All this can be done without detracting from the imperious claims of the gospel upon the conscience of the individual, who transcends every social situation and communal destiny to face the mystery of the divine judgment and mercy. The humble parson who tries to be a mediator of the divine grace and the ordinary services of the church may have a better chance of doing this and presenting the gospel in its full dimension than the professional evangelist, however gifted.

But whatever the church may do to spread the gospel, it must resist the temptation of simplifying it in either literalistic or individualistic terms, thus playing truant to positions hard-won in the course of Christian history. We cannot afford to retrogress in regard to the truth for the sake of a seeming advance or in order to catch the public eye.

The problem we are considering really transcends the question of the validity of highly individualistic evangelism, which the frontier tradition in America has made particularly popular among us. The problem is whether, in the course of our history, the church can absorb what is valid in the modern "liberal" attitude toward history and yet preserve what is valid in the Reformation's rediscovery of the Biblical message of redemption. That message did not make the sharp distinction between the virtues of the redeemed and unredeemed which modern pietism makes. The Reformation knew of the equal need of all men for divine forgiveness. Its interpretation of the Christian faith did not encourage simple answers to the complex questions of social order and justice. It recognized the fragmentary character of all human virtue and the finiteness of all human knowledge. Such a message of Christ is relevant to the perplexities of an atomic age without presuming to offer Christians a simple way out of common human dilemmas. It knows that the ultimate dilemmas are universal and that the judgment of Christ is always relevant to both the righteous and the unrighteous.

THE SECURITY AND HAZARD OF THE CHRISTIAN MINISTRY •

Lesson: I Corinthians 3, 11-15.

I want to speak to you in this climactic hour, in which long and arduous years of preparation for the Christian ministry come to a close for you, on the theme "The Security and Hazard of the Christian Ministry," upon the basis of the Scripture lesson of the evening.

The security is quite obvious. It exists in the foundation or in the words of the text "Other foundation can no one lay than that which has been laid in Christ Jesus." We might spend some time in comparing the gospel of Christ with the religions of the world. But it may suffice to prove the security of this foundation by calling attention to the fact that the answer to the human predicament is more adequately given in the Christ revelation, because in that revelation the freedom of man is given its final norm and the guilt of man is given the final salve and healing.

The gospel of Christ is succinctly expressed in the Cross of Christ. That Cross always represents two dimensions to the eyes of faith. It means on the one hand the perfect love, which is the final norm for this strange creature with such a radical freedom, distinguishing him from other creatures, that no norm can be placed for that freedom but the realization of himself in the love of God and his fellows, even at the expense of his physical existence. The Cross of Christ stands on the very limit of human history and defines the perfect good which is not beyond our possibilities, as the history of martyrdom proves, but which is certainly not within conventional possibilities of our existence. We have thus in Christ as our norm and law, a

• Address delivered at the One Hundred and Twenty-first Commencement at Union Theological Seminary, May 28, 1957.

standard which challenges every achievement and prevents us from taking premature satisfaction in any of the virtues by which men count themselves righteous. But the gospel of Christ is not primarily a norm for our freedom but a balm for the wound of our guilt. The central message of the gospel is that "God was in Christ reconciling the world unto himself" and overcoming the hiatus between his divine holiness and our sinful nature. Morally the gospel of Christ presents us with such indeterminate possibilities that the Christian faith is always threatened with the heresy of other-worldliness. But to capitulate to the search for perfection at the price of responsibility would be to build falsely on the foundation of Christ.

It would be equally false to invest some proximate good, some easily attainable virtue, with absolute sanctity. The long history of Christian legalism and fanaticism proves that many have hazarded to build wrongly on the foundation of Christ and to escape the tension and the relaxation of the tension through the assurance of divine mercy, by the strenuous effort to establish human virtue, in either ordinary or extraordinary terms, as the way of salvation. But if we build truly on the foundation of Christ we escape the evils of both fanaticism and irresponsibility.

To build on the foundation of Christ truly means that we cannot engage in the world flight of Buddhism or the fanaticism of Islam. The world flight of the one is due to a disregard of the whole historical order. The fanaticism of Islam is due to the introduction of false absolutes into history. Historical responsibility and fanaticism are frequently closely related. The one is the by-product of the other. To call attention to these dangers is to introduce the second word of our topic into our thought. The security is in the foundation. The hazard is in the building upon the foundation. For as Paul insists in our lesson, no one can guarantee the way we build on the foundation; it may be "hay, wood and stubble" or "silver, gold and precious stones."

The Yogi and the Commissar

Years ago Arthur Koestler wrote an interesting little book entitled *The Yogi and the Commissar*. The Yogi was the symbol of world flight and the Commissar was the symbol of the fanaticism which is the inevitable fruit of the illusion that we can, from our standpoint, define and achieve history's ultimate good. Koestler did not even consider that the gospel of Christ provides us with an alternative to both Yogi and Commissar because it sets the final good, not in eternity, but in history, though at the very rim of history, and it prevents us from regarding any human virtue or achievement as anything but fragmentary. But we must humbly acknowledge that the long history of Christian fanaticism on the one hand, and of Christian otherworldliness on the other hand, clearly prove that it is possible and perhaps inevitable that man should build falsely on the foundation.

The hazard of the Christian ministry is obviously to build wrongly on the true foundation, to build "wood, hay and stubble," in the words of the Apostle. I should like to analyze these hazards in terms of the two tasks which always confront us. The one is to minister to the perennial needs of men in the light of the gospel and the other is to minister to the peculiar needs of the people of this generation.

As pastors, we must minister to people who go through the natural cycles of life. They grow up, and then they wither and die. And whether in youth or in age, they fall into sin because they have a unique freedom which enables them to make many false starts and false ends. It is one of the blessed forms of the ministry that one is entitled to be a guide and helper to young people as they grow up. The process of growing up is not quite as easy for young people as Karen Horney seems to assume (in her *Neurosis and Human Growth*), for she thinks if neuroses do not interfere, there is a natural development of the potentialities of human nature. Actually the process of growth demands a combination of discipline and freedom, of law and of grace. We build wrongly on the foundations if we interpret the gospel merely in terms of discipline, and particularly if we identify law and discipline with the conventions of society, which partly express and partly corrupt the necessary disciplines of life. One of the besetting errors of Protestant Christianity is excessive conventionality. All laws, and particularly those which are expressed in traditions and conventions, must be subject to the law of love if we are to mediate the discipline of life to growing youth. Excessive legalism and conventionality is wrong, but so is the romanticism which extols freedom as the final good; for the problem for youth and for all men is not how free we can be, but how free we can be, being bound by our responsibilities. Both conventionality and romanticism are false elaborations of a religion of truth and grace, of love and law.

In the course of life young people grow old, and all men go the path of withering and finally dying. It is certainly as difficult to grow old gracefully and to face death with faith and peace, as to grow up. If I have any regret about my early ministry, it is that I was so busy being what I thought to be a prophet of righteousness, that I was not sufficiently aware of the importance of the pastoral ministry to the maimed, the halt, and the blind, in short to all people who had to resign themselves to the infirmities of the flesh and who must finally face the threat of extinction. The "sting of death is sin" declares the Scripture, which is to say, if we center our life within ourself and not in God, if we do not learn the nonchalance which is able to confess "Whether we live, we live unto the Lord; and whether we die, we die unto the Lord, and whether we live therefore or die we are the Lord's," our death and the death of our dear ones will strike us as stark tragedy, though it is the common lot of all men. We build falsely on true foundations if we try to mediate the grace of the Christian faith through slogans and clichés or if we try to quiet anxious hearts through spurious appeals to special providence which is supposed to protect the faithful. For the gospel gives us no special securities or exemptions from the frailties of men and the tragedies of life. We are expected to live life fully but also to be detached from life so that we have everything as if we had it not.

Among the perennial needs of people, whether young or old, is their need as sinners. We have all fallen short and we are all engaged in more or less pathetic efforts to hide that fact. All sentimentality which hides our sin and helps people escape the seriousness of man's predicament, all frantic legalism intended to obscure the fragmentary character of human virtue and to prevent the confession of man's sins and therefore the possibility of real grace is a part of the hazardous, erroneous building on the true foundation. It changes the gospel from a gospel of grace and forgiveness to a sentimental morality which gives simple answers to difficult problems.

Not much evil is done by evil people. Most of the evil is done by good people, who do not know that they are not good. It is one of the true functions of the minister of Christ to puncture the self-deceptions, including his own, by which people try to perpetuate the open secret that we all think of ourselves more highly than we ought to think.

The Problems of the Age

We must help people to face not only the perennial problems of human existence, the problems of growth, of death and sin, but to face the unique problems of our age. The eighteenth and nineteenth centuries were wrong in hoping that history would essentially change the perennial human situation. But within that situation history certainly presents us with some novel responsibilities and predicaments in every new age.

One of these new responsibilities is to preserve the dignity of man and the healing power of true community amid the impersonal and merely technically contrived togetherness of an industrial age. The Christian church in

America has done tolerably well in comparison with other churches in building integral religious communities in our cities. That is the achievement partly of American sectarianism and partly of the immigrant church. But there is something in this achievement which is not in accord with the foundation of Christ. Our churches are friendly, even to the point of being chummy. That is just the point; they are too chummy. They have mixed the natural community of race and class too much with the community of grace. Hence the grievous entanglement of our churches with racial pride in a day when the state leads the church in establishing racial brotherhood. If we want to build truly on the foundation we must mediate the Gospel judgment: "If ye love them which love ye what thanks have ye?"

Community, particularly in an industrial society, requires justice; and justice requires a delicate equilibrium of social forces. To be ministers in our kind of society means to distill the norm of love into norms of justice. If we do not understand the relation between love and justice, our preaching of the gospel of love is bound to degenerate into sentimentality.

But So as by Fire . . .

Finally, we cannot escape the problem as Christian ministers in America, the wealthiest and most powerful of modern nations, of mediating the gospel to the conscience of the nation, involved in all of its responsibilities. A pure individualism and pietism is certainly hay and straw in our day. So is a simple moralism which cannot understand the responsibilities of a nation in a nuclear age, which cannot make war without risking the physical fabric and the moral substance of our civilization and which cannot simply disavow the terrible new instruments of war without risking capitulation to tyranny. To speak the word of truth and of faith in a nation and generation involved in such deep predicaments in which the perennial problems of mankind have reached new dimensions, is certainly a hazardous undertaking. Let us change Paul's metaphor a little. He declares that it is hazardous to build on the foundation of Christ and that if you build wrongly you may be saved "But so as by fire." Let us merely say, you are not in peril of your life. You are only in peril of your soul, but you can be saved "by the skin of your teeth."

PART III: Revelation and the Kingdom

BARTH—APOSTLE OF THE ABSOLUTE

For months, even years, we have been hearing of Barth and the Barthian movement in Germany. But the reports have been fragmentary. None of Barth's books was available to us in translation. It seems the fate of American theology, at least so far as it is developed in the pulpit rather than the theological school, that it must orient itself without any sense of cooperation with German theology. Perhaps that is not so much its fate as its punishment for the superficiality which creates a market for every casual book of sermons while translations of significant theological treatises from other languages are left on the shelves. Let us hope that Douglas Horton's service to the American church, rendered through his translation of Barth's *Das Wort Gottes und die Theologie,* will earn the deserved gratitude of sales so large that other translators may be encouraged. At any rate, we finally have direct contact with this man Barth.

Barth's theology has been described as a kind of fundamentalism. If one means by fundamentalism a theology which rests upon a defiance of the generally accepted results of the historical and physical sciences the description is quite erroneous and misleading. The Barthian school accepts the results of the Biblical criticism and has no magical conceptions of revelation. Neither has it any quarrel with the physical sciences and evolution. But in the sense that it is an effort to escape relativism through dogmatism it is a new kind of fundamentalism or an old kind of orthodoxy. It is, in fact, a revival of the theology of the Reformation, Calvinistic in its conception of God and Lutheran in its emphasis upon the experience of justification by faith.

The Place of Jesus

The simplest explanation of Barthian theology is that it is a reaction to the subjectivism and the relativism of liberal theology. It reacts not only to the theological but to the inevitable ethical relativism of modern thought. The Bible is not, according to Barth, an inerrant revelation but neither is it the history of man's progressive thoughts and experiences of God. It contains the word of God, an absolute in spite of all relativities. The absolute character of this revelation is finally guaranteed by the position of Christ. With Paul, Barth, if he knew Christ after the flesh, wants to know him so no more.

Jesus Christ is not the keystone in the arch of our thinking. Jesus Christ is not a supernatural miracle that we may or may not consider untrue. Jesus Christ is not the goal which we may hope to reach after conversion. . . . He is God who becomes man, the creator of all things who lies as a babe in the manger.

Just what is the significance of Christ and how does he become the center and basis of our religion? Simply that he resolves the conflict between God and man, between man's finitude and his infinite hopes. What damns man is not his sins in specific situations but his sin. The good and evil, the virtues and vices which emerge in historical incident and are determined by the condition of time and place are not man's real problem. What drives man to despair is not the satanic nature of his life when governed by its evil moods but the inadequate nature of his highest morality.

God stands in contrast to man as the impossible in contrast to the possible, as death in contrast to life, as eternity in contrast to time. The solution to the riddle, the answer to the question, the satisfaction of our need is the absolutely new event whereby the impossible becomes of itself possible, death becomes life, eternity time and God man.

A Sense of Guilt

If this does not make sense to a liberal theologian, it might be observed that it does state a problem which liberal religion has sadly neglected. It is the highest function of religion to create a sense of guilt, to make man conscious of the fact that his inadequacies are more than excusable limitations—that they are treason against his better self. It accomplishes this task by revealing sin as a treason against God. "Against thee and thee only have I sinned," cries the psalmist. Barth puts it this way: "To suffer in the Bible means to suffer because of God; to sin, to sin against God; to doubt, to doubt of God; to perish, to perish at the hand of God."

It is quite possible that such a religious consciousness of sin has the moral limitation that it preoccupies the soul with an ultimate problem of life to such a degree that it loses interest in specific moral problems and struggles which must be faced day by day. But the merit of this note of tragedy in religion is that it saves us from the easy optimisms into which we have been betrayed by our moral evolutionism. After all, there is something just as unreal in most modern dogmas of salvation through moral evolution as in the older doctrines of salvation.

Is Progress Real?

Is not the doctrine of progress little more than dogma? Is it not true that history is the sorry tale of new imperialisms supplanting old ones; of man's inhumanity to man, checked in one area or relationship expressing itself in new and more terrible forms in other areas and relationships? Is it not a monstrous egotism and foolish blindness which we betray when we imagine that this civilization in which commercialism has corrupted every ideal value is in any sense superior to the Middle Ages, or that the status of the industrial worker differs greatly from that of the feudal slave? Religion ought to condemn the achievements of history by bringing them into juxtaposition to the "holiness of God." Even if we cannot define the holiness of God without making it relative to our own experiences and hopes, that religious experience will at least help us to see that moral limitation involves perversity, that it is in a sense treason against the highest we have conceived.

In so far as Barthian theology reintroduces the note of tragedy in religion, it is a wholesome antidote to the superficial optimism of most current theology. But we may well question whether it gives us the sense of certainty and the experience of "deliverance from the body of this death" which it imagines, and we may also question whether it does not pay too high a moral price for whatever religious advantage it arrives at.

As to the sense of certainty, having sacrificed the inerrancy of the Bible and even the miraculous in Christ's life, it tries to escape the subjectivism and relativism in which religious knowledge, together with all other knowledge, is involved, by finding one absolute, the Christ-life or the Christ-idea. It is really the Christ-idea that is absolute rather than the Christ-life, for this theology cares nothing for the peculiar circumstances of Christ's life or the historical background of his teachings. It is not even above describing the ethics of the Sermon on the Mount as the definition of the ultimate ethical idea which men can never reach.

How do we know that this Christ-idea is absolute and not subjective: we do not know. That is simply dogmatically stated. The proof that is offered is the proof of human need. Only this kind of an absolute can save man from the cursed paradox of his existence, from an existence which conceives ideals beyond attainments and lives at once in eternity and in time. To accept this absolute is the experience of justification by faith and presumably it gives support in actual life to the dogma. That is, we know this doctrine to be true because it is a doctrine which meets a human need.

The Pathos of Theological Thought

Here we have the whole pathos of this kind of abstruse theological thought. In order to escape the relativism of a theology which is based upon and corrected by biology, psychology, social science, philosophy, and every other field of knowledge, we accept a theology which has no way of authenticating itself except by the fact that it meets a human need. This is a sorry victory. Relativism may be defeated but at the price of a new and more terrifying subjectivism. How do we know that the human need which this kind of religion satisfies is not really a too-morbid conscience? May it not be that the very emergence of Barthian theology at this time comes from the sense of tragedy which the war created, particularly in Germany?

Barth considers that possibility and denies it, dogmatically. There is, as a matter of fact, no way of escaping relativity except through dogmatism or magic. There is always a danger that a religion which makes or has made its adjustments to society, to culture, to science, and to thought in general will degenerate into nothing more than a sentimental glow upon thought and life. In contrast to that kind of insipid religion, Barthian religion has the note of reality in it. But ultimately there is no more peace in dogmatism than in magic. We can escape relativity and uncertainty only by piling experience upon experience, checking hypothesis against hypothesis, correcting errors by considering new perspectives, and finally by letting the experience of the race qualify the individual's experience of God.

The other question to be considered is whether Barth does not pay too high a moral price for the religious advantages of his theology, even if these are real. There is, to be sure, a note of moral realism in Barthian thought which is not found in quietistic theology. The peace which comes to the soul through assurance of pardon, the inner harmony which is realized by overcoming the sense of moral frustration, does not absolve the sinner of his sins. We are sinners still even after we have been saved.

The Moral Price

Let us acknowledge with gratitude that we have here no new escape from the world of reality. The true Christian according to Barth continues to look upon the brutalities of history with wholesome contrition. He knows that he is a part of a world and that his sins have helped create it. Nevertheless, it is inevitable that he should be more concerned with the problem of his inner life than with the effort to protect and advance moral values in society. Even if there is no social progress in the sense that modern liberalism assumes, each generation has the task of defeating its own lusts or of bringing them under some kind of discipline. In our own generation, in which man's expansive desires may be gratified more easily and in which his lusts are expressed with more deadly force than in any previous age, it is particularly important that the humility expressed in the cry, "God be merciful to me a sinner," should result in creative social activity as well as in a religious assurance of pardon.

If religion can help men see that the root of imperialism is the imperialism of the individual and that social misery is in some sense due to the perversity of the individual soul, it has remarkable social and moral function. But if the realization of the tragedy of sin merely busies the sensitive soul with efforts to find theological, metaphysical, and mystical solutions for the problems of our mortality, the poor devils who bear in their bodies the agony of social injustice may be pardoned if they will regard religion with indifference and contempt.

Individual Responsibility

Barthian pessimism is, as all pessimism, the fruit of moral sensitiveness. It is the business of religion to create a sensitive conscience. And there is certainly more religious vitality in such pessimism than in the easy optimism of evolutionary moralism. Yet it is one of the tragedies of the religious life that it is almost impossible to create this kind of moral sensitivity without tempting the soul to despair of history and take a flight into the absolute which can neither be established upon historical grounds nor justified by any strictly rational process, but can only be assumed and dogmatically asserted because it seems morally necessary. What seems impossible must become possible, else the world will have to worry its way out of bloodshed, slavery, and social misery without the aid of the sensitive souls whose very acuteness of feeling incapacitates them for the world's work. It will then have to depend for emancipation upon the morally sensitive souls who have no assurance of God to save them from despair but who develop what moral energy they can while walking always on the narrow ledge at the side of the abyss of despair.

BARTHIANISM AND THE KINGDOM

It is quite obvious that Mr. Homrighausen and I are in agreement at many points in our estimate of Barthianism and liberalism. I think he is quite right in resenting the suggestions that the Barthians are not interested in the social question and in pointing out their social radicalism. He thinks I do not fully appreciate this background of social radicalism. It is at this point that I would part company with him and make a distinction between their social sensitivity and their social vigor. I would say that the Barthian theologians are very sensitive to the iniquities of the present social system and that in this critical attitude they are measurably superior to the liberal theologians who frequently indulge the illusion that the League of Nations, or the latest bank merger, or the last humanitarian campaign are proofs of the imminent realization of the new heaven and the new earth.

The Barthians are very critical of present society but they are also very critical of every effort to improve society. They regard it as necessary but dangerous; dangerous because moral and social activity might tempt men to moral pride and conceit and thus rob them of salvation. If the Barthians are socialists, I think it is not unfair to them to say that they don't work very hard at it. It might as well be pointed out, too, that men like Gogarten manage to combine a social ethic which smells of feudalism with their theology of crisis. That proves that a radical social philosophy does not flow inevitably from Barthian theology. The real fact is that the theology originally emerged from a radical social philosophy which found no possibility of realizing itself in history. I still insist that if the Barthians gave themselves more vigorously to the social task they would not be quite so pessimistic about history, because vigorous moral activity creates its own eschatology.

It ought to be said that the moral sensitivity and the lack of social vigor in Barthian thought flow from the same source, and that source is religious perfectionism. God, the will of God, and the Kingdom of God are conceived in such transcendent terms that nothing in history can even approximate the divine; and the distinctions between good and evil on the historical level are in danger of being reduced to irrelevancies. Mr. Homrighausen himself offers an interesting example of just how this kind of moral logic works. "Should Christians ever fight for their rights?" he asks. "If they do is it not an evil? At least it is not an absolute good. Is a compromise ever good; does the end ever justify the means?"

I am not sure just what he means by fighting for rights. If violence is implied, of course it would be rather easy to rule it out on ethical grounds. But since Mr. Homrighausen is a pretty consistent Barthian I suspect he means more than that. He means that to contend for one's rights is not consistent with a perfect ethic of love which, if followed consistently, leads to complete nonresistance. In terms of this perfectionism he is therefore forced to rule out all types of political, social, and economic pressure by which the weak must oppose the pretensions and exactions of the strong. To be very specific, he would undoubtedly have to frown upon the innumerable strikes which will probably occur this coming winter in order that wage scales may not sink to new minimum levels. From the standpoint of ethical and religious perfectionism such strikes are undoubtedly unethical. Yet I am persuaded that they may help to keep society from reaching new depths of inhumanity.

Of course they represent compromise. All history is compromise. But the "nicely calculated less and more" with which we must deal when we deal with the ethical problems of history is really important. Any religious idealism which absolves us of responsibility for finding the best possible means to the highest possible social end is dangerous to the moral struggle. That does not mean that it is not also helpful. There is always a touch of the sense of the absolute in vital religion, and in so far as the Barthians have this sense they are religiously superior to the liberals who have been so completely lost in the relativities of history that every slight eminence in the landscape of time seems to them to be a final mountain peak of the Kingdom of God.

True religion does save man from moral conceit in the attainment of his relative goals. But if the sense of the absolute and transcendent becomes so complete an obsession as it is in Barthian theology all moral striving on the level of history is reduced to insignificance. It is good to survey history occasionally *sub specie aeternitatis,* but it is not wholesome to the moral vigor of a people to make the eternal perspective the perpetual vantage point. It is because the Barthians do this that they cannot give themselves with great fervor to any social program, however certain they may be that society is in need of reorganization and however clearly they perceive what steps must be taken for its redemption. In Barthianism, religious vigor first creates and then devours ethical passion.

BARTHIANISM AND POLITICAL REACTION

The Barthian theologians began as frustrated and disappointed socialists. Brunner and Barth both acknowledge their indebtedness to Ragaz, Kutter, and the Christian socialists who were believed in the prewar period to have established an effective relationship between Christianity and socialism. The First World War convinced Barth and his followers that the hope of the establishment of a Kingdom of God on earth was an idle dream, and they returned, therefore, to the emphasis of orthodox Christianity upon the perennial sinfulness of the world and the need of a salvation which transcended the whole sphere of socio-ethical relationships. Neither human nature nor society could be redeemed in ethical terms. All that was possible was to accept the grace of God and to know oneself "justified" in a world of sin.

Logically this emphasis need not preclude rigorous social, ethical, and political activity looking toward the alleviation of the world's injustices and inequalities. Barth and Brunner remain socialists who insist that capitalism must be destroyed even though a good Christian does not give himself to the utopian illusion that the socialism which is substituted for capitalism represents either the Kingdom of God or even a proximately just society. As a rational and ethically sensitive person, declare both Barth and Brunner, the Christian is bound to seek a social order which will throw the most effective restraints about the sinfulness of man and establish the most tolerable communal life. But all this is fairly inconsequential in the light of the real problem which faces the Christian, that is the distance between the human and the divine, between time and eternity, and the necessity of appropriating the grace of God by which that chasm is bridged.

Serving Social Reaction

Though a modified social radicalism is thus compatible with the neo-orthodoxy which Barth has created, it is becoming increasingly apparent that the emphases of the new theological conservatism are being exploited in the interest of political reaction to a greater degree than in the interest of social liberalism and radicalism.

Various elements in Barthian orthodoxy lend themselves to this use by political reactionaries, even though, in the case of Barth, the conception of the transcendence of God is so absolute that it is impossible to use either religious dogma or religious emotion for the purpose of supporting or sanctifying any particular political program, either conservative or radical. Among his followers this is less true. Gogarten in particular has developed a political ethic from the Barthian theology which finally ends in the bog of a reactionary feudalism.

The first element in the Barthian orthodoxy which can easily become grist for reaction is its revival of the Lutheran theory of the *Schoepfungsordnung*—the "order of creation." By this, the natural relations of life, family, state, vocation, and race are designated. It is maintained that both the rationalistic individualism of the nineteenth and the rationalistic collectivism of the twentieth century do violence to these relations which God has ordained. There is probably some truth in this charge. The Russian attitude toward the family and the generally critical attitude of socialism toward the sentiment of nationality may be regarded as a too consistently rationalistic attitude toward natural sentiments and relationships.

Finding Social Institutions "God-Given"

Perhaps it is true that the imagination of religion can deal more adequately with the organic character of life than a rationalism which reduces organism to mechanism and reacts against a mechanistic individualism with an equally insupportable mechanistic collectivism. However, there is only one step from the religious sanctification of the order of creation to the religious support of particular types of social organization which the theologian regards as "God-given." Thus Gogarten sets a feudalistic conception of a social order, which smacks of serfdom, against rationalistic equalitarianism in the name of a religious conception of vocation (*Beruf*). The world of nature, it is argued, is full of inequality and the rationalist is trying to coerce this world into equality.

The same theory of the order of creation gives a new support to the idea of statehood, and many a Barthian epigone is using it to justify the state absolutism which is setting itself up in Germany. In the same way the anti-Semitism of the Hitler movement is justified because it is supposed that the reality of race belongs to an order of creation to which rationalists are trying to do violence. It is interesting to note that the new dualism of Barthian theology works in paradoxical fashion here. In one moment the world is a world of sin which cannot be redeemed. In the next moment it represents a "God-given" order which must not be violated.

An Orthodoxy that Breeds Indifference

Thus some of the modern theological reactionaries manage to combine all the weaknesses of both religious dualism and monism, of a too rigorous separation between God and the world and a too consistent identification of the two. The National Socialist Lutheran preacher who argued at a meeting of the German Christians that when the Apostle

Paul declared "in Christianity there is neither Jew nor Greek" he did not mean that this ideal was to be realized in a world of sin but that he meant it for a world of the resurrection, was thus drawing a possible though not a necessary deduction from the new orthodox emphasis.

Another emphasis in the neo-orthodoxy of Barthianism which may be appropriated by the reactionaries is its good Lutheran emphasis upon "justification by faith." Brunner, in his recent book, *Das Gebot und die Ordnungen,* derives some valuable insights from this doctrine. He recognizes, for instance, that political action cannot be "Christian" in any exact sense and that the effort to have a Christian socialism or a peculiarly Christian approach to any cultural or political problem will destroy that unity between Christian and non-Christian action which is necessary for the success of any secular enterprise. The idea that the Christian is "justified" in doing the things which must be done in an imperfect world enables him to deal realistically with all current problems and to regard various ascetic and semi-ascetic withdrawals from the world as "parasitic" efforts to establish purity at the expense of other people's sins.

But the same doctrine of justification also persuades Brunner that a judge who administers a bad law should not worry too much about it since God will justify him in enforcing a bad law in an imperfect world. The judge must not be too anxious about the imperfection of the law, particularly since it is worth remembering that "any given law" is better than no law at all. In all this Brunner forgets completely that no law is a fixed quantity and that judges are making law constantly by their interpretation of previous laws. One can be thankful, therefore, that Oliver Wendell Holmes and Justices Brandeis and Cardozo have never heard of Brunner's theory of justification by faith.

Complacency to Social Injustice

Perhaps this tendency of Barthianism to sharpen the contrast between the human and divine in one minute so that all the world lies in hopeless sin and in the next minute to "justify" the hopeless world in its imperfections has no greater dangers than the liberal tendency to find the divine in every little human virtue. But its dangers seem equally great. What can be done with this kind of doctrine was clearly revealed in Germany recently when a group of Lutheran clergymen suggested that it was impious to hope for a social order in which wages would be commensurate with human needs since human sin made such justice impossible and since the expectation of it denied "the necessity of Christ's salvation."

Here religious absolutism which begins by making the conscience sensitive to all human weakness ends in complacency toward social injustice. The selfishness of privileged groups who are trying desperately to prevent the organization of a social order in which all men will have basic security is confusedly identified with human selfishness in general, and the workers are told that they must suffer from injustice as punishment for the sins of mankind. The harassed unemployed may well express their scorn for these theological subtleties and insist that they are at least entitled to a world in which all men suffer equally from the consequences of human sin.

The new emphasis upon the natural law in Barthianism as a method of holding the sinful world in check is a revival of the doctrine of the natural law which has characterized Christian orthodoxy until the rise of modern liberalism. Liberalism erroneously imagined that the law of love could be made authoritative for the world of politics and economics and it thereby merely substituted unconscious compromise for conscious compromise. Perhaps there is nothing more important in the ethical reorientation of modern Christianity than a new study of the doctrine of natural law. Love perfectionism is clearly no specific guide for the detailed problems which arise in human society. No society has ever existed without some degree of coercion and it is better to recognize that fact than to obscure the realities with idealistic phrases which permit privileged people to benefit from covert coercion while they stand in abhorrence of the overt resistance of the underprivileged.

Aids of Reaction

On the necessity of coercion, men like Brunner and Gogarten speak with clarity and persuasiveness. But on the whole the doctrine works out completely to the advantage of political and economic reaction. In Gogarten this is obviously true. In Brunner the reactionary tendency is less marked but nevertheless real. First of all, the state is given a new emphasis. It is the instrument which God uses to hold a sinful world in check. All the epigones of Barthianism are using that doctrine to justify the efforts to establish a state absolutism in Germany under Hitler.

Brunner is more circumspect. But his pessimism about human society finally drives him into the camp of reaction in spite of his avowed socialism. He thinks capitalism ought to be destroyed. But since any political order is better than no order at all, and since the state is a "dyke" against the final consequences of sin, and since any effort to remodel the dyke might possibly result in an inundation of the world in sin, it follows that the Christian can countenance change only if it can be achieved without interruption (*Pausenlos*). Brunner presses that point so strongly that one does not see how a Christian can possibly countenance adequate measures of social change, since no conceivable method can be guaranteed to achieve its goal without some social dislocations and convulsions.

Conscious or Unconscious Conservatism

Without being unfair to Brunner one must come to the conclusion that a genuine religious absolutism is unconsciously compounded in his social theory with the fears which a bourgeois world harbors of the consequences of a revolution. If we are to have a new theory of natural law we ought at least to have one which will justify necessary coercion in favor of a new social order as much as in favor of the status quo. With the possible exception of Barth himself, who refuses to permit the premature application of his theology to any political problems, the other Barthian thinkers are either consciously adjusting themselves to political reaction (as in the case of Gogarten) or they are being appropriated for that purpose by their lesser disciples.

As one who bears a few wounds from doing battle against complacent liberalism, I must confess that this appropriation of Barthian thought by reaction almost persuades me to return to the liberal camp as a repentant prodigal. Fortunately there are alternatives which make it unnecessary to embrace liberal illusions for the sake of avoiding orthodox confusions. One must not make the mistake of ascribing Hitlerism to Barthian theology. Barth himself is one of its most determined foes. But Hilter's type of reactionary politics, including his anti-Semitism, finds altogether too much abettance in this new theology to justify the confident prediction of some European theologians that they have found a way of extricating the Christian church from its too intimate relationship with capitalistic civilization into which liberal Christianity supposedly enmeshed it. Rather than escaping from this slavery, too many of the alleged emancipators have turned out to be minions of the oppressor.

MARX, BARTH, AND ISRAEL'S PROPHETS

We hear much today about two types of dialectic thinking, dialectic materialism and dialectic theology; about the secularized religion of which Karl Marx is the author and the extreme reaction to it associated with the name of Karl Barth. Both of them are derivatives of a much older dialectic—that of the Hebrew prophets. Marxism is a secularized version of the prophetic interpretation of history, and Barthianism is a highly sophisticated version of the religious thought which insists upon the absolute transcendence of God. In the one case, the prophetic idea of God as working in history and giving it meaning is reduced to the idea of a logic in history which works toward the final establishment of an ideal society not totally dissimilar from the messianic kingdom of prophetic dreams. In the other case, it is denied that God works in history; the world of human history is a chaotic and meaningless thing until it is illumined by the incarnation; since all human actions fall short of the perfection of God it is denied that human actions can in any sense be instruments of God; the hope of a better world in prophetic eschatology is transmuted into a consistent otherworldliness which simply promises doom for man and all his works, as far as man is a creature of nature.

In both of these types of dialectic thinking, the true dialectic of Hebrew prophecy and the Gospels is destroyed. The significant fact about Hebrew thought is that it neither lifts God completely above history nor identifies Him with historical processes. It is, in short, neither pantheistic nor dualistic, as all Greek thought inclines to be. The God of Jewish prophecy is a transcendent God. Before Him "the nations are as a drop of the bucket, as small dust in the balances—it is he that sitteth on the circles of the earth and the inhabitants are as grasshoppers before him." The idea of the transcendence of God is perhaps most beautifully and adequately expressed in Isaiah 40.

The Prophet's God

The idea of God's transcendence seems to have been arrived at in Hebrew thought through ethical insights. The prophets denied that God was limited to his chosen people or that he depended upon their pride and success for his glory. Faith in a completely transcendent God was, in other words, their victory over polytheism and tribalism. Since everything in history is partial, relative, and imperfect, it follows that any God worthy of genuine adoration must transcend history. The God of the Hebrew prophets was transcendent as both the creator and the judge of the world, as both the ground of all existence and as its goal and end. Jewish prophecy thus rested upon the idea of creation (in which God is both distinguished from and related to the world) and it made religion dynamic by seeing the will of God not only as the ground of existence but as its ultimate fulfillment.

For the Hebrew prophets this transcendence of God never meant that the world of historic existence was meaningless or sinful as such, and that the realm of meaning and goodness was above the world. The transcendent God worked in history, and the prophets pointed out how He worked. Evil and injustice would be destroyed and good would be established. History was a constant revelation of both the judgment and the mercy of God. The insistence of modern ethical naturalism that history is meaningful, and the whole liberal idea of progress, is an essentially Hebrew concept revived to counteract the dualism of Christian orthodoxy.

The Religious Realism of Marx

But at one significant point it failed to achieve the depths of Hebrew prophecy. Its logic of history was a simple logic and not a dialectic. It saw history as a realm of creativity, but not of judgment. In its appreciation of the fact of judgment and catastrophe in history, Marxism is undoubtedly closer to the genius of Hebrew prophecy than liberalism, either secular or religious. The idea of Marxism that unjust civilizations will destroy themselves is, in fact, a secularized version of the prophecies of doom in which the Old Testament abounds.

The Marxians pride themselves upon their scientific realism by which they claim to have arrived at this knowledge. But such knowledge is the product of religious rather than scientific realism. It is only because life is moral and men feel that an unjust civilization ought not to survive that the scientific evidence can be finally adduced that it will not survive. But on the other hand, the prophets were too realistic to share the illusion of modern rationalism that men would desist from evil once they had discovered it. They know that evil must sometimes destroy itself in a terrible catastrophe before men will cease from their rebellion against God and His laws of justice. This pessimism is obvious in the words of Isaiah: "Make the heart of this people fat and their ears heavy—and I said, O Lord how long and He answered until their cities are wasted and without an inhabitant." In this pessimistic analysis of the stubbornness of human egoism and sin modern radicalism is, again, much closer to the prophets than most of our modern religion.

The mercies of God, for both the prophets and Jesus, were also revealed in nature and history and were not, as in later Christian orthodoxy, revealed purely in supernatural acts. Jesus pointed to the impartiality of nature, "which visits with equalest apportionment of ill, both good and bad alike," as a revelation of God's mercy; and the prophets pointed to the slowness of historical processes as an evidence of the longsuffering of God. He destroys evil but he "is slow to anger and plenteous in mercy." There is always chance for repentance, though the prophets realized that men do not usually avail themselves of the chance.

The prophetic insistence upon the meaningfulness of human history is a natural consequence of the Jewish conception of the unity of body and soul. There is no suggestion in Hebrew thought of a good mind and an evil body, an idea which is the bane of all Greek ethics. Greek thought may begin with the naturalism of Aristotle but even in it the highest ethical attitude is the rational contemplation of pure being, which is a form of rational existence, transcending the historical world. The dualism of Plotinus and neo-Platonism is thus implicit in the naturalism of Aristotle and invariably works itself out. In this connection the difference between the love doctrines of the Stoics and of Jesus is significant. For the Stoics, the perfection of love is a rational achievement from which all emotions of pity have been subtracted. In Jesus, love is the achievement of the total psyche. There is in genuine prophetic ethics no moral distinction between emotion and reason or between body and mind. For this reason the Jews never had a doctrine of the immortality of the soul, but only a hope of resurrection.

Prophetic Rejection of Dualism

It is clear, therefore, that where modern naturalism protests against the dualism and idealism of Greek thought and Christian orthodoxy, it is in line with prophetic thought. It seems to be equally clear that the unqualified distinction in Barthian thought between the finite and the infinite is a heresy from the standpoint of prophetic religion and that, in spite of important distinctions, it really falls into the errors of neo-Platonic dualism.

On the other hand, the strong insistence in prophetic thought on the transcendence of God distinguishes it from all forms of modern naturalism, whether liberal or radical. For it, historic reality is never self-explanatory or self-sufficient. Both the ground and the goal of historic existence lie beyond itself. The weightiest ethical consequences flow from this emphasis. It is never able to make an unqualified affirmation of the ultimate moral significance of any movement in history. It cannot, as democratic idealism did, identify the democratic movement with the Kingdom of God. Neither can it, as modern radical Christianity does, identify the Kingdom of God with Socialism. The Kingdom of God, the final ideal, is always beyond history. What is in history is always partial to specific interests and tainted by sin.

A stronger hold on prophetic essentials would have saved liberal Christianity from committing the error of identifying bourgeois democracy with the ethics of the Sermon on the Mount. Religious knowledge often anticipates the knowledge gained by painful experience. Through many disappointments and disillusionments we are now discovering to what degree the democratic movement was the instrument of the middle class interests and perspectives. A genuine prophetic religion would know that *a priori*. In the same way modern radical Christians incline to an identification of the Kingdom of God with Socialism. Some of them persist in regarding Russia as a paradise long after it is apparent that, no matter what the genuine achievements of Russian Communism, the ideal society is being relativized there by the inertia of history and the necessities of politics.

The Relativity of History

It is this relative and imperfect character of every historical movement and achievement which persuades the dialectic theologians to counsel Christians to abstain from politics as Christians, though of course they recognize the necessity of acting in an imperfect world. The dialectic materialist thinks it is possible to affirm the proletarian movement as an absolute in history. The dialectic theologian is unable to affirm anything in history as really good. But the moral defeatism of his perfectionism is as foreign to prophetic religion as is the utopianism of orthodox Marxism. In prophetic religion there is a more genuine dialectic in which the movements of history are in one moment the instruments of God and in the next come under His condemnation. Thus Babylon and the king of the Medes are regarded by the prophets as the instruments of vengeance in God's hands. But that does not mean that they are better than others and that they will not be cut down in time. They pronounce doom upon Babylon as well as upon Israel. Their attitude toward Israel is perhaps the perfect illustration of this dialectic. They do not deny that Israel has a special mission from God ("You only have I chosen"). But this same Israel stands under the judgment of God and must not make pretensions. God's hands are in the destiny of the Ethiopians, the Syrians, and the Egyptians as well as in the history of Israel. John the Baptist warns his contemporaries, when he finds them complacent in their sense of destiny, that God is able to raise up children of Abraham from the stones.

This interpretation of ancient history has a very direct relevance to modern social problems. The Dutch and other Calvinists were not wrong in affirming the democratic movement as against monarchical reaction. Democracy was in its day an instrument of God. It was modern liberal Christianity which was wrong (having lost faith in the transcendent God) in making an easy moralistic identification of democracy and the Kingdom of God, without a religious reservation. Modern radical Christians are not wrong in affirming the fateful mission of the victims of injustice in our present civilization. The prophets and Jesus blessed the poor, not because they were morally superior as individuals to the privileged, but because they are by virtue of their position in society the forces of progress and creativity in it.

Change Comes from Below

The privileged classes of society form an "upper crust." This phrase is literally accurate. It is a crust they form. No matter how good privileged people may be, they will be inclined to defend their interests and with it the old society which guarantees and preserves them. The destructive and constructive force must come from below. Any religion which, in its perfectionism, wipes out this insight and destroys all criteria for the religious evaluation of political movements will become, for all of its talk of perfection, an instrument of the classes which are afraid of social change. If we live in a society which is unable to establish justice (as I think we do), it becomes a Christian duty to seek a just society and to appreciate the fateful mission of those whose hunger will create that society more than it will be created by our ideals. That is our duty, even if we know as Christians that human egoism and collective will-to-power will reduce the justice actually achieved by every new society to something less than perfect justice.

A Christian socialism in our day could find an adequate theology and an adequate political strategy by a return to the dialectic of prophetic religion. If it fails in that, the Christian religion will on the one hand become a little conventicle of dualists who find human history meaningless and historic crises irrelevant to the real meaning of human life; on the other it will capitulate to a secularized radicalism and to naturalistic substitutes for religion. These will have vigor and social energy and they will undoubtedly succeed in the long run in establishing a new society. It will probably be a better society than the one in which we now live. But it will not be just as it might be if it is established by fanatics who have no idea how relative all human ideals are. Utopianism is the perennial disease of all naturalism. In one moment naturalism protests against God and in the next it exalts some movement in history into its God. It is thus not only subject to perpetual disillusionment but tempted to perennial self-righteousness and to the cruelty which flows from all self-righteousness.

It is idle to hope that, even at best, a prophetic religion could completely stem the tides of dualistic otherworldliness on the one hand, and of naturalistic utopianism on the other. But it is still possible to create and, above all, to reclaim a prophetic religion which will influence the destiny of our era and fall into neither defeatism nor into the illusions which ultimately beget despair.

KARL BARTH AND DEMOCRACY

In writing to a theological professor in Prague just before the European crisis reached its climax, Karl Barth said: "Has the whole world come under the bewitching power of this huge serpent? Must the postwar pacifism really end in such a terrible paralysis of the courage needed for decisions?—I still dare to hope that the sons of the old Hussites will show sloppy Europe that some real men still exist in this world. Every Czech soldier who will then fight and suffer will fight and suffer for all of us and—I say this without reserve—also for the church of Jesus Christ which in the midst of such Hitlers and Mussolinis will either decline into ridicule or will be wiped out."

We find these judgments astonishing, though we agree with them politically. They are astonishing because they come from a man who has spent all his energies to prove that it is impossible to mix relative political judgments with the unconditioned demands of the gospel. Nothing discredits Barth's major theological emphasis more than his complete abandonment of his primary thesis in the hour of crisis. Just as Einstein's two per cent pacifism was discredited when he called for a war against Nazi Germany. We agree neither with Barth's previous separation of the gospel from fateful political and historical decisions which we as men must make, nor yet with his present identification of the Czech soldier with the liberty of the church of Christ. Surely Barth ought to be the last man to believe that the church "will be wiped out" if the Hitlers and Mussolinis are not defeated. It may be forced into the catacombs, but the more the ridiculous Caesar-gods rage the more apparent it will become that Christianity is true and that it is the ultimate truth. The majesty of God is most perfectly revealed in the moment when the Christ is crucified. The gates of hell cannot prevail against this church.

But the church against which the gates of hell cannot prevail is not any particular historical institution. Nor is its future determined by whether men will save democracy against Fascism. On the other hand, it is quite true that the fate of a Christian civilization may well be decided or could have been decided by Czech soldiers. There is a difference between a civilization which seeks to build itself on the gospel foundations and one which explicitly defies the gospel. This difference is tremendous and it is worth fighting for. Those who believe that Greek culture would have survived if the Greeks had not defeated the Persians at Salamis have never been able to present very plausible arguments for their convictions. A culture lives in a civilization, and a civilization is a physical thing which can be destroyed and can be saved. But a culture is nothing more than a rationalization of a civilization if it is not also the fruit of a religion which is not primarily concerned about the future of cultures and civilizations.

Here again Barth, the exponent of dialectical theology, has proved himself to be not sufficiently dialectical. In all the years before this crisis his "no" to the problem of culture and civilization was too unreserved, and in the hour of crisis his "yes" is too unreserved.

KARL BARTH ON POLITICS

We called attention earlier to the fact that Karl Barth had written a letter to a Czech professor of theology in which he declared that Czech soldiers would be fighting for the church of Jesus Christ if they fought against Hitler. The letter has had interesting repercussions. The Nazi press has published it widely to prove that Barth's opposition to it was informed by political animus rather than religious scruples from the very beginning. More interesting still, Barth has published a pamphlet on "The Church and the Political Question of Today" in which he elaborates systematic conclusions from the position he took in the Czech crisis.

The pamphlet is important because it really brings to an end what has been known as Barthianism; for Barthianism in its pure form declared political questions to be irrelevant to the gospel. Barth conceded that Christians must indeed make choices between political alternatives, and that his own common sense judgments were on the whole socialistic, but he did not relate these decisions with the content of the gospel, which is solely a declaration of the mercy of God to men who are and remain sinners, whatever side of a political controversy they may choose.

In this pamphlet Barth declares that Nazi politics must be opposed from the standpoint of Christian faith for two reasons. The first reason given by him is not revolutionary from the standpoint of his own thought. The reason is that Nazi politics is not merely a political program but a religion and that it promises a salvation which is diametrically opposed to what Christians believe about man, God, and the relation between man and God, and to the need which all sinful men have of the mercy of God in Christ. He compares this Nazi religion with the Mohammedanism against which Luther admonished the faithful to pray and act. He declares that he sees no reason why Nazi religion should be placed in any other category than that of a political religion like Islam.

The second reason is more revolutionary from the standpoint of orthodox Protestantism. He declares that Christians must oppose National Socialism because it is not a "Rechtstaat," that is, a state based upon justice, but that it is "tyranny qualified by anarchy and anarchy qualified by tyranny." He thinks it important from the Christian standpoint to know that this government came into being through a "gigantic fraud, the fraud of the Reichstag fire," and that it is not supported by the German people as a whole but by a "small clique" who conduct "fraudulent elections" to maintain the semblance of popular support. The tyranny is attested by the fact that "no one is safe against arbitrary arrest, arbitrary court procedure, conviction, imprisonment, cruel mistreatment, death ending by being returned to one's family as content of a funeral urn." This kind of tyranny, he holds, absolves the Christian of the obligation of obedience to the state as enjoined in Romans 13, the fateful Romans 13 which has had such a decisive influence upon Continental Christianity and has so frequently given the state a sacrosanct character beyond any possible justification. "It is impossible to pray for the preservation of the government of National Socialism," he declares, "without outraging one's Christian confession and making one's prayer meaningless."

Perhaps the most interesting section of his pamphlet is devoted to the proposition that this conviction is not merely a personal opinion of his but that it follows inevitably from his Christian faith. He holds that he has both the right and the duty to present this conviction in the community of the faithful as "not merely a political opinion" but as a "compulsion of his faith in Christ." What then shall those do who do not agree with him? Since we are not Catholics, but Protestants, he asserts, we have no business to wait upon some official utterance of the church. It is our business to testify to our moral convictions in the light of our faith. Let those who disagree with us also bear testimony in the light of their Christian faith. Let them prove in the light of the Scriptures that they have a right to say "yes" to National Socialism and "no" against our unequivocal "no." We will leave the ultimate issue to the work of the Holy Spirit in the church.

These are exactly the principles for which we as Christian Socialists have stood, though of course we would extend the range of political judgments beyond those envisaged by Barth. We have insisted that we have no right to declare that only socialistic political convictions are compatible with Christian faith but that we have both the right and the duty to insist that they are binding upon us and that they are organically related to our Christian faith; and that we have the right and the duty to challenge those who do not agree with us to validate their political convictions in the light of their faith. The church must not be a mere forum of diverse political opinions. It is important that those who speak from within the church should speak in terms of their faith. It is also important that our convictions should not be bound by any official position of the church, but that they should be bound by a common faith.

If Barth had arrived at his present convictions ten years earlier the history of central Europe might be different, considering how powerful his influence was in accentuating those tendencies of Lutheranism which make it politically neutral. The one weakness of his pamphlet is that he does not admit that he has changed his basic position. He admits only that the pressure of the years has changed his emphasis. This is a little too much like the Communist strategy which never admits obvious changes in the party line. In spite of this weakness, however, Barth's new standpoint may have far-reaching significance in the religious life of Europe, assuming that he still retains the degree of influence on the continent which once was his. It may for instance have immediate political significance in Switzerland, where the problem of Fascism is a very pressing one.

It is significant that the ministry of education in Berlin immediately answered Barth's broadside against Nazism by a decree, stipulating that no German student shall be allowed credit for any work done at the University of Basle, as long as the university continues to retain Barth as professor.

WE ARE MEN AND NOT GOD

Beyond the traditional differences between confessions at Amsterdam the most marked theological contrast, apparent at the first Assembly of the World Council, was between what was frequently described as the "Continental theology" and what was with equal inaccuracy known as the "Anglo-Saxon approach to theology." Both designations were inaccurate because many Continentals did not share the first approach, and the second was "Anglo-Saxon" only in the sense that beyond all denominational distinctions in the Anglo-Saxon world, delegates from that world seemed united in their rejection of the Continental position.

Issues Raised by Barth

This position might best be defined as strongly eschatological. This does not mean that it placed its emphasis primarily upon the hope of the culmination of world history in the second coming of Christ, the final judgment, and the general resurrection. If the position is termed eschatological it must be regarded as a form of "realized eschatology." Let Karl Barth's words explain the emphasis, since he was the most persuasive spokesman of the position.

The assurance, declared Barth, that "Jesus Christ has already robbed sin, death, the devil and hell of their power and has already vindicated divine and human justice in his person" ought to persuade us "even on this first day of our deliberations that the care of the church and the care of the world is not our care. Burdened with this thought we could straighten nothing out." For the final root of human disorder is precisely "this dreadful, godless, ridiculous opinion that man is the Atlas who is destined to bear the dome of heaven upon his shoulders."

No Christian would quarrel with the affirmation that the church finds the true and the new beginning of life and history in the revelatory and redemptive power of our Lord's life, death, and resurrection. The questions which arose at Amsterdam were about the conclusions which were drawn from this article of faith. Did not these conclusions tend to rob the Christian life of its sense of responsibility? Did they not promise a victory for the Christian without a proper emphasis upon repentance? And did they not deal in an irresponsible manner with all the trials and perplexities, the judgments and discriminations, the tasks and duties which Christians face in the daily round of their individual and collective life?

The Testimony of St. Paul

The first conclusion which Barth drew from the Christian certainty that Christ has already gained the victory over sin and death was that "the care of the church is not our care." We must rather commit the church unto the Lord "who will bring it to pass." He has called us to be his witnesses but not to be "his lawyers, engineers, statisticians, and administrative directors."

One is a little puzzled about this complete rejection of differentiated functions, since the precise point of St. Paul's classical chapter on the church as the body of Christ in I Cor. 12 is that there are not only "diversities of gifts" but also "differences of administration" and "diversities of operation" within the church. And St. Paul does have a "care" about the church, which is very relevant to our present ecumenical task. His care is lest diversities of gifts and differences of administration tempt "the eye to say to the ear, I have no need of thee." In other words, he is afraid that special gifts and functions within the church may become the occasion of the isolation of one member from another, rather than the basis for their mutual growth in grace. It is in this way that sin enters the church and divides it. If these divisions are to be overcome, must there not be a contrite recognition of the sinful pride in our special gift or function by which we have become divided?

What is that but "care" about the church? It is the basis of the "dying with Christ" without which, according to the Scripture, there can be no new and triumphant life with him. The real weakness of this unvarying emphasis upon what we cannot do and upon what Christ has already done is that it tempts the Christian to share the victory and the glory of the risen Lord without participating in the crucifixion of the self, which is the Scriptural presupposition of a new life, for the individual, the church and the nation.

Decrying the Prophetic Function

We are warned with equal emphasis that the "care of the world is not our care." We are to beware lest we seem to present a kind of "Christian Marshall plan" to the nations. This is a wholesome warning against the pat schemes of Christian moralists. But does it not annul the church's prophetic function to the nations? Must not the church be busy in "the pulling down of strongholds, casting down imaginations and every thing that exalteth itself against the knowledge of God and bringing into captivity every thought to the obedience of Christ"?

In such a day as this we are particularly confronted with the fact that nations and empires, proud oligarchies and vainglorious races have been "wounded" by the divine wrath in the vicissitudes of history and "have not received correction." It is a sobering fact that judgment so frequently leads to despair rather than to repentance. It is not within the competence of the Christian church to change despair into repentance. That possibility is a mystery of divine grace. But it *does* belong to the "care" of the church for the world that it so interpret the judgments under which nations stand, and so disclose their divine origin, that there is a possibility of repentance.

If the gospel is made to mean merely the assurance of God's final triumph over all human rebellion, it may indeed save men from anxious worries. But does it not also save them prematurely from their own perplexities? It prevents them from indulging in the vainglorious belief that they can create the Kingdom of God by their own virtue. But does it remind them that they are "workers together with Him"? Is this not, in short, a very "undialectical" gospel in which the "Yes" of the divine mercy has completely canceled out the "No" of the divine judgment against all human pride and pretension?

What Help for Christians?

The second question one is forced to raise about this emphasis is whether it has any guidance or inspiration for Christians in the day-to-day decisions which are the very woof and warp of our existence. Barth insists that we have no "systems of economic and political principles to offer the world." We can present it only "with a revolutionary hope." This emphasis has its limited validity. Christianity is too simply equated by many with some simple system of "Christian economics" or "Christian sociology." But Barth's teachings seem to mean that we can, as Christians, dispense with the principles of justice which, however faulty, represent the cumulative experience of the race in dealing with the vexing problems of man's relations to his fellows.

We ought indeed to have a greater degree of freedom from all traditions, even the most hallowed, as we seek to establish and re-establish community in our torn world. But freedom over law cannot mean emancipation from the tortuous and difficult task of achieving a tolerable justice. It is certainly not right for Christians to leave it to the "pagans" of our day to walk the tightrope of our age, which is strung over the abyss of war and tyranny, seeking by patience and courage to prevent war on the one hand and the spread of tyranny on the other, while the Christians rejoice in a "revolutionary hope" in which all these anxieties of human existence, and the particular anxieties of our age, are overcome proleptically. It is particularly wrong if we suggest to these pagans that we have no immediate counsel in the present perplexity but that we will furnish a "sign" of the "coming Kingdom" by some heroic defiance of malignant power, if the situation becomes desperate enough. We will not counsel any community that this or that course might lead to tyranny. We will merely prepare ourselves to defy tyranny when it is full blown.

"Crisis" Theology Gone to Seed

Here there are suggestions of a "crisis" theology, but not in the connotation originally intended. It is only fair to Barth and to those for whom he speaks to acknowledge gratefully the great contributions which this theology made to the struggle against tyranny in recent decades. Its interpretation of the Christian faith helped to create a heroic heedlessness, a disposition to follow the Scriptural injunction, "Be careful in nothing." This resulted in a very powerful witness to Christ in the hour of crisis. But perhaps this theology is constructed too much for the great crises of history. It seems to have no guidance for a Christian statesman for our day. It can fight the devil if he shows both horns and both cloven feet. But it refuses to make discriminating judgments about good and evil if the evil shows only one horn or the half of a cloven foot.

There is a special pathos in the fact that so many of the Christian leaders of Germany are inclined to follow this form of flight from daily responsibilities and decisions, because they are trying to extend the virtue of yesterday to cover the problems of today. Yesterday they discovered that the church may be an ark in which to survive a flood. Today they seem so enamored of this special function of the church that they have decided to turn the ark into a home on Mount Ararat and live in it perpetually.

Barth is as anxious to disavow any special responsibilities in our debate with a secular culture on the edge of despair as in our engagement with a civilization on the edge of disaster. We are not to worry about this "godless" age. It is no more godless than any other age, just as the evil in our day is neither more nor less than that of any previous period. We seem always to be God rather than men in this theology, viewing the world not from the standpoint of the special perplexities and problems of given periods but *sub specie aeternitatis*.

Have We Nothing to Say?

In any event, says Barth, we are not to enter into debate with the secularism of our age. With a special dig at his old opponent Brunner, who had analyzed the "axioms" of secularism to prove that they were filled with idolatry, Barth warned that we had nothing special to say to the godless people of our age which we would not have said in any age. What we have to say to them is that "Jesus Christ died and rose again for them and has become their divine brother and redeemer."

Does this mean that St. Paul had no right to analyze the meaning of the yearning of his day for the "unknown God" and prove its relevance for the gospel? When Julian Huxley, for instance, writes a book, *Man in the Modern World*, in which he manages to distil every error of modern man about himself and his destiny, his virtue and his wisdom, is the Christian apologist to refrain from every apologetic assault upon some of the absurdities of these modern beliefs? Is he merely to assure Mr. Huxley that Christ died for him, even though Mr. Huxley could not, in his present state of belief possibly understand why anyone should need to die for us?

One sees that the church is as rigorously prohibited from turning a furrow in the field of culture as in the field of social relations. Let the church remain an ark, ready to receive those who are fleeing the next flood. If meanwhile weeds should grow in the garden of either culture or civilization that is not surprising, since the church knows *a priori* that weeds grow in every human garden.

With the fullest appreciation of what this theology did to puncture the illusions of churchmen, theologians, and moralists, one must insist that this is not the whole gospel. It warned the church rightly that it must bear witness, not to its own power but to the power of God, not to its capacity to build the Kingdom but to the Kingdom which has been established by divine grace.

But the Christian faith, which can easily degenerate into a too simple moralism, may also degenerate into a too simple determinism and irresponsibility when the divine grace is regarded as a way of escape from, rather than a source of engagement with, the anxieties, perplexities, sins, and pretensions of human existence. The certainty of the final inadequacy of the "wisdom of the world" must not be allowed to become the source of cultural obscurantism. The Christian must explore every promise and every limit of the cultural enterprise. The certainty of the final inadequacy of every form of human justice must not lead to defeatism in our approach to the perplexing problems of social justice in our day. The possibilities as well as the limits of every scheme of justice must be explored. The certainty that every form of human virtue is inadequate in the sight of God must not tempt us to hide our talent in the ground.

One of the tasks of an ecumenical movement is to prevent a one-sided statement of the many-sided truth of the gospel. "Narrow is the way which leadeth unto life." There is an abyss on each side of that narrow way. Anyone who is too fearful of the abyss on the one side will fall into the abyss on the other side. We "Anglo-Saxons" who object to this one-sided emphasis may be corrupted by many Pelagian and semi-Pelagian heresies. We stand in need of correction. But we also have the duty to correct.

We are embarrassed about our correction because we cannot deny that this "Continental" theology outlines the final pinnacle of the Christian faith and hope with fidelity to the Scriptures. Yet it requires correction, because it has obscured the foothills where human life must be lived. It started its theological assault decades ago with the reminder that we are men and not God, and that God is in the heavens and that we are on earth. The wheel is come full circle. It is now in danger of offering a crown without a cross, a triumph without a battle, a scheme of justice without the necessity of discrimination, a faith which has annulled rather than transmuted perplexity—in short, a too simple and premature escape from the trials and perplexities, the duties and tragic choices, which are the condition of our common humanity. The Christian faith knows of a way through these sorrows, but not of a way around them.

AN ANSWER TO KARL BARTH

Karl Barth's irenic reply to my criticisms of his Amsterdam address must naturally elicit an answer in kind. He rightly suspects that it is difficult to avoid presenting the opponent in caricature. I hasten to confess that at one point my argument was subject to a misinterpretation. I suggested that the emphasis of his Amsterdam address might encourage certain tendencies in the German church to regard the church as a perpetual ark and make a home in it on Mount Ararat. I certainly did not tax Barth himself with such a tendency, for as he rightly insists he bore eloquent testimony against religious irresponsibility, particularly during the war years. He may be sure that the so-called Anglo-Saxon world is not unconscious or unappreciative of his creative relationship to the resistance movements of Europe.

Not Always in Crisis

In the light of this relationship it may seem completely unjustified to suggest that the temper of Barth's address at Amsterdam tends to support an attitude of irresponsibility toward the immediate and pressing decisions which Christians must make from day to day. It could be proved, nevertheless, that a theology which illumines the pinnacles of the Christian faith and nerves men to heroic action in a day of obvious crisis may yet be less than adequate in guiding their conscience in the prosaic tasks of every day. After all, Barth's disciples were inclined, before Nazism was revealed in its full demonic dimensions, to see little difference between it and other forms of political evil. In like manner Barth seems inclined today to regard the differences between Communism and the so-called democratic world as insignificant when viewed from the ultimate Christian standpoint. But we are men and not God, and the destiny of civilizations depends upon our decisions in the "nicely calculated less and more" of good and evil in political institutions.

Attitude toward Bible

Barth thinks that the real difference between the thought which he represents and the Anglo-Saxon world lies not at the point where I placed the main emphasis but at a point of minor emphasis in my criticism, namely, in our contrasting attitudes toward the Bible. He thinks that the Anglo-Saxon world does not take the authority of the Bible seriously enough, spinning its theologies and theories without reference to Biblical texts and their context. We, on the other hand, charge the Continent with Biblical literalism. Perhaps it would be profitable therefore to waive debate on the first issue and survey this second one.

In doing so we must begin by admitting that it would be foolish to speak of a single "Anglo-Saxon" or a single

"Continental" attitude toward the Bible. Both regions are naturally filled with various contrasting and contradictory tendencies. It is nevertheless true that, very broadly considered, there is a difference between them in attitude toward the Bible. Continental thought, particularly as influenced by Barth, seeks to establish Biblical authority over the mind and conscience of the Christian with as little recourse as possible to any norms of truth or right which may come to us out of the broad sweep of a classical, European, or modern cultural history. In Anglo-Saxon thought there is a greater degree of commerce between culture in general and Biblical faith.

It might be well to begin by admitting the errors to which we are led by this procedure on the Anglo-Saxon side. For these errors are obvious not only in what Europe knows as American liberalism; they are obvious, though expressed in a different way, in the characteristic Anglican thought of Britain. There is no doubt a great deal of preaching in the Anglo-Saxon world in which Biblical faith is corrupted and supplanted by the current credos of our culture. Sometimes Biblical faith is identified with bourgeois individualism, and the message of the Bible is reduced to the concept of the "infinite worth of the individual" or to confidence in the value of a "free society." Recently an appreciative layman sent me a sermon by his pastor which was in his opinion better than the pronouncements of the World Council at Amsterdam. The pastor declared that the struggle of our age was between Christianity, which believed that "the state must serve the individual," and Communism, which believed that "the individual must serve the state."

How Protect Purity of Gospel?

There is obviously no engagement between the Holy God and sinful men in such expositions of Scripture. There is neither need nor knowledge of a divine judgment or mercy. One is reminded of Thoreau upon his deathbed who, when asked whether he had "made his peace with

God," declared that there had never been any alienation between himself and God. One cannot deny that much of what passes for Christianity in the Western world is no more than a simple confidence that God is our ally in our fight with Communism even as he was our ally in our fight with Nazism. And isn't it nice that God is always on our side! Let us not forget to pay tribute to Barth's influence in the Anglo-Saxon world in extricating the Christian faith from the idolatries of our day.

In performing this work of reformation Barth believes, however, that it is necessary to protect the purity of the gospel by destroying every possible commerce or debate between the Christian faith and the philosophical and ethical disciplines. One must not enter into a debate with modern culture to prove that its analysis of the plight of man is mistaken and that its proffered redemptions are illusory; one must preach the gospel and wait for the Holy Spirit to validate it. Neither must one relate the ethical demands of the gospel to any ethical insights which may have come to mankind in classical or modern currents of thought. One may champion justice in the political order provided one does not appeal to "natural law" and is careful to find warrant for one's conception of justice in the Scripture. One may even have to torture Biblical texts in order to arrive at a preference for a democratic society without making any appeal to non-Biblical sources of insight.

If this procedure meant that one regarded, as Luther did, the mind of Christ as the final criterion of Scripture as well as the final norm of law one would have a creative freedom over all law, including the positive law of states, the "natural law" so dear to Catholic thought, and even Scriptural laws as concocted by Protestant literalism from various ethical injunctions embodied in the canon and representing various levels in relation to the law of love. But it does not seem to mean this.

What is "Time-Bound"?

Barth accuses us for instance of regarding the Pauline word, "In Christ there is neither male nor female" (Gal. 3:28), as more authoritative than such texts as: "For the man is not of the woman; but the woman of the man. Neither was the man created for the woman; but the woman for the man" (I Cor. 11:8-9); or "Wives, submit yourselves unto your own husbands, as unto the Lord. For the husband is the head of the wife, even as Christ is the head of the church" (Eph. 5:22-23).

I am informed that Barth dismissed the authority of the Pauline injunction that women must not pray in church with their head uncovered. He regarded that injunction as "time-bound." But as far as I know he did not give a criterion for determining what is time-bound and what is timeless in these Scriptural injunctions. I should certainly regard St. Paul's absolute subordination of woman to man as more obviously time-bound than the word, "In Christ there is neither male nor female." It may have been influenced by the second creation story, according to which God fashioned Eve from Adam's rib. It is certainly colored also by the traditional standards regulating the relation between men and women in every pretechnical culture.

Or does the modern Continental conception of Biblical authority exclude the possibility that echoes and accents of the culture of an age appear in the Scripture? If this is excluded, Biblical authority may indeed emancipate us from the prejudices of our own age, but at the price of binding us to the prejudices of bygone ages. Furthermore, the Bible may thus become the instrument of, rather than the source of judgment upon, the sinful pretensions of men— in this case of the sinful pretensions of the male toward the female. Some of us remember very well how the very texts which we are asked to take as seriously as the word, "In Christ there is neither male nor female," were used by Biblical literalists to prove that women did not have the right of suffrage in the state.

The Jewish Question

Barth uses one other example of Anglo-Saxon indifference toward the Scripture. He thinks we try to solve the Jewish question without having recourse to the wisdom of Romans 9-11, where St. Paul yearns over his own people and hopes "that they might be saved." He does not say just what light these chapters shed on some of the vexatious issues of our day. Among Biblical literalists I know there is a division of opinion between those who support Zionism on the ground that the Jewish state will hasten the culmination of the whole of human history and those who oppose it as a nationalistic corruption of the messianic hope.

Barth himself has rendered a great service to the Lutheran world in recent decades by extricating the Lutheran conscience from the grip of another Pauline text—Romans 13:1: "Let every soul be subject to the higher powers . . . the powers that be are ordained of God." No one can deny that this single text without reference to the "consensus" of Scripture, and therefore without the reservation of the many Scriptural judgments upon the pretensions and corruptions of political authority, induces an uncritical reverence toward political authority. Fortunately later Calvinism softened the authority of this single text, a service which was not performed in German Lutheranism early enough to prevent the misuse of the text for generations.

There are in short very good reasons for preferring some texts of Scripture to others and for judging them all from the standpoint of "the mind of Christ." We do that at our hazard of course; but the hazards of Biblical literalism are certainly greater.

Cultural Facts Affect Insights

Sometimes the rigorous distinction between Scriptural and other moral insights leads to a roundabout discovery of certain moral insights in Scripture, without due acknowledgment of what the culture of the age has contributed to the insight. Thus Barth in the volume of his *Dogmatik* devoted to the Biblical concept of creation writes pages upon pages of very excellent exegetical commentary on the simple word of Genesis, "Male and female created he them." This commentary has made Barth the champion of women's rights within the church on the Continent, though he seemed at Amsterdam at times to deny the women in the name of St. Paul what he granted them in the name of Moses. But the simple word from Genesis was the weapon with which he triumped over the priestly minds who insisted that only a man could be a priest in the church for the reason that only a man could represent a male Christ.

I would not wish to deny that all that Barth has found in this simple word of Genesis is actually implied there. I think it is implied. But it is also true that the Christian ages did not find it there for centuries. Why not? Perhaps there is a kind of enmity "between the priest and the woman," vividly displayed in the "Code of Manu" but operative in all religion, though overcome in the Christian faith whenever the "love of Christ" operates to challenge every social convention and tradition which encourages pride rather than mutual respect between persons.

But the Christian church is a religious community, subject to certain characteristically religious aberrations which stand in contradiction to the mind of Christ. The enmity of the priest toward the woman is one of them. If this theory seems speculative, the fact is certainly not speculative that it was a secular age which granted women fuller recognition as persons, and that even now the religious communities lag behind the civil communities on this standard of ethics.

When, therefore, we expound the word of Genesis, "Male and female created he them," it behooves us not to take a prestidigitator's delight in pulling rabbits out of a hat which every previous exegete regarded as merely a hat. We ought rather to admit contritely that we understand the full implication of the Scriptural word that God created both man and woman in his design of the human person because we are the heirs of a spiritual history which includes a secular revolt against religion. We shall continue to reject the exaggerated forms of feminism which a highly rationalistic culture breeds, even as we shall continue to bear witness against all illusions and idolatries of a secular age. Yet we will admit that God "is able of these very stones to raise up children unto Abraham." It is not the first nor the last time that a facet of the full truth in Christ has been clarified and restored by heresy after being obscured by orthodoxy. There are certain insights about the political order which come to us in the same way from modern secularism, despite its libertarian or equalitarian illusions.

The illustration of the attitude of the church toward women has been chosen as an example of contrasting attitudes toward Biblical authority in the Anglo-Saxon and in the Continental world, not only because Barth chose some of his examples from this realm but also because his discussions on the subject at Amsterdam illustrated so nicely both the power and limitations of his method.

No one has the right to speak for the "Anglo-Saxon" or any other portion of the Protestant world. Yet it is, I hope, not too presumptuous to say that there are many in the Anglo-Saxon world whose gratitude for Barth's profound interpretations of our Biblical faith will yet not beguile them into accepting his method of preserving the purity of that faith from corruption. They believe that it easily leads to two errors. One is the introduction of irrelevant detailed standards of the good, when the Christian life requires a great deal of freedom from every kind of law and tradition, including the kind which is woven together from proof-texts. The other is that it fails to provide sufficient criteria of judgment and impulses to decisive action in moments of life when a historic evil, not yet full-blown and not yet requiring some heroic witness, sneaks into the world upon the back of some unobtrusive error which when fully conceived may produce a monstrous evil.

WHY IS BARTH SILENT
ON HUNGARY?

The whole world has been thrilled by the spontaneity and the stubbornness of the Hungarian rebellion against Russian despotism. As George Kennan and Bedell Smith predicted, the monolithic structure of Communist tyranny cracked first in the satellite nations, where patriotism united with love of freedom to offer resistance; and Poland and Hungary were the first to offer resistance. We need not now go into the details of the difference between the Poles, who were able to contain their revolution within peaceful Titoist limits, and the Hungarians, who were so outraged by the Russian guns turned on peaceful demonstrators that their hatred of the oppressor knew no bounds. They sought absolute freedom from Russia; and their revolution was suppressed in a bloodbath which has destroyed permanently whatever prestige still adhered to the Communist ideology in Eastern Europe and among the intellectuals and neutralist theologians of the Continent. It is enough to record that the régime in Hungary, which seemed to have the uneasy acceptance of the people, was proved by recent events to have been so oppressive that it piled up resentments, resulting in a heroic defiance which astonished and thrilled, as well as saddened, the whole world.

I

Our purpose is to analyze the record of Europe's most famous and imaginative theologian, Karl Barth, in relation to recent Hungarian history. Nothing in that record can dim the theological achievements of this man, who was the chief instigator of the neo-Reformation theology, which challenged the liberalism in religious and secular society that had reigned in Western culture in the nineteenth century and was finally destroyed by the historical realities culminating in the First World War.

Nor can Barth's record on Hungary change the glory of his relation to the resistance movements in the Nazi period, though it is now obvious that that resistance was dictated by personal experiences with tyranny and not by the frame of his theology, which was, before Hitler as now, too "eschatological" and too transcendent to offer any guidance for the discriminating choices that political responsibility challenges us to. Barth was the theologian of the anti-Nazi resistance in the whole of Europe. In his famous letter to Hromadka (who is ironically involved with him now in the toils of neutralism), he went so far as to say that a Czech soldier fighting the Germans would be serving Christ. His partisanship was probably too extreme, as his neutralism now is too undiscriminating. But let past history stand. Karl Barth will of course be properly scornful of any attempt to judge his theology by its political fruits; he would have it judged by its adequacy in interpreting "the Word of God." But let us be Scriptural and follow the axiom, "By their fruits shall ye know them," remembering that political justice and wisdom must be one of the fruits by which any system of thought is to be judged.

What has all this to do with Hungary and its revolution? The link is established by Barth's intimate connection with the Reformed Church of Hungary and by the confusing advice he offered it. Barth was, in fact, a kind of unofficial pope of the Hungarian Reformed Church. When the church adopted a new constitution it submitted the articles to Barth for approval. When the Communist government dismissed Bishop Ravasz and suggested the election of Bishop Bereczky, the church leaders asked Barth whether it was correct to elect a bishop favored by the government. Barth answered that the favor or disfavor of the government should be irrelevant to the church if the opinions of the bishop were theologically correct. Bereczky was in fact a devout, theologically correct, and timid man. So he was acceptable to both Barth and the Communist government, and so he was elected. That government, it should be recalled, was headed by the notorious Rakosi, who had contrived the execution of the other leader, Rajk. Both men were implicated in "Titoism"—a crime in Stalin's eyes— and Rakosi saved himself by sacrificing his partner. Rakosi was dismissed just before the revolution in the vain effort to appease the wrath of the Hungarian people.

Another bishop was appointed—John Peter, who was certainly not "theologically correct" because he has since confessed that he was a Party member; but it is not recorded that Barth gave him the imprimatur. Peter did represent the church at Evanston, though the state department kept him under surveillance, knowing his now confessed record, as the church leaders did not. Needless to say, Bishop Peter gave Evanston some very pious accounts of the church in Hungary; and, also needless to say, he confused some church leaders outside Hungary. But he did not confuse the faithful pastors and people of the Hungarian churches. Many of these have since perished in the revolution and thousands of them have fled their fatherland.

Barth had a rather triumphant tour in Hungary, and all his thoughts about the issues of church and state in a tyranny are faithfully recorded in his collection of occasional writings entitled *Against the Stream* (1954). A Hungarian Christian asked him, for instance, whether it was right for a Christian to co-operate with a Communist government. Barth answered: "We shall never see a state either in its pure form as an ordinance of God or in its complete diabolical perversion. These are the two frontiers between which history moves." Thus the possibility of a diabolical government's appearing in history was excluded in principle. This did not change the fact that the Hungarians had direct experience of the demonic in their own government.

If one inquires why a man of so wise and robust a mind as Karl Barth should have come to such false conclusions in a specific historical case, and why he should have been so sure of himself that he did not inquire of the Hungarian Christians instead of lecturing to them, one must look for the answer in the confidently held theological frame of reference, and also in the lower political frame of reference. One must inquire about the latter as well as the former, for even a theologian who thinks he can solve everything by drawing on the wisdom of the "Word of God" is a man who makes his decisions about proximate ends according to his political presuppositions.

II

Karl Barth's theological framework is defective for wise political decisions for two reasons. The first is that he is too consistently "eschatological" for the "nicely calculated less and more" which must go into political decisions. In his essay "The Christian Community and Political Change" he declares: "The goal toward which we are moving is the second coming of our Lord Jesus Christ. The message of the church is a message of hope for everyone. Alternations in political systems must stand in the light of this great change, which is called Jesus Christ. It would be curious if the church, which knows of this one great change, could not accept with a certain calm certain smaller changes."

The "certain smaller changes" which are to be accepted with calm are, for instance, the change from comparative political freedom to despotism. Not being a theologian, I can only observe that if one reaches a very high altitude, in either an eschatological or a real airplane, all the distinctions which seem momentous on the "earthly" level are dwarfed into insignificance. Since Barth had much to do with the eschatological theme of the World Council of Churches' Evanston assembly, one wonders whether his presence at Evanston would have changed the atmosphere and made the eschatology more relevant to the unimaginative and common-sense "Anglo-Saxon" mind.

The second defect in Barth's theological approach to political and moral problems is his extreme pragmatism, which disavows all moral principles. In answering Emil Brunner's question, "Why do you not oppose totalitarianism now, as you did then (in the Nazi period)?" Barth declared: "The church must concern itself with political systems, not in terms of principles but as seen in the light of the Word of God. . . . It must reject every effort to systematize political history and must look at every event afresh." Without the guidance of principles and looking at every event afresh in the light of the Word of God, Barth comes to the capricious conclusion that Communism is not as bad as Nazism because it is not anti-Semitic. "It is a question," declared Barth, "whether it was the totalitarianism, or the barbarism, nihilism, and anti-Semitism, which was the chief sin of Nazism." A little concern for "principles" would have instructed Barth that some of the barbarism of Nazism was derived from the same monopoly of irresponsible power from which the barbarism of Communism is derived. Looking at every event afresh means that one is ignorant about the instructive, though inexact, analogies of history which the "godless" scientists point out for our benefit.

A Catholic theologian has defined the Barthian approach to the political order as "designed for the church of the catacombs." The description is accurate: Barth's view makes no provision for discriminating judgments, both because of its strong eschatological emphasis and because of the absence of principles and structures of value.

"The Christian church," Barth writes, "is independent of all political changes, inasmuch as it is grounded in the Word of God and committed solely to his word. It can therefore see ancient and modern political systems as nothing but halting and restricted human efforts, the furthering or opposing of which it must not confuse with its proper mission." This advice would be more palatable if Barth were not so interested in passing political judgments while he constructs a theology which disavows political responsibility in principle. He has a framwork for these political judgments, which can be discerned below the level of his theological framework.

An unkind critic might suggest that the framework of an arrested nineteenth century Marxism, by which he judges between "capitalistic" and "socialistic" nations; a kind of

Marxism that, despite Barth's theological avoidance of "systems," is not sufficiently alert to the fresh constellations of history to realize that the capitalism of the West may have corrupted, but did not destroy, democracy, while the "socialism" of Communism did produce absolute despotism. But this criticism would not be fair, because Barth is no Christian Marxist. He disavows the Marxist creed resolutely, as does his fellow-traveling Czech disciple, Hromadka. The Marxist creed is in his subconscious but not in his conscious approach to things.

Thus in reporting on his trip to Hungary Barth wrote:

> I did not find a single outright believer in the new system in Hungary. . . . Enthusiasm for the Red Dean (Hewlett Johnson of Canterbury), who visited Hungary before my visit, aroused astonishment among the Reformed Christians. . . . But the Reformed church also resisted the opposite temptation of Rome—that of entering opposition as a matter of principle. I met no responsible Reformed Christian who thought that one ought to take the line of political resistance as a matter of political principle.

In fairness to Barth it must be said that, while he obviously did not meet in Hungary the kind of Reformed Christians who not only resisted as a matter of principle but suffered heroically in doing so, his approach to things has been more creative in East Germany, where political resistance is absolutely impossible because of the weight of Russian military upon that Soviet outpost. There Barth's eschatological emphasis has inspired a kind of religious resistance which has permitted the East German Christians to bear witness to their faith and to assert their dignity as men, without raising false hopes and fears in the political realm.

III

Some of the political framework of Barth's judgments is furnished by his ill-disguised anti-Americanism and by what he regards as our "worship of the dollar." Some of it is given by his belief that the struggle is not between Communism and democracy but between Slav and German. In his lecture on the "Church between East and West" he declared: "Russia signifies not only Communism but the resurgence of the Slavonic races, which thrust back the German thrust toward the east." But the political struggle between the East and West, according to Barth, is complicated by another factor: the struggle between America and Russia. "Russia and America," he declares, "are both in different ways children of Europe. . . . They have both suddenly grown into giants, who each in his own way would like to be patron, benefactor and protector of Europe. Both are afraid of encirclement by the other." Then Barth adds a final word which certainly does not follow from the "Word of God," for he declares: "One must concede that the anxiety of the Eastern giant is better founded than that of the Western giant, when one considers the total ring of Western bastions."

One is amazed by the number of technical, strategic, and political presuppositions which entered into these hazardous judgments. We are men and not God, and all our political judgments are bound to be hazardous. If we are also theologians we ought to have the grace to repeat the Pauline warning from time to time: "Thus say I, and not the Lord," so that our hearers will not regard a stray political opinion as a deliverance *ex cathedra.*

One could forgive Barth many things because he is a creative and imaginative theologian, who is also interested in politics. One could even forgive him his many capricious judgments in politics, though one might well wish that he would study the realities of the political order a little more if he is going to speak about them so much. But the one failing that is difficult to forgive is that he has not modestly confessed himself in error about Hungary. He seemed to know so much about Hungary, and history has refuted his judgments so absolutely.

The godless existentialist Jean Paul Sartre has broken with Communism and denounced its actions in Hungary. Even the lowly party hacks in the Communist parties of Britain and France have been shocked. But Barth's Czech disciple Hromadka has issued a pathetic defense of the Hungarian government, and Barth himself has remained silent. Surely one could have expected as much of the world's most eminent Protestant theologian as of the assistant editor of the *London Daily Worker*, who publicly disavowed all his former illusions.

BARTH ON HUNGARY: AN EXCHANGE

If the ardent young English-speaking disciples of Karl Barth are really interested in "mutually helpful criticism" they might begin by refraining from flagrant misinterpretation of my criticisms of the master. Let me enumerate some of them.

1. I did not insinuate that Barth was a "Communist sympathizer." On the contrary, I quoted his biting criticism of the "Red Dean" of Canterbury to refute this charge.

2. I did not criticize Barth for not advising a revolution in Hungary either eight years ago or now. I criticized him for adopting a complacent attitude toward Communist tyranny, particularly in Hungary, by many devices, including the observation that no government in history is absolutely good or absolutely evil. I did not challenge the theological correctness of the Christian truth that no government is absolutely evil, but merely observed that the young Hungarians must have found it morally and politi-

cally irrelevant when they found a despotism, particularly a foreign one, absolutely insufferable.

3. I did not criticize the most eminent theologian of our day for remaining silent, out of indifference for the important theological pursuits in which he is engaged. I was speaking of a man who enjoys an unparalleled theological eminence in our generation but who has not dwelt in an ivory tower. He has spoken rather consistently on political issues; and during the Nazi terror he was the religious inspiration of the anti-Nazi movement. In our engagement with the Communist tyranny he has taken the opposite position and has been the inspiration of European neutralism. He has not remained quiet on these new issues but has spoken as consistently in defense of neutralism as in his anti-Nazi days. All my quotations were taken from the collection of his political and theological essays entitled *Against the Stream*. My criticisms of Barth were particularly relevant in regard to Hungary because so much of that volume is devoted to his dialogue with the church in Hungary.

4. I did not expect him to admit to the same errors to which Sartre admitted. I only observed that this atheistic existentialist admitted his error and that Barth might have admitted the error of judgment in which he refused to equate or compare Nazi and Communist tyranny on the ground that it was still an open question whether the Nazis were so bad because they were totalitarian or pagan or anti-Semitic. Events in Hungary were ample proof that we must have enough regard for "systems" and "principles" to recognize that an absolute monopoly of irresponsible power creates grievous injustices under any system. My point was that "looking at every event afresh in the light of the Word of God" defrauds us of the lessons from the analogies and experiences of history. Not theology but common sense and historical experience ought to persuade us that Cromwell's protectorate was a despotic form of government resulting in many grievous injustices, even though Cromwell was not a pagan but a very devout Christian. I think this criticism is particularly relevant in

the light of Barth's observation that none of the Hungarian Reformed Christians were tempted to the "Catholic error of opposing the régime out of principle."

In addition to these misrepresentations of my position I must call attention to some very ludicrous misinterpretations of the historic situation. Barth, these young gentlemen declare, did not speak during the Hungarian crisis because of his "reluctance to encourage Switzerland and the rest of the righteous 'free world' to undertake a holy war against Russia at the time when the West had effectively dirtied its own record at Suez." One can only be astounded at this interpretation of recent history. Who in addition to neutral Switzerland was spoiling for a "holy war"? Our own country united with Russia in disciplining the three invading nations in Egypt, and so rigorously refrained from supporting the Hungarian revolution that we have earned the disrespect of many Europeans.

The young gentlemen report that Barth's position was less anti-American than that of most of his Swiss countrymen. That is a comfort, though not surprising, since we were not engaged in a holy war. I am intrigued by the anti-Americanism of the Swiss as reported by the young men. Did they criticize us because we slapped the British and French down in Egypt or because we failed to support the Hungarians? At any rate, nothing that could have been said could possibly have aggravated the danger of a holy war, since there was not the slightest inclination to such a war either among the Swiss or in America. There was only revulsion against the Russian cruelty in Hungary.

The young men's final excuse for Barth's silence (and they do offer an excuse despite their insistence that a theologian, as contrasted to an "anthropologian," is not required to speak on the issues of the day) is that the "dubious role played by Cardinal Mindszenty in the revolution" has validated Barth's reserve. I know that the Communists' boss, Khrushchev, has used Mindszenty's alleged role to prove that they were dealing with a Fascist uprising. But have the young men not heard that this was the most spontaneous uprising of a resentful people in recent history? And that the Cardinal had no more to do with it than that the Nagy government, in the brief moment of his freedom, unwisely allowed him to hold a press conference which he unwisely exploited?

Perhaps I might offer a parting word of advice for the young and ardent disciples, and that is that there is no substitute for common sense, even for theologians, whether budding or eminent.

PART IV: *The Catholic Heresy*

ARROGANCE IN THE NAME
OF CHRIST

Writing about the excesses against the church during the civil war in Spain, the Archbishop of Westminster, primate of the Roman Catholic church in England, recently interpreted the sufferings of the church as follows:

Christ foretold that his followers should suffer and be known by the mark of the cross. He pronounced them blessed when reviled and ill-treated for His Name's Sake. St. Peter writes, "Think it not strange the burning heat which is to try you as if some new thing happened to you." The church of God is no stranger to the violence and hatred of the "gates of hell," but the patience of Christians under persecution does not justify indifference to the fate of our country and our Christian civilization. We have ordered the following prayer from the Missal to be said daily in the diocese till further notice, "Almighty and everlasting Lord in whose hands are all the might and the lordship of the kingdoms of the earth; look upon and help Christendom and with the power of thy right arm crush the heathen peoples whose trust is in their ferocity. Through Christ our Lord."

The Archbishop closes his appeal in behalf of the Spanish church by quoting an English priest in Spain who objects to the use of the phrases "government forces" and "the rebels" in the foreign press. "They should say," declares the priest, "'the rabble' and 'the forces of Christian law and order.'" Evidently the strong condemnation of rebellion in orthodox Christianity can be easily overcome if the church happens to be on the side of the rebels. It need only insist that the government forces are "rabble" and that the revolutionists are "forces of Christian law and order."

This comment and exhortation of a Catholic hierarch upon the tragic events in Spain is an interesting commentary upon the perils in which the church always stands in its relation to the world. It is in the world and always, to some degree, of the world; but in the moment of crisis it claims an absolute identity with the Christ, whose purity is above the world. Thus the Archbishop identifies the sufferings of Spanish priests with "the cross" and suggests that the vicissitudes, which the revolution has brought upon them, conform to the promise and prediction of Christ, "Blessed are ye if men revile you and speak all manner of evil against you falsely."

The Height of Spiritual Arrogance

This is spiritual arrogance of the worst type. This is the very arrogance which proves that the most grievous sin of pride is always committed by religion and in the name of Christ, the sin of identifying sinful human purposes with the perfection of Christ. The Archbishop does not utter a word of penitence over the grievous relationship between Spanish Catholicism and the decrepit feudalism, now in its last stages of decay in Spain. He does not admit that the Spanish peasants, now in revolt in Spain, have suffered for ages from the most corrupt form of landlordism in Europe and that the injustices from which they have suffered have piled up a terrible increment of vengeance in their souls. Nor does he evince contrition for the fact that the hierarchy and the priests of the church have been in intimate league with landlordism, monarchism, and reaction in Spain not only before but after the revolution. The church in Spain is, in other words, a political instrument, and one which is committed to reactionary politics without reservation.

Considering these facts the revolutionary and radical

forces have been fairly generous toward the church until the moment of this present reactionary rebellion against the democratically chosen left government. The effort to overthrow this government and to return to the oppressions of the past has naturally aroused the fury of the new Spain and of all of the forces fighting for its preservation. It is regrettable that the passions of conflict never know discrimination and that radical defenders of the government should vent their vindictive passions upon pious and self-sacrificing nuns. Some innocent priests are undoubtedly also victims of the furies unleashed by civil conflict. In political conflicts individuals are unfortunately treated as symbols rather than as persons. Thus innocent individuals are made to suffer for the sins of the institutions.

One might wish that revolutions were otherwise and that the passions of conflict were more restrained. But it ought to be the first task of a profound religion to deal realistically with the causes of these terrible passions. Perhaps it is even more important to deal contritely with them and to recognize what action or attitude of the self has been responsible for such destructive hatred in the soul of the other. We find instead the Catholic church, wrapped in the cloak of self-righteousness, calling God's curse upon the "heathen peoples whose trust is in their ferocity" and speaking of rebels against constitutional authority as "the forces of Christian law and order." The force of religion is used, in other words, exclusively to increase rather than to mitigate the natural self-deception and pretension of the human heart.

Perhaps there is no more crucial test of the genuineness of a religion than its effect upon human pride and pretension. It is because religion may issue in either a contrite subjection of all human ideals to the holiness of God or in a false identification of those ideals with the divine perfection that it is impossible to regard any religion as good *per se*. The final and most sinful pretension of the human spirit is always expressed religiously. Just as the final effort to overcome the pretension is religious. It need hardly be said that both within and outside of Christianity the former consequence is a more frequent fruit of religion than the latter. That is why social radicals are, broadly speaking, right in regarding religion as a bulwark of social reaction, but are nevertheless wrong in their total appraisal of the place of religion in life.

The Church Clings to a Dying Feudalism

In the case of the Spanish church we see again an almost unqualified identification of Christ with a particular set of social values, in this case those of a dying feudalism. Spain is the last modern nation to go through the process of decaying feudalism. Her church has evidently learned nothing from the history of Europe during the last three hundred years. As in France of the eighteenth century and in Russia two decades ago, the church is once again defending a "Christian civilization" against the "rabble." It is too blind to see that it is defending a corrupt and unjust civilization against a rising passion for justice. The pathos of all human sinfulness is revealed in this self-deception of the church. To claim the moral prestige of Christ's "blessed are ye if men revile you" for sufferings incurred in a sordid political struggle is a consistent expression of religious pride and sinfulness.

This is, of course, no reason why Protestants should regard the error committed by the Spanish church as uniquely Catholic in its defects. To assume that would be to close our eyes to the universal character of the temptation to sinful pride and arrogance. Protestantism is sometimes as intimately enmeshed in the evils of capitalism as Catholicism is with feudalism. It must be admitted however, that the Catholic theory of the church as divine institution lends itself particularly to the temptation of confusing relative with eternal values. Since the church is the incarnation of Christ it is supposed to incarnate the spirit of Christ in every historical situation. This theory lacks the proper reservations such as are found in the more consistent Protestant views of the church. It does not do justice to the fact that though the church may delight in the law of God after the inward man, there is a law in its members which wars against the law that is in its mind. That war is an eternal one in the life of the church. Whenever the church imagines that the battle has been won, its very confidence will prove it to have been lost.

PIUS XI AND HIS SUCCESSOR

What will be the effect of the Pope's probably imminent death on Vatican policy? Catholics may regard the question as slightly premature, not to say impious, but they will hardly question its importance, particularly since the Vatican has taken such an intransigent line in the disturbed affairs of the contemporary world. Will its present policy, in which Catholicism is becoming more and more an unqualified ally of Fascism, be changed? Does the selection of a new pope offer at least the possibility of some deviation from this line?

To judge from the casual conversation of non-Catholics, two presuppositions, both of which are very dubious, usually underlie speculations about the future. One is that the present Secretary of State, Cardinal Pacelli, is the probable successor of Pius XI. The other is that Vatican policy at the present moment is the personal policy of either the Pope or his Secretary of State and might therefore be appreciably altered in a new reign. The first supposition is almost certainly false and the second requires many qualifications. Cardinal Pacelli is not likely to be the new pope. If precedent should be violated and he should be raised to the papal throne, the present policy would certainly be continued; for it is his policy. There is, however, a long tradition against elevating the secretary of state to the highest eminence, in spite of the prestige which he acquires during his secretaryship. The simple reason for this is that he makes too many enemies during his period of authority to be able to command a majority in the electoral college.

The hierarch with the greatest chance of success is always the one who is not too definitely committed to any particular policy and not too closely identified with the various divergent and sometimes conflicting influences, particularly monastic influences, within the church. Our own presidential conventions offer interesting parallels to this tendency.

A brief survey of the reigns of recent popes clearly proves the point. The secretary of state for the "angelic" Pope Pius IX, who reigned from 1846 to 1878, was the reactionary Cardinal Antonelli; but Pius's successor was not Antonelli. His successor was the diplomatic and slightly liberal Leo XIII. Leo had several secretaries, the last of whom, Cardinal Rampolla, gained a great reputation in Europe. His election to the papacy was vetoed by the Emperor of Austria. Whereupon a very simple and pious man, who prided himself upon his simplicity and whose gifts were in marked contrast to those of Rampolla, was elected and reigned as Pius X. Pius chose a man much shrewder than himself as secretary, the Spanish cardinal, Merry del Val. When Pius died in 1914 many assumed that his secretary would succeed him. But Rampolla finally came into his own, for a disciple of his was chosen. The new pope reigned as Benedict XV. He chose Cardinal Gasparri as his secretary. Gasparri gained wide fame and potent influence during the days of the First World War. But he did not succeed his master, though he probably determined the choice of the successor. The election fell upon Cardinal Ratti, who had come into prominence through his negotiation of the concordat with Poland after the war. He had been a cardinal for only a short time when he was elected to the papacy in 1922.

Unlike Pius X, the present Pius is a man of diplomatic training and may therefore be presumed to be the author of his own diplomatic policy to a larger degree than was the previous Pius. Nevertheless, there are evidences that his Secretary of State, Cardinal Pacelli, has been the real driving force behind the present papal diplomacy, particularly in the recent years of the Pope's declining strength. Any speculation about a possible change in this policy may well be prefaced by a short description of it. A description of this kind cannot be entirely accurate, however, because Catholic discipline prevents the serious tensions within the church from being aired in public. Some very honest Catholics even deny that they exist. Yet the evidences of these tensions, not to say conflicts, are clear enough to the outside observer.

The present policy of the papacy, a policy for which Cardinal Pacelli is probably more responsible than the Pope, is first of all to favor the hierarchy against lay Catholicism. By "lay Catholicism" the present writer is designating something which Catholics have probably never named but which nevertheless exists. At times it has expressed itself in Catholic political parties, for example, in the German Center, in which such lay leaders as Chancellors Marx and Bruning achieved a greater authority over their followers, at least in the realm of politics, than was held by the bishops. The term "lay" Catholicism is not entirely accurate, however, for it ought to include certain liberal political movements, such as that led by the Italian priest, Don Sturzo. Many village priests, as distinct from the hierarchy, have been active in similar movements. It would be difficult to give an exact description of the political tendencies of these movements, but it is quite clear that they were economically more liberal and politically more daring than anything ventured by the hierarchy. They expressed the common man's discontent with the status quo. In Germany the policies of the Center party managed to be a bridge between socialism and bourgeois conservatism, a not inconsiderable achievement considering that Catholicism is traditionally rooted in feudalism.

In every case the policy of the papacy in the now closing pontificate was to the disadvantage of these movements. The concordat with Mussolini completely destroyed Don Sturzo's movement. The concordat with Hitler was concluded in defiance of the advice of the effective leaders for the German Center party. It was an agreement between the Catholic hierarchy and the German Nazis in which the hierarchy sacrificed the lay forces of the church for the sake of preserving the freedom of the religious institution within a totalitarian state. Many who were leaders in the now defunct Center party must find it difficult to suppress an "I told you so" when they realize how little the bishops gained in their bargain with Hitler, and how little they have been able to improve the terms of the bargain by pleading with Hitler to accept them as equal allies in the fight against Communism.

The tremendous emphasis upon "Catholic Action" societies in the present pontificate belongs to the same policy. Catholic Action places the lay forces of the church directly under the bishops and thereby establishes a more perfect hierarchical control over all Catholics. The final effect of this process is the establishment of greater papal control over national units. This, despite the accusations of rabid anti-Catholics, has not been the unvarying policy of the papacy. Certainly the tendencies toward centralization of authority have increased in recent years. Among other things they led to an understanding between the church and Hitler in regard to the Saar plebiscite which violated the convictions of 90 per cent of the Catholic population in the Saar.

The other side of present papal policy is more difficult to deal with justly because of the universal reticence of all parties affected by it. Broadly speaking, it could be designated as the continued ascendancy of Jesuit influence at the Vatican over the milder and more spiritual tendencies of other monastic groups. The Benedictines and Franciscans are less anxious to play the political game than the Jesuits and are less deeply involved in political activities. Particularly since the Spanish crisis the Jesuit influence has been accentuated. For Spain is the classic nation of the Catholic counter-Reformation, and Jesuitism is the driving force of that movement.

Any speculation about a possible new policy in regard to Fascism and radicalism after the present Pope's death therefore revolves around the question: Is the intimate alliance between Catholicism and Fascism a consequence of Jesuit influence or is it the product of tendencies within Catholicism deeper and more far-reaching than any particular influence? The answer to that question would seem to be that Jesuit influence has merely accentuated a tendency which Catholicism is bound to express. If, therefore, a new pope stood less directly under Jesuit influence, one might hope for a less unqualified alliance between Catholicism and Fascism; but one could hardly hope for a reversal of the policy. The change is bound to be slight, but even a slight qualification of the policy might have important consequences in world affairs.

Catholic political policy is determined by fateful forces in modern history. The most important is the intimate historical connection between Catholicism as a civilization and feudalism. This bond sometimes gives Catholicism a certain degree of impartial perspective with regard to capitalism, such as was revealed, for instance, in the politics of the German Center party. But it puts it at a complete moral and spiritual disadvantage where there is a dying feudalism, whether in Spain or in Latin America. In such a situation the feudal relation between church and state, or more particularly between the church and the army and the feudal landowning caste, is so strong that the instincts of Catholicism to preserve itself as a social system overpower any possible moral scruples which may inhere in Catholicism as a religion and to which the more spiritual monastics may give occasional voice. Fascism, except in Spain, is of course not feudalism but the effort to press the forms of feudalism upon a technical civilization, a procedure which results in consequences even worse than those of feudalism.

Catholic policy is determined by the irreligion of radicalism as much as by the feudalism of Catholicism. The avowed intention of radicalism to destroy institutional religion naturally drives religion into the camp of reaction, particularly if the religion is rooted in a historic institution. The radical will be unable to see anything in this opposition to his cause but proof of his thesis that all religion is counterrevolutionary. He will never know how many purer religious souls in a historic religious movement are really defending their faith and not a civilization. Nor do the purer religious souls realize to what degree the irreligion confronting them is not the decadence which they imagine it to be but a protest against the religious sanctification of social injustice.

There is a peculiar pathos in the present Catholic anti-Communist campaign, with its admissions that the church does not like Fascism but prefers it to Communism because Communism tries to destroy it while Fascism merely embarrasses it. Since German Fascism is as anti-Christian as Communism, the Catholic choice is reduced to a preference for a lower-middle-class type of modern religion over the proletarian variety. The total situation is determined by forces on both sides too deeply rooted in history and too inexorable in their logic to permit the hope that a change in reigning popes will greatly affect the issue. All historic religions have tended to become so intimately related to the civilizations of which they were part that they have been driven to defend them against just as well as unjust judgments and to die with them if the judgment of history was a death sentence. Catholicism is particularly tempted to this identification and confusion because it was the architect of medieval and feudal civilization. There is good reason to estimate the achievement of medieval civilization more generously than the modern liberal or radical rationalist is inclined to do, but such a generous estimate increases the pathos of the present situation. This pathos is accentuated even more by the recognition that religion is never so simple a rationalization of a given social order as the radical believes, and that within the pale of Catholicism today there are many pure spirits who long for a better world and seek higher justice.

The radical will not learn to estimate the perennial and basic character of this tragedy of modern Catholicism in particular and of organized religion in general for centuries. He will learn it only when, three hundred or five hundred or a thousand years from now, some group of creative spirits challenges a decadent Russian society in the name of a higher conception of society. It will be seen then that this decadent society can offer stubborn resistance because its official spokesmen derive moral self-respect from the memories of Russian sovietism in its creative period and have appropriated the moral prestige of Lenin's disinterestedness.

THE CATHOLIC HERESY

It is becoming daily more apparent that the Catholic church has cast its lot with Fascistic politics. In Germany the church is reduced to the pathetic role of begging the Nazis kindly to let it co-operate in their anti-Communist campaign, since the Pope hates Communism as much as Hitler does. Many a liberal Catholic, particularly in America, does not like Fascism. Politically liberal Catholics do not deny that their choice of Fascism is a hard alternative. They justify it by the assertion that Fascism does not intend to destroy the church while Communism does. One might answer that Fascism intends to destroy Christianity if it should not succeed in corrupting it and making it serve its purely national purposes. But that does not make an immediate contribution to the problem. The Catholic might answer that sufficient unto the day are the evils thereof. For the moment only German Fascism is avowedly anti-Christian. In Austria Fascism is completely clerical and in Italy it has made a cynical bargain with the church.

Grounds Not Purely Political

The real problem is whether the Catholic position is justified from the Christian standpoint. In order to understand the problem correctly it must be appreciated that Catholicism takes its stand for other than purely political reasons. It is not simply a rationalization of economic interests. It would be foolish to deny, of course, that some aspects of Catholic policy can be understood only in terms of the intimate historic alliance between the church and the feudal order. The position of the church in Spain is partially determined by the historic affinity of interest between the clerics and the feudal aristocracy. This same relationship is making the church the primary source of Fascistic politics in French Canada. It also explains the role of the church in South America. Nevertheless, there are democratic and progressive Catholics in nonfeudal nations, who are forced into political support of Fascism in defiance of all their political convictions and instincts. Their plight is pitiful. What is the basis of their position?

The cynic might explain their position by attributing it to the necessity of obedience in an authoritarian church, the heart and center of which is involved in feudalism, though some of its members are not. The iron authority of the church prevents them from extricating themselves from political policies which they personally disavow. But even this explanation is too simple. The real basis of the Catholic position in modern politics lies in the most characteristic of all dogmas of the church, its identification of the church with the Kingdom of God. For the Catholic the church is an unqualifiedly divine institution. It is Christ on earth and in history, as the pope is the vicar of Christ. Any attack upon the church is therefore unqualifiedly evil because it is an attack upon Christ. In the recent letter of the Spanish bishops they speak of the blasphemies of loyalist troops, their profaning of sacred mysteries and finally of the act of a trooper in pointing his revolver at the "sacred host." This is regarded as a final revelation of the "hatred of Christ" which animates "our poor Communists" and can be explained only by the ascription of it to "diabolical" influences. It seems never to have occurred to these bishops that a radical soldier might profane a church not because he hates Christ but because he hates a historic institution with all of its dubious involvements in the political struggle on one particular side. The Spanish bishops incidentally do not see or confess a single mistake of the church in its relation to the social struggle, though American Catholics, like Father Ryan, have said some very critical words about the Spanish church.

This perfect complacency of the Spanish hierarchy, its confidence that its enemies are the enemies of Christ and its pathetic belief that hatred toward it can be explained only in terms of diabolical inspiration, is the natural fruit of a dogma which identifies a human, relative, and historic institution with the divine. The consequences of this dogma are so baneful in all human history that we have new reason to emphasize the Protestant doctrine that the church is not unqualifiedly the Kingdom of God but rather that place in human society where the Kingdom of God is known and where the judgments of God are felt to be pointed at all human actions and institutions, including the church itself.

Not that the Roman church is alone guilty of this heresy. In the Greek Orthodox church divinity is ascribed not so much to the hierarchical institution as to a body of sacred tradition. But the general effect is the same. At the Oxford Conference last summer, one of the most brilliant exponents of Greek Orthodoxy, Father Bulgakoff, insisted again and again that modern history must be interpreted as a conflict between Christ and anti-Christ, and he attributed the antireligion of radicals to the mysterious working of anti-Christ as prophesied in Scriptures. There is a peculiarly pathetic aspect in this charge of anti-Christ. It fails to recognize that a great deal of protest against historic religion is prompted not by the devil but by a wholesome reaction to the divine pretensions of very human institutions and very imperfect priests. That is, the alleged anti-Christ is actually objecting to what is really anti-Christ in the religious institution. The Scriptural definition of anti-Christ is one who blasphemes against God by lifting himself above measure. Anti-Christ, in other words, is one who pretends to be Christ. This is what led Luther to give the pope that name. In this connection it is instructive to note that in many Catholic nations it is a legal offense, defined as blasphemy, to speak contemptuously of the church. The true Protestant would say that blasphemy is precisely the pretension of the church to be so divine that it cannot repent and ought not to be criticized.

Catholic Heresy Not Confined to Rome

The Catholic heresy is not confined to Rome, nor yet to Rome and Orthodoxy. Anglo-Catholicism is also seriously infected with it. At the Oxford Conference a not too impressive Anglo-Catholic archdeacon protested that the continued call of the conference for the repentance of the churches was absurd. The church could not repent because the church was Christ. This particular archdeacon was not the most intelligent representative of his group. It is instructive therefore to turn to one of the finest spirits of Anglo-Catholicism, V. A. Demant. Writing in the English journal, *Christendom,* the organ of the Anglo-Catholic social movement, Demant, who has a very profound understanding of current social issues, declares that on the whole he is forced to choose "left" rather than "right" in most of the political issues which confront him "because in that (leftist) tradition I find some link with my prejudices— which have their roots in the civilization of Christian Europe." With this general orientation Demant proceeds to discuss what he ought to do if faced with an antireligious movement, and declares:

> Where formal atheism and anti-Christian paganism is at issue, however much in line with Christian justice the aims of the secular movement may be, and however oppressive, corrupt, superstitious and servile the church may be—I will not allow the sins of the Christian bodies to prevent my siding with those who uphold the church against those who would destroy it. It would be a tragic and unholy choice, but it would have to be made, because the essential content of the Body of Christ is a more ultimate thing than the most perfect system of social justice.

In my own soul this confession of Demant has had a most shattering effect, all the more so because I hold him in such high esteem. It revealed to me the tremendous importance of the Protestant principle. It is the "essential content of the Body of Christ" which is to be preferred to the "most perfect system of social justice"! The power of God is thus restricted to the "Body of Christ." Does the church not know that if it is the Body of Christ, it is collectively under the fate which St. Paul confesses as an individual, namely that "there is a law in my members which wars against the law that is in my mind"?

The Protestant Inheritance

Is this complacent assumption of the church that God can work only through it any different from the complacency of preprophetic Israel and does it not stand under the prophetic condemnation, "Are ye not as the children of the Ethiopians unto me?" Is it not this sin which John the Baptist castigated when he insisted that God would be able "out of the stones" to raise up "children unto Abraham"? Is it not this sin which has made the vice-regent of Christ, at his worst, a kind of priestly and ghostly Caesar who has claimed for Caesar's dubious imperial ambitions the ultimate sanctities of the spirit of Christ?

We do not want a new crusade of anti-Catholicism. But the relevance of this theological issue to contemporary political problems might well prompt us to a new understanding of what is involved in the genius of Protestantism. It must be admitted of course that our Protestant inheritance disintegrates into secularism much more easily than Catholicism does. It must also be admitted that many of our Protestant radical minorities allow themselves to be used as catspaws and allies of antireligious radicals without any sense of responsibility toward their religious inheritance and with no sure hold upon the truth which divides them from secularists. They stand against Roman Catholicism but are in danger of becoming enmeshed in Stalin's catholicism. For Stalin is but a secularized version of the pope. He also believes that anyone who opposes him is an incarnation of the very principle of evil. (In Communist mythology that means that he is a Fascist.) He also believes this because he claims ultimate sanctity for the dubious, though probably necessary, compromises of Russian statecraft. He, like all priests of an established religion, is unable to distinguish between a heretic who would undermine the faith and the one who seeks to purify it of its corruption. He, like all priests who have become kings, claims a more ultimate sanctity for his power than ordinary kings who have only a borrowed divine aura.

The danger that radical Protestantism may become a too servile ally of secular radicals can be avoided only if our criticism of the Catholic heresy is made, not from the standpoint of secular cynics but from the standpoint of Protestant Christian faith. We will resist all temporal divinities, whether they call themselves popes, kings by divine right, or commissars. We will not be under the illusion that we can get rid of this tendency toward self-deification by getting rid of the Catholic faith or the Christian religion. We recognize in it the very quintessence of sin, the tendency of man to make himself God. That we should discover the Christian church itself as a potential vehicle of this sin will make us the more circumspect in our claims and the more certain that the majesty of God may reveal itself in the destruction of historic Christian churches as well as in their preservation.

THE POPE'S CHRISTMAS MESSAGE

The annual message of the Pope at Christmas time is significant for the fact that it has become increasingly a statement of the relevance of the Christian faith to the various social and political problems which vex our world. The statement last month was more unequivocal than any previously made. The Pope rightly condemned theories which "claim for particular nations or races or classes the juridical instinct as the final imperative from which there is no appeal" and also the philosophies of state absolutism which regard the state as "an absolute and supreme entity" which is "exempt from criticism and control." The condemnation of Marxism is remarkably restrained in the latest papal message. The Pope is content to declare: "Always moved by religious motives the church has condemned the various forms of Marxist socialism and she condemns them today." But this condemnation is merely a prelude to the statement that "the church cannot overlook the fact that the worker . . . is opposed by a machinery which not only is not in accordance with nature but is at variance with God's plan and with the purpose he had in creating the goods of the earth." Here he restores the ancient teaching of the church, once very influential, according to which all the treasures of the earth should be made available to all men. The Pope draws distributist, rather than communist conclusions from the religious idea of a divine ownership of all property. He thinks that private property should be a privilege of all men and that a propertyless worker is condemned to "economic dependence and slavery." He wisely observes that this kind of slavery is possible either "through the exploitation of private property or through the power of the state."

It is not possible to do justice to the full program of social justice for individuals and nations which the Pope elaborated in his Christmas message. It must certainly be regarded as superior to many secular and Protestant analyses of social problems, which ignore one or another aspect of the complexities of social justice. There is a remarkable balance in this Catholic statement.

Its primary defect is derived from a general defect in all Catholic social theory. It is based upon the assumption that there are in two sources, the natural law of justice and in the Scriptural law of love, exact and precise definitions of every problem of justice. It assumes that universal principles of justice have been challenged primarily by positivists and relativists who "give a deceptive majesty to purely human law" and who "leave the way open to a fateful divorce between law and morality."

This is a Catholic thesis which every Catholic teacher has been expounding in recent years. According to it the explicit egotism of Nazi politics is but the final product of a pragmatism which rejects the standards of universal law for the sake of laws of expediency. According to this thesis the secular world has undermined law and order by its moral cynicism. On the whole this is a false polemic of Christianity against secularism, in which many Protestants have also participated.

There is indeed a decadent cynical, relativist, and nihilistic fringe of secular culture. But on the whole modern culture is utopian, universalist, and moralistic. It believes in the possibility of establishing universal justice, and universal culture. It has rejected Christianity because it thinks it knows of simpler methods of saving both men and nations than Christianity proposes. The real fact is that both Catholicism and modern culture have one thing in common. They know much too exactly just what justice is. Modern rationalism and Catholic rationalism both have too great a confidence in the ability of reason to state the laws of justice. Both fail to understand the full interplay between reason and interest and passion in man's social life. The most sophisticated moderns draw cynical conclusions from this taint of interest in all historic justice and declare that there is no justice. But the more naive moderns are agreed with Catholicism in estimating the ability of man to define the eternal laws which govern society. Only the moderns would allow the scientists, rather than the church, to define the laws. And they believe that the knowledge of the law is sufficient to guarantee its fulfillment; while Catholicism takes human sin more seriously than that. It believes that only an infusion of grace will enable man to fulfill the law which transcends his own interests.

Simple moralism, rather than moral cynicism, has brought us so close to disaster in the modern world. Not many moderns are Nazis who believe that there is no good but "my" good. But there are many moderns, both Christian and secular, who believe it easy to define the good without corrupting the definition by "my" interest; and to realize it without compounding it with self-interest. We dare not disavow general standards of justice. But neither must we give ourselves to the illusion that they are either easily defined or simply realized. Some of our worst social evils are derived, not from the cynics, who acknowledge no standard but their own, but from the fanatics who acknowledge an absolute standard but fail to detect the corruption of self-interest in their definition of the absolute.

THREE ELEMENTS IN PAPAL LEADERSHIP

The Pope's address to the College of Cardinals on June 2 is a remarkable document and also a very typical one; for it combines three elements which are characteristic of Roman Christianity. It pleads for the city of Rome; it makes the traditional claims for the primacy of the Bishop of Rome over all of Christendom; and it makes some thoroughly Christian observations on the conduct of the war. Thus it combines the Roman, the Papal, and the Christian elements which constitute Catholicism as we know it.

In regard to Rome the Pope declares: "If at the moment our anxiety is especially for Rome it is because such sentiments are evoked by the pitiable conditions in which a large part of the population of the city, which is also our diocese, finds itself." This special anxiety is natural enough, though the conditions in Rome are probably no more pitiable than those under which the Pope's children, let us say, in Poland, suffer. This may be put down as local patriotism which qualifies the Pope's universal loyalties.

The genuinely Christian observations on war policies are expressed as follows:

In many is born the impression or the fear that there may not be, even for the peoples and nations as such, any alternative but this: A complete victory or complete destruction. When once this sharp dilemma has entered men's minds, its baneful influence is a stimulant for the

prolongation of the war. Even among those who by natural impulse or for realistic considerations would be
disposed to a reasonable peace, the spectre of the alternative and the conviction of the real or supposed will of
the enemy to destroy national life to the very roots,
smothers all other reflections and instills in many the
courage of desperation.

This is the Pope's wise criticism of the Allied policy of
"unconditional surrender." It is a pertinent criticism and
is informed by genuine Christian presuppositions.

It is rather strange and interesting how the papal address combines with these immediate concerns the presentation of the ancient claim of the primacy of the Holy See.
The argument is, as usual, that the Pope has inherited from
Peter the promise of Christ that he would build his church
upon this rock. "Between Christ and Peter," declares the
Pope, "there reigns from the days of the promise near
Caesarea Philippi—a mysterious but eminently real bond
which was affected once in time but draws its roots from
the eternal counsels of the Almighty." The entire papal
argument is a proof of the fact that in all debates, the
important point is the presuppositions upon which the
conflicting arguments proceed. Granted that the words of
Christ were meant personally for Peter, and granted that
Peter was the first bishop of Rome (a particularly questionable presupposition) and granted that there is a mystical and magical bond between the first and last Bishop
of Rome, the argument may seem irrefutable. It is of course
implausible to all who are unable to accept the presuppositions.

For the Pope no unity of Christendom is possible, if all
those who "profess themselves Christians" do not accept
this papal claim. There is something rather pathetic about
the papal hope that he may persuade errant Protestants to
accept this claim; for it proves how little he understands
the irrevocable character of certain historical events, which
have made these ancient papal claims implausible.

"How much more potent," declares the Pope, "would be
the influence of Christian thought and life on the moral

substructure of the future plans for peace and reconstruction if there were not this vast dispersal and division of religious confessions, that in the course of time have detached themselves from the Mother Church!" We are not so sure. The Christian gospel validates itself finally not so much by the unanimity of its contemporary witness as by the profundity of its appeal. An authoritarian unity is always a peril to this profundity, for it achieves harmony by sacrificing facets of the gospel testimony which do not fit into the prevailing scheme. Suppose all of Christendom were now united under the Pope! Would then not the whole of Christendom be committed to the proposition that the integrity of the church must be the first consideration of statecraft; and would we then not support any government which allows the church to live and attack every government which is inimical to the church, no matter how important its collaboration for a peace system might be?

THE POPE ON PROPERTY

In his radio address, commemorating the anniversary of the beginning of the Second World War, the Pope made many very commendable observations on the method of reconstructing the world, on the necessity and the limit of force in building a world organization and on the obligation of the wealthy nations to come to the aid of those whose lands have been ravaged by war.

In dealing with the property issue the Pope was obviously prompted by the fear that Europe would be subject to radical political movements with collectivist property concepts. He reiterated the general Catholic distributist idea of property. Property should not be abolished but as widely distributed as possible, because it is a form of security which all men desire and deserve. "The church," he declared "does not intend in principle to protect the rich and plutocrats against the poor. On the contrary ever since its beginning the church has protected the poor and the weak against the tyranny of the powerful." One might say in passing that such a statement betrays the usual inability of Catholic thought to distinguish between the principles of an institution and what it does in fact. In principle the church desires to protect the poor; but in fact it has often been the ally of the landlords against the peasants, of the aristocrats against the rising middle classes and of the monarchs against the rebellious democrats.

But to return to the Pope's ideas of property, the primary weakness of Catholic property ideas from Aquinas to the present Pope is that it does not preserve the original Christian idea that property may be necessary in a sinful world, in order to give men security against the ambition of others, but that it must be regarded as a necessary evil which must not be given an absolute sanction. The justification of property in Catholic thought has become as absolute as in eighteenth century thought.

Catholicism does, of course, teach that property should be morally and politically controlled. The Pope declares, "When the distribution of property is an obstacle (to justice) the state should in common interest intervene, regulate its activities or issue a decree of expropriation with suitable indemnities. Small holdings in agriculture, the arts, trade and industry must be guaranteed and supported."

The general philosophy behind the papal pronouncement is that which informs our own antitrust laws. The Pope refuses to admit that technical advances make the socialization of large-scale industry necessary. He declares, "The suggestion should not be put forward that technical progress is toward the establishment of gigantic concerns which must inevitably cause the collapse of a social system, based on private property." But he does not explain how large-scale concentrations of wealth are to be brought into the scheme of his philosophy of distribution. He merely observes that "technical progress must not prevail over the common good but must be governed by it and subordinated to it."

The papal philosophy of property is half right and half wrong. It is right in seeking to maintain a distribution of property as one method of preserving an equilibrium of social power in opposition to an omnipotent state. He calls attention to the fact that the ideal of the socialization of property may in actual history produce "a dictatorship of a political group, that as a ruling class will control the means of production." He understands in other words that the complete socialization of property may compound economic and political power and thus destroy liberty.

But the papal policy has no program, but moral exhortation for one aspect of the modern property issue. A technical civilization creates centralized forms of economic power which must be socially owned because they can neither be perfectly controlled, nor can the wealth and property in them be divided in such a manner as to give every one an individual share in the power and security of the property.

The papal pronouncements on property are on the whole superior to those of the Protestant churches who have usually not thought out a consistent attitude toward the issue; so that the conservative part of the church usually accepts the liberal ideas of property uncritically while the radical minority of the church subscribes to Marxist ideas without qualification. Catholic property philosophy is consistent but nevertheless inadequate for the problems of our day. It recognizes that property is a legitimate form of security in one of its aspects; but it has no answer for the problem when property becomes inherently so powerful that it becomes a threat to security and justice.

OUR RELATIONS TO CATHOLICISM

The acrimonious relations between Catholics and Protestants in this country are scandalous. If two forms of the Christian faith, though they recognize a common Lord, cannot achieve a little more charity in their relations to each other, they have no right to speak to the world or claim to have any balm for the world's hatreds and mistrusts. The mistrust between Catholics and Protestants has become almost as profound as that between the West and Communism. A little editorial note in this journal, raising questions about the advisability of the Protestant position on the school bus question produced more correspondence than any other recent editorial comment. Catholic journals, some of which are wont to label every liberal Protestant utterance as "Communist" suddenly hailed us as a font of wisdom. The Knights of Columbus who had condemned our articles on the Catholic position in South America, gave us an embarrassing embrace. Most of the Protestant clergy were highly critical of our position. A surprising number of Protestant laymen on the other hand wrote in commendation and expressed their embarrassment over the degree of animosity which exists between Protestant and Catholic clergy. We know of Catholic laymen who have the same sense of embarrassment and who long for a better understanding between Protestantism and Catholicism. There is incidentally an untapped resource of democratic common sense among laymen in all churches, which clerical leaders might draw upon to their advantage.

What is written in these pages is by no means an official utterance of *Christianity and Crisis.* The editorial board of this journal has never threshed out this issue and we have no way of knowing whether any degree of unanimity on the issue could be achieved. This word is a purely personal venture, which has the hopeful but probably futile purpose of putting the debate between Catholics and Protestants on a different level.

We should like to present three propositions, the first of which applies to both Protestants and Catholics, the second to Catholics, and the third to Protestants. The first proposition is that there is an unfortunate inclination in the human heart, which Christians should, but have not, mastered, to be more concerned with the sins of others than with our own sins. Thus democrats frequently increase the peril in which a democratic civilization stands by heedlessness toward the internal corruptions of this civilization and preoccupation with either the Nazi or the Communist external danger. Communists, on the other hand, are even more self-righteous, being informed by a secular religion which knows nothing of the sinful corruption, which appears in every human endeavor and which foolishly equates all historic evil with capitalist corruption. In the same way a good deal of Protestantism is little more than anti-Catholicism; and Catholicism is very fond of historic theories which ascribe all the ills of our generation to the destruction of a Catholic civilization by the force of the Protestant Reformation and modern secularism. This inclination to find the root of all evil in the sins of the other and not in those of the self is as wrong as it is natural. There ought however, to be some resource in the Christian church to counteract it; for the Christian faith insists that the primary encounter in human life is not between good and evil men, nations, or institutions, but between all men and God. "Whosoever thou art that judges," declares St. Paul, "thou thyself doest the same thing." The mistrust and hatred of others which affronts us, always has greater similarities with our own mistrust and hatred than we would like to believe. The root of all Christian charity lies in the contrite recognition of the common need of all men for the divine mercy. Charity, particularly the charity of forgiveness is not something which can be demanded or learned. It springs from the heart of those who know themselves to stand under a more ultimate judgment than any of the judgments by which they judge their foes and their foes judge them. If there is not something of this ultimate insight informed by faith, in the Christian life, it is a salt which has lost its savor. Catholics may boast of the superiority of their discipline and unity; and Protestants may boast of their superior liberty. But without charity the virtues of each become corrupted by an intolerable self-righteousness. The virtues of each have, indeed, become thus corrupted.

Since we are men and not angels we do, of course, have our various loyalties and causes to which we have a responsible relationship, which we seek to protect against various perils and which we judge favorably in camparison with other causes and values. Catholics thus feel under the compulsion of protecting their kind of Christian civilization against what seems to them the anarchy, and sometimes the secularism of Protestantism. Protestants on the other hand do have a certain common interest with secular democratic idealism in protecting the values of liberty against what seems to them to be the encroachment of an authoritarian and an officially intolerant creed. This brings us to the second proposition which refers particularly to Catholics.

The Catholic bishops have the practice of rushing to the public and to print, every time Protestants call attention to some form of official Catholic intolerance, with the assertion that it is Christ himself who is under attack and that only disloyalty to Christ could have prompted the criticism. There is a curious pathos in this performance; for the bishops could hardly understand that from the Protestant standpoint it is precisely this unqualified identification of Christ with the historic church which is the root of all Catholic heresies and the cause of Catholic intolerance. We should like to report, for the benefit of our Catholic friends, that our Protestant army chaplains, returned from their army service, have become to a large degree anti-Catholic.

Only a few were able to report the achievement of anything like a sense of spiritual comradeship with Catholic chaplains. Where such comradeship was established it was accepted with such gratitude that we may assume a much wider desire for it than gratification of it. Mostly the Protestant chaplains resented "being pushed around." This "pushing around" consisted in various Catholic efforts to establish special privileges in the army which frequently succeeded because officers tended to yield to the persistent and consistent pressure of Catholic authorities while they had nothing to fear from divided Protestantism. We could give chapter and verse on these charges of Protestant chaplains and it may yet be necessary to do so.

In the same way Protestants are inclined to be unyielding on problems of the public school because they suspect the hierarchy, at least, of being inimical to the whole idea of the public school system, which Protestants, as well as our secular democrats, regard as one of the foundation stones of our democracy. Protestants are, furthermore, not at all certain that the Catholic hierarchy really accepts the fundamental separation of church and state, to which American democracy is committed. The position of the late Archbishop Ireland, affirming the Catholic acceptance of this principle and insisting that the Catholic church had prospered under it, has been frequently disavowed in recent years.

We have been told again and again that Catholicism must insist on the obligation of the state not only to teach religion but to teach the "true religion." This means that Catholicism accepts our constitutional principle "that Congress shall pass no laws respecting the establishment of religion" only provisionally, that is so long as it is powerless to alter it. We have been assured of course that a mere majority would not give the church the right to alter this principle. It would seek its alteration only if the Catholic population achieved an overwhelming majority.

The remoteness of this prospect is, according to the late Monsignor Ryan, supposed to allay our fears. But it can hardly change our convictions that Catholicism would, if it could, seek the establishment of a particular religion. We Protestants oppose this not only because the condition of religious pluralism in America makes it quite unfeasible but also because we believe that monopoly in anything, including monopoly in religion, is a source of corruption.

It is a particular source of corruption in religion. Institutions of religion should be politically powerless, if the true principles of our religion are to achieve political influence.

We could multiply these charges of official intolerance. Catholic bishops have sought to eliminate Protestant institutions from community funds, if they sanctioned birth control clinics. The bishops probably honestly believe that the prohibition of birth control, according to the "natural law," is so absolute that violation of the prohibition is the proof of un-Christian conduct. But thoughtful Protestants have some basic questions about these supposed absolute requirements of the "natural law." It is the very character of Catholicism to be unable to recognize the honesty of such scruples.

It simply regards skepticism in regard to any of its "self-evident truths" as the mark of the moral nihilist. It is in short not easy to deal charitably with an officially intolerant religion. It is usually certain, not only that it is right but also that those who are wrong are so for unchristian motives. It cannot understand what Oliver Cromwell meant by the robust warning: "Remember, by the bowels of Christ, that you may be mistaken." Upon the understanding of that warning depends the appreciation of the moral legitimacy of a democratic civilization.

Despite the genuine difficulties which we face as Protestants in dealing with a form of the Christian faith which is officially intolerant we have lacked charity as much as have Catholics, partly because we fail to appreciate the genuine grace of personal religion within this system of official intolerance. Furthermore, we fail to appreciate the real concern for religious values which underlies the Catholic insistence on religious instruction. Protestantism is erroneously branded by Catholicism as merely another version of secularism. But on the other hand Protestant faith lacks sufficient robustness to understand that an absolutely rigorous separation of church and state does mean the secularization of the community; for the state is the organ of the community in regulating its common concerns.

Our constitutional fathers quite obviously and quite rightly wanted to prevent the establishment of religious monopoly. That is the clear meaning of the First Amendment. It is not at all clear that they sought to prevent the state's support of religion absolutely, provided such support could be given equitably to all religious groups. Whether this should be done is a question of policy upon which we may have different opinions. It may well be that the religious heterogeneity of America is such that the state support of religion is not advisable.

But we ought not to prejudge that issue in the name of a principle of "separation of church and state" which in exact constitutional terms goes no further than the prohibition of the establishment of one religion and the suppression of others. It is not at all irreverent to suggest that our highest court, in interpreting this simple prohibition of the constitution, inclines to "follow election returns" as Mr. Dooley once suggested, in the sense that it inevitably not only interprets what our constitutional fathers intended but also mirrors what we now intend. That is the existential character of the judicial process.

We will, as good Americans, abide by the decision of the court, but we must also recognize that its decisions over a period of decades and centuries, accurately reflect what the American people believe their democracy to be. The present tendency to make the separation of church and state as absolute as possible is a reflection not only of the prevailing secularism of our culture but of the Protestant fear of Catholicism.

This fear may seem in one sense justified. But in another sense it is an effort to cover up by political action, the weakness of Protestantism in the field of religion itself. The anarchy of Protestantism, its lack of spiritual discipline, its ridiculous tensions between obscurantist versions of Protestantism on the one hand and of liberal versions on the other, its half-secular sentimentalities, all these weaknesses are more responsible for its sense of insecurity than anything that Catholicism may do politically.

Let us defend ourselves against any political actions of Catholicism which tend to encroach upon our liberties; but let us achieve a greater consciousness of our own weaknesses and our tendency to cover our weaknesses by our apprehensions about a religious foe or competitor. It is not a very nice fact about human nature that religious communities should be in conflict with one another, partly for the same reasons that there is hatred between racial communities. In each case inner insecurities and a guilty conscience are transmuted into social hatreds. But in the case of religious hatreds these fears of the other are doubly reprehensible because the faith which should cure us of our fears is made into a bearer of them.

THE GODLY AND THE GODLESS

The National Catholic Welfare Council has made a statement entitled "The Christian in Action," which has the primary purpose of challenging the Supreme Court decision which outlawed the "released time" religious program in the public schools of Illinois. The bishops centered their criticism on the reliance of the Court upon Jefferson's metaphor "the absolute wall of separation between church and state." This metaphor, according to the Catholic bishops, cannot clarify the First Amendment which enjoins that "Congress shall pass no laws respecting the establishment of religion or the suppression thereof," since the meaning of the amendment is perfectly clear. It means that there shall be no "established church" no "state religion" and, therefore, that no religion shall be given preferential status by the state. It does not, therefore, prohibit cooperation between church and state so long as this is done in terms of complete equality.

This journal has previously outlined a similar criticism of the Supreme Court decision and expressed the conviction, stated in the dissenting opinion, that "a rule of law cannot be drawn from a metaphor." We are perhaps a little more sensitive than the Catholic bishops to the fact that it is very difficult to achieve a policy which will be regarded as fair by all religious sects and by those who have no religious loyalty. It is clear, for instance, that Catholics would hope ultimately to secure the public support of parochial schools under their interpretation of the First Amendment. This would be regarded as unfair by most of the Protestant sects which have no parochial schools. If complete fairness were to be achieved it would mean the establishment of parochial schools by various Protestant sects, a policy which would wreck the unity of our public school system. It would, granted the religious pluralism of the American culture, also endanger the unity of the people. We do not believe that the increased secularization of our culture ought to be the price of that unity; but we do have some understanding of the viewpoint of those who fear religious divisiveness in our community. Despite these apprehensions it is important that Protestant agreement with the Catholic position should be expressed, as far as that agreement runs.

It is equally important that we should, from the standpoint of the Protestant faith, express our disagreement with a basic presupposition of the Catholic position. The bishops express that presupposition in these words: "The failure to center life in God is secularism, which . . . is the most deadly menace to our Christian and American way of living." There is a great truth but also a considerable error in this simple condemnation of secularism. The truth is that secularism, in both its liberal and its Marxist variety, promised the world a utopia of perfect justice, if only the irrational prejudices of religion could be eliminated. This utopia was not realized, not only because the Western world is involved in a deadly conflict between the two versions of secular idealism, but also because each misinterpreted the human situation. Each believed that the evils of human nature and the injustices of society were due either to a simple remedial ignorance which more education would eliminate; or to the institution of property, which the abolition of that institution would overcome. Neither recognized the profoundly idolatrous tendency in the heart of man, the tendency to set himself up as God and to defy the common good. Catholicism usually makes the mistake of regarding secularism as morally cynical, that is, as acknowledging no law except the good of each individual or nation. Actually only a very subordinate strain of secular thought is morally cynical. Nazism was the final fruit of that strain of thought. Most secular thought is morally sentimental. It believes in generally valid principles of justice; but it underestimates the recalcitrance of the human heart. It does not know that though men may "delight in the law of God after the inward man," there is yet a "law in their members which wars against the law that is in their mind."

In our Christian apologetic against secularism it is, therefore, not enough to teach men that there is a God; but rather that the true God with whom all men are ultimately engaged, is our enemy before he is our redeemer. We cannot know His mercy if we do not acknowledge His judgments upon the inclination of all men and nations to set themselves up as God. But this God, who is revealed to the Christian through Christ, is not simply an ally of the Christians against the secularists. His judgments fall as severely upon Christians as upon secularists, precisely because the Christian faith in God is no guarantee against the corruption of using God as an instrument of our interests and of claiming the "law of God" or the "natural law" as a rationalization of our claims against the claims of others. That is why Jeremiah insists that the judgments of God fall upon both the "circumcised and the uncircumcised" and why John the Baptist warns against the complacency of those who think they are virtuous because they are "the children of Abraham" and suggests that "God is able of these stones to raise up children unto Abraham." Translated this means, that the "elect" must have some contrite recognition of the fact that the truth of God is frequently stated by those who do not know God against those who claim they do.

No Christian polemic against secularism can be truly Christian if it does not recognize that liberal secularism was partly informed by a sense of justice which found the religiously sanctified social forms of the feudal order intolerable and that Marxist secularism is partly informed by a sense of justice which found the religious and secular justifications of middle-class justice intolerable. If these facts seem to belong to another age one need only mention Spain and possibly Italy and some Latin American countries to prove their relevance to contemporary scenes. One might also mention the simple identification of bourgeois interests and Christianity in the Calvinist political parties of Holland.

A Christian apologetic must not simply be a defense of God against the godless but a disclosure of the Majesty of God against the pretensions of the godly and the godless and a promise of mercy to those who truly repent, whether godly or godless. The godless must know God before they can repent. Sometimes the "godly" have greater difficulty in repenting. For they have to unlearn their prayer: "I thank Thee God that I am not as other men."

CATHOLICS AND DIVORCE

A debate, which has developed in New York state with reference to its divorce laws, illustrates one of the difficulties in the relations between Protestants and Catholics. The state of New York has not changed its divorce laws since the eighteenth century. According to these laws adultery is the only ground for divorce. Meanwhile a culture has developed in a modern urban secular community in which divorce for many other causes is publicly approved or condoned. The inevitable consequence is that the law is circumvented. The form of circumvention, discovered by the district attorney of New York, is "faked" testimony proving adultery, even though neither party has been guilty of it.

This situation prompted a demand for a liberalization of the divorce laws. Catholic authorities, however, declared that this development proved the necessity of making divorce laws more stringent and eliminating even adultery as ground for divorce. One Catholic dignitary, preaching in the Cathedral, declared that divorce was the evil fruit of "apostates from the Catholic faith who call themselves reformers." The belief of Catholics that a rigorous insistence on the indissolubility of marriage can be preserved merely by legal sanction in a community which lacks every presupposition for such a standard, reveals a shocking reliance upon law as the basis of morals. Protestants were guilty of this same error during the Prohibition movement. Both Catholics and Protestants ought to know that no moral standard can be enforced by the police power of the state if the overwhelming portion of the population does not abide by it voluntarily. Police power can deal only with the recalcitrance of a minority.

We may well question Catholic legalism even when it is exercised within the church itself. We may ask whether the sacramental character of the marriage relation can be preserved by law when the disloyalty of one or both partners has in fact violated the sacrament. From the Protestant standpoint, Catholicism places too great a reliance upon law, even within the Christian community. There are certain ideal standards of personal conduct and of human relations which may be preserved by grace but not by law. If grace is lacking no legal sanction can make such standards either possible or sufferable. But so long as Catholic legalism is limited to its own religious community we do not have the same concern about it as when it seeks to enforce impossible standards upon a whole civil community.

This problem represents one of the many instances where Protestant Christianity must develop its own middle ground, distinguished from both the Catholic and the secular position. Such a ground requires that we seek to preserve the sacramental conception of marriage in opposition to the secular community's concept of marriage as a mere social contract, in which only the two contracting parties are engaged. But it also involves opposition to the Catholic effort to preserve by legal sanction what can only be maintained by every resource of grace. The decay of American family life is a shocking aspect of a general moral decay. A thoughtful judge recently expressed the opinion that half of all cases of child delinquency are caused by broken homes. Stringent laws may be necessary to protect the rights of children in the home as much as possible. But law does not have the power to prompt incompatability to be transmuted into compatibility by forgiveness, or to induce the kind of patience and mutual forbearance which makes intimate relations sufferable. There is a certain Catholic nation permitting no divorces on any ground, in which, according to report, half of all homicides are committed by irate husbands and wives upon their spouses. There is a lesson worth pondering in those statistics.

CATHOLICS AND MOTIVES OF ACTION

"Everyone knows," declared the Pope in his allocution, "that the Catholic Church never acts from worldly motives."—"The diplomacy of the Soviet state," declared Foreign Minister Molotov, "bases itself firmly on the scientific analysis of objective reality. . . . Soviet diplomacy always adheres strictly to principles. It is alien to combinations promoted by the situation at a given moment, to unscrupulous transactions, intrigues, intimidations or to disguising real tendencies by false formulae."

We know how distasteful it will be to many readers to place these two pretentious claims in the same paragraph and thereby suggest that they have any similarity. The Catholic church claims never to act from worldly motives, because any policy by which it defends, protects, and extends the influence of the church in the rough struggles of history is for the sake of an institution which is more than an historical institution. It can, therefore, not grant that the difference in its attitude toward a Fascist régime, which is merely perverting justice, and a Communist régime, which seeks to destroy the church, is determined by the anxious survival impulse of an historic institution. Whatever treasures of grace are born in the earthen vessels of this historic institution cannot, however, completely hide from the critical, or even from the sympathetic, observer that very human and sinful human motives express themselves in this struggle for survival. One might mention the rather hysterical sermon of Cardinal Spellman on the Mindszenty trial, to which Professor Bennett refers in the leading editorial, as a case in point.

It will be remembered that the eighteenth century thought with Condorcet that all fanaticism could be abolished from human civilization if we could only get rid of "priests and their hypocritical tools." The rationalists of the eighteenth century rightly discerned that the root of fanaticism lies in the unwillingness of finite men to admit the conditioned character of their perspectives and the interested character of their judgments. It correctly saw a fruitful source of the illusion of the absolute in religion, but it erroneously regarded traditional religion as the only source of it.

It did not foresee to what degree "the scientific analysis of objective reality" would take the place of priestly absolutism as the source of fanaticism. It did not foresee that a Stalinism would arise, which would justify the most intolerable injustices, the most ruthless diplomacy, and the most cynical subversion of juridical procedures on the ground that all Communist tactics spring from devotion to the laws of "objective reality" discovered by a Marxist-Leninist science. Evidently it is possible to pretend to stand above the ambiguities of human existence without the benefit of clergy. The resulting pretensions are even more monstrous. In so far as they are more monstrous we must more rigorously resist them. While doing so, we will shed a tear, however, over the plight of a civilization caught in a controversy between a Caesar who knows nothing about Christ and a vicar of Christ who is a little too sure of the complete identity between his own and Christ's purposes.

THE RISING CATHOLIC-PROTESTANT TENSION

Both Catholics and Protestants must admit the deep pathos of the fears and prejudices which exist between the two communities of Christendom, making a mockery of the common elements in their faith, more particularly of their common profession that "love vaunteth not itself, is not puffed up, doth not behave itself unseemly, seeketh not her own, is not easily provoked, thinketh no evil." The fact is that we do think evil of each other and are easily provoked.

The political struggle over the Federal Education Bill has become so acrimonious that it threatens the social peace of our nation. We have had some fairly serious waves of anti-Catholic hysteria in this country, the repetition of which we must seek to avoid at all costs. But that requires moderation and forbearance on both sides. If a Roman Catholic cardinal regards an honest difference of conviction between himself and Mrs. Roosevelt on provisions of the education bill as proof of "anti-Catholic prejudice" on Mrs. Roosevelt's part, it would appear that there is no possibility of proving oneself free of "prejudice" except by agreeing with him. Such a simple solution of the problem of "prejudice" aggravates every issue in a religiously plural- istic nation such as our own. Not only on matters of reli- gious controversy but on almost every other issue of life, the preservation of community in a free society requires that we have some degree of respect for the motives of people who differ with us seriously, who "love what we hate" and desire that which we abhor. We must take for granted that on all social issues we are not discarnate minds, arriving at our positions without presuppositions, that is, without prejudices. But if we have any measure of

charity we will remember that we are in the same position
as our competitor or foe. In the words of a Puritan divine
of the seventeenth century, "my reasons are as dark to
thee as thine are dark to me until the Lord enlighten all
our seeing."

On the particular issue of tax support for parochial
schools the Protestant or the secularist is usually unable to
comprehend the sense of injustice which the Catholic tax-
payer feels, when contributing to the support of public
schools to which he does not send his children and then
paying an additional amount for the support of his own
schools. This seems like rank injustice to him. His sense of
injustice is not assuaged by the argument that our national
solution of the problem of religion and education is the
only possible democratic one. He knows that there are
democratic nations in which public funds are used for the
support of religious schools or for religious education in
public schools. The Protestant, as distinguished from the
secularist, might also bring some measure of sympathy and
understanding to the Catholic for his efforts to give a
religious content to education and for his recognition of
the fact that the public school, which is at best religiously
and culturally neutral, is at its worst, a religious school in
which a secular-religious scheme of redemption is taught.

But there are certain aspects of this problem which our
Catholic fellow-citizens have not considered sufficiently.
The complete secularization of the public school and the
prohibition of state support for parochial schools may not
be the only possible democratic solution of the problem of
the religious pluralism of America; but, it has become an
established solution. Established solutions, which work
tolerably well, are not easily challenged by abstract concepts. Some of us agree with Catholic critics that there is
not much evidence that the constitutional phrase "Congress
shall pass no laws respecting the establishment of religion
or the suppression thereof" does not mean, in terms of either
logic or historic intent, the same as the "absolute wall of
separation." But surely our Catholic friends must know that
history makes and interprets laws even in nations in which
there is a written constitution, and that in this case the

Supreme Court has been the voice of history or more exactly the voice of the American people. The jealousy for the inviolability of the public school in its present form may be wrong in some absolute court of judgment; but there are no such courts in history. Catholics may believe that it is an expression of the secularism of our age, but they hardly do justice to the instinct for community and social peace which is expressed in it. Should we allow the public support of private schools in this country, ethnically and culturally less homogeneous than any country of the world, we would ultimately duplicate in our schools what we already have in our churches—namely, the institutionalization of ethnic and cultural divisions in the community. Can a nation such as ours afford this? Such problems are not settled by abstract concepts of "natural law" but by a wise and statesmanlike weighing of a dozen imponderables, all of which differ from nation to nation and from age to age.

It is necessary furthermore to assure our Catholic friends that the doctrine which has gained prevalence in Catholic circles in recent decades on the question of toleration (and which is, indeed, the traditional position of the church) has hardened the hearts of non-Catholics in this country. More precisely it has filled them with fear. We refer to the position expounded by various Catholic teachers that ultimately the church must hold the state responsible for the support of "true" religion, meaning the Catholic religion, even though it is ready to accommodate itself to something less than this provisionally. Even Catholic reassurances that only a nation, overwhelmingly Catholic, would fulfill the necessary conditions for such a venture has not quieted non-Catholic fears. We know that the orthodoxy of this position is being challenged by able Catholic theologians today. They maintain that it is not, according to Catholic doctrine, the business of the state to be concerned with the salvation of souls but only with the common welfare; and that it is therefore not its business to give special support to "true" religion. We do not know to what degree this second doctrine has found acceptance in Catholic circles. We hope it will find wide acceptance. We do know that Ryan and Boland's exposition of Catholic doctrines, according to which Catholic toleration of minorities would seem to be only provisional and tentative, has had much to do with the "camel's nose" theory held by non-Catholics. This theory is that we must not yield to Catholic demands at any point since any demand is merely the nose which is threatening us with the whole camel of authoritarian religion in our tent.

One further point must be considered in weighing the charge of "bigotry" made against those who disagree with the Catholic position on any question. Have our Catholic friends ever thought how much patience is required when our own convictions are constantly challenged as obvious violations of the natural law, and as, therefore, in conflict with the expressed will of God?

We do not agree with Catholics in their effort to validate the sacramental character of marriage by seeking to compel the state to render marriage indissoluble by legal enactment. Nor do we agree that there is a "natural law" which proves contraception to be a sin against God and nature. In many a community we are challenged by Catholic prelates with threats of nonco-operation if institutions in which birth-control information is available, are included in a community chest. We are, furthermore, given public reprimands for being involved in the "moral nihilism" or the moral "relativism" of our age, if we fail to accept the Catholic theory of an inflexible natural law, which regulates even historically contingent moral norms.

If Protestants have any degree of charity, they will know that these positions are matters of faith for Catholics and that they cannot yield them. But it takes a considerable degree of charity to remember that and not to interpret these attitudes as merely the fruit of a graceless attitude toward those who differ from us. A pluralistic world like our own, indeed any democratic world, requires a certain degree of relativity on some points of moral practice if not on points of moral doctrine. "Remember, by the bowels of Christ, that you may be mistaken," declared Cromwell to the sectarian absolutists of his day who threatened the unity of his army by their religiously inspired convictions.

It requires a great deal of forbearance, to be consistently confronted by men and institutions who are never mistaken but always have the law of God on their side.

We have presented as honestly and with as little malice as possible some of the reasons which make non-Catholics apprehensive about Catholic theories and practices. Resentments thus bred, may easily be fanned into flames by such ill-considered charges of bigotry as Cardinal Spellman makes with greater and greater frequency.

Having said all this, we would like to suggest that the school aid question might be settled if non-Catholics would allow federal scholarship or other educational aid, to go to scholars in any school, provided it is to the scholar and not the school. We have already accepted this policy in the G.I. Bill of Rights and there is no reason why it could not be extended. On the other hand Catholics ought not to regard such a policy as merely one step toward the direct tax support of parochial schools. They mistake the temper of this country if they imagine that such a policy could be given legal sanction without decades of the most acrimonious controversy. Furthermore, the fear of this ultimate demand now endangers every viable compromise.

It might be added in conclusion that there is not now in this country a meeting ground where representative leaders of various faiths can sit down together and exchange convictions upon these weighty matters with some degree of mutual trust. We will not apportion the blame for this situation. But it is a scandal. We meet each other only vituperatively in the public prints. As long as this is so, the secularists may plausibly contend that a society can be saved from the fury of the theologians only by its secularization.

THE POPE'S DOMESTICATED GOD

Every Protestant who seeks to mitigate the hatreds and fears of Rome, which so easily disfigure the heart and countenance of Protestantism, is periodically either implored by his Catholic friends to join the true church or assured that he is not far from being worthy of being included in its membership. The wide advances of Catholicism since the war have made Catholics even more confident than hitherto that Protestantism is a heresy or defection which must ultimately disappear, since its dismal anarchy compares unfavorably with the impressive inclusiveness and unity of the Roman church. Even so wise a Catholic theologian as Father J. Courtney Murray, in a recent debate with W. Russell Bowie, expressed the opinion that Protestants had a sense of inferiority, not because they were afraid of becoming second-class citizens in America but because they had a secret fear that they might be second-class Christians.

Intolerable Pretension

All these hopes and illusions come to mind as one reads the Pope's Christmas message. Nothing that has recently emanated from Rome has revealed so clearly the great gulf which lies between Rome and those of us who are not bound to the Holy See. We often define the difference between us in terms of our varying attitude toward freedom. We persuade ourselves that we Protestants would rather run the risks of anarchy for the sake of spiritual freedom than gain the boon of unity and order at the price of spiritual tyranny. But that was only one issue in the Reformation. A more important issue was derived from the Reformation conviction that Catholicism was involved in idolatry because it allowed the church to usurp the majesty of God. It pretended that the church could mediate the divine mercy and judgment without itself standing under that judgment or requiring that mercy. It was, in short, involved in an intolerable pretension.

This pretension is expressed or implied in almost every paragraph of the Pope's Christmas message. Pius XII begins by expressing the feeling that millions of faithful are imploring him as they once implored the Redeemer, "Give us a sign from heaven." "Well then," answers the Pope, " 'today you will know that the Lord will come and at dawn you shall see his glory.' The sign you are waiting for shall be announced to you today . . . when by our hands the mystic door is to be removed once again, thus opening the entrance to the greatest temple of Christendom." In short, the Pope will furnish the "sign from heaven" by initiating the holy year.

The Pontiff expresses the hope that "divine providence may deign to work in (this year) and through it the marvels of his mercy." But this is more than a hope. It is guaranteed by his own assurance. "We ourselves," the Pope continues, "to whom divine providence has reserved the privilege of proclaiming it and granting it to the whole world, already foresee its importance for the coming halfcentury."

After reading these words one turns to Matthew 24 where Christ warns against those who try to point too definitely to the signs of redemption: "Then if any man shall say unto you, Lo, here is Christ, or there; believe it not. For there shall arise false Christs, and false prophets, and shall show great signs and wonders; insomuch that, if it were possible, they shall deceive the very elect." Thus one almost instinctively repeats the polemic of the Reformation against Rome. At the risk of the charge of "intolerance" one must confess that the words of the Pope strike a non-Roman as blasphemous.

Pope Pius proceeds to analyze the political, spiritual, and moral miseries of our day and ascribes them to the "rebellion" of the modern world. "Just as the modern world has tried to shake off the sweet yoke of God," he says, "so it has rejected with it the order he established, and with the selfsame pride that moved the rebel angel at the beginning of creation, has pretended to set up another of its own choice." This is the familiar doctrine of Catholicism that Reformation, Renaissance, nationalism, and industrial revolution are all caused by man's rebellion against the order of God, as established in the heyday of medieval culture. It does not take into account to what degree the new vitalities which were expressed in these various movements could not be fitted into "God's order" as the church conceived it, precisely because the order was too narrowly conceived. Nor is there any understanding here for the fact that the irreligion of some of these movements was derived from resentment against a too simple identification of the will of God with the contingent circumstances of a feudal civilization. There was undoubtedly some of the pride of the "rebel angel" in these movements. But the same pride was in the culture and the church against which they rebelled.

Papal Pride

Some of the same pride is in fact betrayed in the words in which the Pope generously welcomes back the erring "children." Among these he includes not only the secularists, whom he rightly accuses of espousing either too individualistic or too collectivistic forms of social life, but also, the adherents of "schism," namely ourselves. "Why," he asks, "are there still separations? Why are there still schisms? When will all the forces of the spirit and of love be united?" One answer is that this will certainly not be possible if the voice which invites us to union speaks with no more humility than the Pope's voice. In several paragraphs one must read twice before being certain whether the Pope is speaking of God or of himself. His invitation reads: "We extend a welcome from the heart of a father whose fatherhood in the inscrutable design of God has come to us from Jesus the Redeemer." Here the Pope is obviously speaking of his own paternal heart.

In another passage the meaning is not quite so clear but in the end it becomes apparent that he is still speaking of himself. "We expect then," he writes,

> a great homecoming during this year of extraordinary grace; great because of the number of children for whom we reserve a most affectionate welcome; great because of the distance some of them will come . . . May all our sons and all men of good will lovingly undertake not to disappoint the hopes of the common Father [yes, capital F] who holds up his hand to heaven in prayer that the new outpouring of divine mercy upon the world may surpass all expectations.

The Pope fondly regards himself as the successor of St. Peter. It will be remembered that St. Peter, after a healing miracle, asked, "Why look ye so earnestly on us, as though by our own power or holiness we had made this man walk?" One looks in vain for any such modesty in this papal pronouncement.

Authentic Christian Teaching

Not only is the grace of God thus bound to the Holy See but the mysteries of divine mercy are related to the holy year. Not absolutely, of course. "Let the holy year then be chiefly a year of repentance and expiation. Interior and voluntary repentance together with expiation are the indispensable prerequisites of every human renovation," the Pope writes. There are some moving Christian exhortations in the statement, not only on the necessities of repentance but upon the need of forgiveness of our foes. On that particular issue the Pope has spoken consistently in words of gospel truth and power. "Whoever would be a sincere Christian," he declares, "must know how to forgive. 'Thou wicked servant,' is the rebuke of the Gospel parable, 'was it not thy duty to have mercy upon thy fellow servant, as I had on thee?' "

One mentions these words of Christian truth gratefully because they prove that there is Christian content in the

Roman Catholic church, as there are no doubt many manifestations of grace in its life. Some time ago at an ecumenical discussion with Catholic theologians in France they advanced the theory that we might be able to approach each other with greater charity if we recognized "remnants of the true church" in each other rather than "branches of the one church." They felt that they would be able to see some "remnant" of the true church in any church in which Biblical truth led to a life of grace. We ought to be able to say as much when we look upon the Roman church. Catholics will, of course, find it offensive if we are able to find only remnants of the true church in this papal statement. But we will not be driven by our resentments to withhold this recognition. By the same token, we cannot be forced by premature hopes of unity to desist from registering a profound disquiet over the temper of the statement as a whole.

Exaltation of Rome

There is an ironic quality in the conclusion of the papal statement. It would almost seem as if the Pope felt that he had not sufficiently bound the grace of God to a particular institution and thought he had to underscore the place which the city of Rome, as seat of the Holy See, has in the divine plan. "Every Christian," he writes, "can and should say, 'Rome is my fatherland.' Here God's supernatural providence over souls is more particularly in evidence; here the saints acquired the norm and inspiration of their heroism . . . Here is the immovable rock to which your hopes are anchored." A more persuasive voice constantly intervenes to challenge these cadences: "If any man shall say, Lo, here is Christ, or there, believe it not."

We are living in tragic times and have no certainty that a suicidal conflict can be avoided. We are not even certain that the health of Western civilization can be preserved. We cannot even be sure that the Catholic party in Italy will grant land reform quickly and thoroughly enough to prevent a further spread of Communism in that country.

Our anxieties are aggravated by the fear that nations, peoples, and institutions may not be adequate for this time of testing, that they have not been sufficiently shaken in their pride and self-esteem to do what is necessary for their salvation. We would be more secure if the Roman Catholic church were anxious with us under the divine judgment and not so anxious about us. We would be willing to dispense with the assurance of its fatherly forgiveness toward us if we were certain that it sought divine forgiveness with us for the evils in which we have been jointly involved.

The Elder Brother of the Parable

"The venerable father of the Gospel story," declares the Pope, "is waiting anxiously on the threshold of the holy door for the contrite return of the prodigal son." But when the Roman church is not usurping the place of the Divine Father it seems to assume the place of the elder brother who does not need repentance. If the mercy of the Father were not so great, the elder brother could drive every prodigal back into the wilderness.

The Roman church has a favorite explanation of all the ills of modern life. They are due to mankind's departure from "God's plan" as incorporated in the church. We have an equally plausible explanation, not for all the ills of the modern world but for a serious aggravation of all our difficulties. The animosities of modern men are exacerbated on the one hand by the priest-kings of a secular religion who make ridiculous pretensions of omniscience and omnipotence from the Kremlin; and on the other hand by priests of a true religion who give the final glory to God but meanwhile are too certain that they are privy to his counsels and the sole dispensers of his grace.

"Those who are whole have no need of a physician, but those that are sick," declares Christ in a deeply ironic word. Could it be that this word is meant for the church as well as the world? Might it not mediate the healing power of the true physician more surely if the church acknowledged its complicity in the world's ills?

THE INCREASING ISOLATION
OF THE CATHOLIC CHURCH

Recent developments in the Catholic church must be disturbing to all non-Roman Christians, even if we have not, as some Anglo-Catholics, cherished the hope of a possible ultimate reunion with Rome. For these developments increase the isolation of the Roman church from the rest of Christendom. They widen the moat of pretension and heighten the wall of contradictory dogma which separates Rome from other Christians.

The first shock came with the Vatican announcement that the Pope would, on November 1st, declare the assumption of the Virgin Mary to be a dogma of the church, which all members of the church are bound to believe. Thus the Pope invokes for the first time the doctrine of papal infallibility which was established in 1870; and at the same time he incorporates a legend of the Middle Ages into the official teachings of the church, thereby placing the final capstone on the Mariolatry of the Roman church.

In some respects the papal encyclical of August 21st is even more disturbing. This is a very carefully worded document which will have as fateful an influence upon the thought of the church as the encyclical on modernism in the last century. In fact, it brings theological tendencies, first expressed in that encyclical, to their logical conclusion. But it is not modernism which is proscribed in the encyclical. The theological tendencies against which the Pope warns are thoroughly orthodox from the Biblical standpoint. They are questionable only from a strict Thomistic standpoint. The Pope's warnings are obviously intended against theological movements in England, France, and Germany which have won the respect of Christian thought beyond the confines of the Roman church.

The strict Thomism of the encyclical is directed against both Protestant thought and against tendencies in modern philosophy. The Pope warns against the "eirenism" in some sections of the church which seeks to "reconcile differences in dogma" between Roman and non-Roman churches. More specifically this means that Augustinian, as distinguished from Thomistic forms of thought, frequently lead to conceptions of the relation of faith to reason, in which Protestants and Catholics are able to agree. In refutation of this position the encyclical frequently reasserts the Thomistic position which makes faith not so much the presupposition of reason as the correction of reason which has "been hampered both by the activity of the senses and the imagination and by evil passions arising from original sin." "Absolutely speaking," the encyclical asserts, "reason can, by its own natural force and light, arrive at the true and certain knowledge of the one personal God."

The Thomistic position is also asserted against tendencies in modern Catholic thought to regard various philosophies as compatible with the Christian faith, a thesis eloquently defended recently in the current issue of an English Catholic journal. The Pope criticizes those who think "that our perennial philosophy is only a philosophy of immutable essences while the contemporary mind must look to the existence of things and life which is ever in flux." This section of the encyclical seems almost specifically directed at the thought of Christian existentialists such as Gabriel Marcel.

For reasons which are not quite clear in the encyclical, the Pope also warns against the preoccupation of some Catholic theologians with early Christian thought. "What is expounded in the encyclical letters of the Roman Pontiffs is habitually neglected by some with the idea of giving force to some notions (*sic*) which they profess to have found in the ancient fathers, especially the Greeks." This portion of the encyclical would seem to have serious consequences on some very significant patristic studies, particularly in France.

In addition fruitful Biblical studies are restricted because some of the Catholic Biblical scholars have evidently traced (as all good Biblical scholars do) the relation of Biblical to non-Biblical historical material. The Pope asserts that the Genesis chapters on creation, etc., must be accepted as simple history and nothing must be taught which might imply that our "ancient sacred writers" are not superior to "the ancient profane writers."

In every section of the encyclical the kind of freedom which true scholarship requires, is restricted in the interest of a strict Thomism. One has no right to speculate from the outside just what sort of forces inside the church move toward the production of such a document. But one rather suspects that the practical hierarchs who want everything in neat and exact form, have expressed themselves in this encyclical against some of the most creative theologians in the Roman church.

Perhaps the most serious aspect of the encyclical is not so much in the particular restrictions which it places upon thought, as its insistence that all encyclical utterances are generally binding.

"If the Supreme Pontiffs," declares the Pope,

in their official documents purposely pass judgment upon a matter up to that time in dispute, it is obvious that the matter, according to the mind and the will of the same Pontiffs, can no longer be considered a question open to discussion among theologians.

The papal absolutism takes one further step and the ossification of dogma is furthered to one more degree. Non-Roman Christians cannot but view these developments with profound regret, particularly in an age in which so many lights of freedom are snuffed out.

CATHOLICS AND POLITICS:
SOME MISCONCEPTIONS

Most American non-Catholics have a very inaccurate concept of Roman Catholic political thought and life. In this concept, it is assumed that if Catholics anywhere had their way, they would at once build a political structure as much like Spain's as possible.

This kind of reasoning is highly damaging to the mutual understanding upon which a democratic society must rest. Democracy requires more careful and discriminate judgments about friend and foe, particularly since a political foe upon one issue in the vast welter of issues may be a friend on another. Some forms of deduction proceed from the assumption that on every and any question a religious group's political attitude is dictated by its basic creed. Others do not even bother to start with the group's actual basic tenets but with tenets the group is imagined to hold.

Thus it is argued: Catholicism is an authoritarian religion. All forms of authoritarianism are (a) hostile to democracy and (b) are brothers under the skin to totalitarianism. It follows that Catholicism is antidemocratic and totalitarian. A simple syllogism then leads with seeming logic to an extravagant question: Is Catholicism any better than Communism? Even that is frequently answered without allowing common-sense evidence to muddy the clear stream of our deductive process.

Religion and Democracy

There is a story about Garibaldi during his campaign for the political unification of Italy. He was told that he must expect the opposition of every village priest. He declared that he would not assume this to be true until it had been proven. He had the reward that comes to every good empiricist: It proved untrue.

I write upon this subject as a Protestant theologian who has his own misgivings about Catholic politics. They can be stated in three propositions:

In the first place, I don't like religious political parties as they exist on the Continent of Europe. I believe that one great achievement of Anglo-Saxon democracy is that it has no religious parties. Religious parties are dangerous because they tend to identify the moral ambiguities of politics (and every political position contains some moral ambiguity) with eternal sanctities. The result is that almost any kind of struggle can be interpreted as a contest between Christ and anti-Christ.

Second, I think that the Catholic church tends to identify the historic church with the Kingdom of God, and too often its final criterion is what a political movement promises or does not promise to the historic church. It is therefore forced at times to give preference to movements which deserve plainly to be condemned on grounds of justice. The relation of the Catholic hierarchy to Peron in Argentina is a case in point.

Finally, the reasoning of Catholic political moralists is too dependent upon deductive and intuitive "rational propositions" for my taste. I do not believe that the only escape from moral nihilism is to be found in the inflexible propositions of "natural law"; particularly not when these propositions become very detailed and commend some principle (such as prohibition of birth control or the absolute prohibition of divorce) as a moral standard fixed by God's eternal law. No one could convince me that birth control would not be advantageous, in Italy, India, and some other overpopulated nations.

Catholicism in Industrial Society

After this confession of prejudices, I can proceed to challenge too simple judgments about Catholic politics.

The worst defect is that Catholicism is often judged solely as it shows itself in old (and decaying) feudal structures, whether in Spain or South America or even in French Canada. People who argue this way usually ignore the relationship of Catholicism to the political life of modern industrial society. Catholicism is at its least impressive in feudal-agrarian societies, where it frequently seeks desperately to hold onto special powers and privileges which were essential in the Middle Ages but are so no longer. Catholicism is most creative in highly developed industrial communities.

It seems completely unknown to American critics of Catholicism that the "middle ground" of European democracy is now being held, and has long been held, primarily by a combination of Catholic and socialist parties. For obvious reasons, the alliance has never been easy. Yet for two reasons cooperation has been possible. Catholicism has always believed that "the state has the moral authority to control economic life." In a sense, therefore, Catholicism, which may have been too tender with the weaknesses of feudalism, has never capitulated to pure capitalism. It has never believed that justice would be an inevitable by-product of the free play of economic forces.

In the second place, Catholicism's relation to European labor has differed from that of Protestantism. Protestantism lost the laboring masses almost completely. Catholicism lost them too—tragically, as Pius XI admitted. But Catholicism has recently regained an organic relationship with labor; its labor organizations have become genuine trade unions and have influenced the policies of the Catholic parties. In effect, unions have formed the bridge which has made the Catholic-socialist alliances possible.

The Protestant Default

In the Germany of the Weimar Republic, the Prussian state government was controlled for over a decade by a Catholic-socialist alliance. In contrast to the Republic itself, the Prussian régime preserved a remarkable stability. What little stability the Weimar Republic had also depended upon this overt and sometimes covert alliance.

It must be observed that the old German Center party did not include the Bavarian Catholics. They had their own Bavarian People's party for the simple reason that their kind of agrarian conservatism did not fit into the policies Catholics had developed in the highly industrialized German Rhineland. Unfortunately, these two parties have since the war become one. The result is that the Adenauer government is considerably more conservative than the old Center. A few years ago some left-wing Catholics in the British Zone tried to reorganize the Center, but it was no more than a splinter group.

The differences betwen Catholicism in Bavaria and in the Rhineland are roughly typical of the differences between the expression of the Catholic ethos in agrarian and in industrial situations. In industrial Europe, Catholicism has had a more creative approach to politics than Protestantism because the latter (particularly in Lutheran countries) tends to be too individualistic and too eschatological (that is to say, preoccupied with ultimate religious issues) to be capable of discriminate judgments in the endless complexities of politics.

Situation in France

Since the Second World War, Catholic influence upon politics in western Europe has grown perceptibly, and only the bigoted or unrealistic could ascribe this to Vatican machinations. In France, the Popular Republicans, the M.R.P., emerged as the first strong Catholic political party in the history of the French Republic. It was heir to, and formed by, a long and distinguished line of Catholic "social" thinkers. In the first elections it won 30 per cent of the vote, but this strength proved to be ephemeral. What happened was that everyone who would have liked to back the old parties of the right, which had been discredited by Vichyism, went along with the new party. It has steadily lost both to the older "liberal" parties and to the Gaullists, until now it commands only twelve per cent of the electorate. But it still is a very important political force. Its greatest individual contribution to French politics is perhaps the perpetual French Foreign Minister, Robert Schuman. Its left wing is eager to remove the purely religious cleavage in European politics and to work for a just social order under modern industrial conditions. It is indicative of the temper of French Catholicism that two years ago, when the Pope said it was impossible to be both Catholic and Communist, the French bishops interpreted the papal word so that it would be clear that the church did not imply a Catholic preference for capitalism. The bishops called attention to previous papal encyclicals to show that the church did not accept the doctrine of an unregulated economic life. (Perhaps some Americans will remember that Franklin Roosevelt, in his first campaign, justified his New Deal by appealing to Catholic political theories based on Pope Leo XIII's teachings and expounded in this country by the late Father John Ryan. Roosevelt pointed out that the "Social Creed" of the Federal Council of Churches was in substantial agreement with these teachings.)

At Home

It is hardly necessary to expound the realities of the American scene. Fortunately we do not have religious parties. But it would be well for Protestants who talk about the "reactionary" tendencies of Catholicism to remember that, in religious terms, the main political struggles in America would appear to be between Jews and Catholics who are left of the Center and Protestants who are right of it.

The alliance between Republicanism and Protestantism is, as in Europe, prompted by the affinity between religious individualism and the political individualism of the farmer on the one hand and the businessman on the other. Catholics do not have their own trade unions in America, but no one can question that they have a sounder relation to the unions than Protestants, as such, do. This is partly due to the fact that our farmers and business people have been largely Protestant, while industrial workers, at least in the North, are predominantly Catholic and, in certain sections and trades, Jewish. The imbalance is no doubt related to the historic pattern of migration to our shores. A good deal of Catholic politics in America is strictly "lay Catholicism." The fact is that the best Catholic politics in Europe is also "lay," or so it seems at least to an observer who has anti-clerical prejudices.

This does not mean that sharp distinction can be drawn between clerical conservatism and lay progressivism. Some of the more radical tendencies in European Catholic politics emanate from neither lay nor clerical sources but from various Catholic orders. There are individual bishops in every Catholic country—even in Spain—who cannot be branded conservative. Take as an example the recent un-explained tension in Quebec between an archbishop, who had ordered collections in the churches for some strikers, and the very conservative Quebec government under Pre-mier Duplessis. The archbishop resigned—no one knows just why. It would seem unlikely that a politician could defeat an archbishop in the counsels of the Vatican. But, in the absence of any authoritative explanation, many Canadian observers draw the conclusion that, in this case, this did happen.

Freedom in Catholicism

In international politics, there is the same need for cir-cumspection. A favorite theory of anti-Catholics is that the Pope is scheming for another world war because of Cath-olic losses in lands behind the Iron Curtain, particularly in Poland and Hungary. Catholic prelates have indeed made statements which seem to support a "preventive" war. When a pious Catholic secretary of the navy voiced such sentiments over a year ago (sentiments which were subse-quently repudiated by the administration), the case seemed to be complete for the theory that American Catholic leaders want a preventive war.

Yet there is strong evidence that the Vatican is strongly opposed to the idea. There is certainly no question that the Catholic statesmen and clerical leaders of Western Europe are opposed to it. They are also very critical of what one of them has called the "sterile anti-Communism" of some American Catholics. The Pope's Christmas message with its "plague o' both your houses" note should help refute the usual concept of Vatican foreign policy.

Incidentally, there is no evidence of simple unanimity among clerical leaders of America on problems of international politics. We tend to assume that the position of the most vocal cardinals is generally accepted. This assumption may be false, but those of us who accept it are not altogether to blame. For Catholic leaders do not criticize each other in public. Nor do they publicly disassociate themselves, although they may privately, from Catholic positions in other nations—Spain, for instance. Thus they are partly responsible for the myth of a monolithic Catholic party, speaking with the same voice throughout the world.

Still it is dangerous for all of us to give the myth credence. Catholicism naturally has a greater unity of discipline than other religious communities. But it has the freedom to relate itself to various national situations. It also has many moral and spiritual resources which can act creatively in a free and responsible society.

PROTESTANTS, CATHOLICS, AND SECULARISTS ON THE SCHOOL ISSUE

Elsewhere in this issue we are publishing an article by Will Herberg on the Protestant-Catholic tension in education, which originally appeared in the monthly *Commentary*. Mr. Herberg, an influential leader among the religiously minded Jews, who has a great influence among

Christian and Jewish college youth, is concerned that the Protestant opposition to Catholicism on the school question plays into the hands of the secularists, who want to eliminate religion from education altogether. We agree with Mr. Herberg, but it is important to call attention to the fact that the Protestant church can not easily choose sides in this controversy because both Catholics and secularists advance claims in the name of democracy which are incompatible with democratic pluralism. The Catholic position is democratic in two senses of that term. It resists the claim of the state to enforce uniform education in the name of the right of parents to give their children an education according to their convictions. It is also democratic in the sense that a Christian viewpoint emphasizes the true dimension of the individual, as having his ultimate authority and fulfillment above the political community and the social process in which he is involved. Without this emphasis man is easily debased into a mere instrument of a social or political process and is left powerless to defy the majesties of the world with a rigorous: "We must obey God rather than man."

But it is only fair to note that our schools are secular not only because of the pluralism of Protestants and the inroads of secularism, but also because the Catholic church objects to religious instruction in the schools under any but Catholic auspices; furthermore the impulse to do justice to Catholics, by permitting them to gain the fringe benefits of buses, luncheons, and textbooks, is lamed consistently by the refusal of Catholics to promise that the granting of those benefits will not be the entering wedge for larger demands, ending in the state support of Catholic schools. But such a disposition of the vexing school question would lead to the endless elaboration of parochial schools by every sect; and this would no doubt seriously impair the unity in a nation which is religiously as pluralistic as we are. The absolute claims of Catholicism are, in short, not easily fitted into a democratic framework.

On the other hand, the secularists make even more absolute claims in the name of democracy. Instead of valuing the various religious traditions they would annul them all in the name of the unity of the democratic community and their secular viewpoint, which is, in effect, another religion with a total and consistent outlook upon life; this violates what Christians and Jews feel to be the truth about man and his destiny. In the one case, the resource of democratic individualism is impaired by an ecclesiastical institution. In the other case, a so-called democratic community is made into an idolatrous center of meaning which violates the rights of the individual which it must be the business of democracy to guard. In this situation there is obviously no consistent line of policy out of the difficulty; the supposition that a mere emphasis upon the separation of church and state will solve all difficulties contributes to the total secularization of our national culture, as Mr. Herberg observes.

Catholics and Protestants ought to realize that the mutual fear and mistrust in which they live is an offense to Christian charity and a scandal in the sight of scoffers and unbelievers. They ought to take steps to make contact between the two communities, at least as intimate as those which exist in the German Rhineland, for instance. They must, furthermore, take practical steps to liquidate the specific controversy in regard to education, more particularly the federal education bill. The most obvious solution of this problem is for Protestants to give up their opposition to federal aid to Catholic children and for Catholics to disavow public aid for the maintenance of parochial schools. To accomplish this result both sides will have to be more flexible in defining the standards to which they appeal. The Catholics ought to realize that no abstract standards of justice can overcome the historic prestige of an established institution, such as the public school. The Protestants must learn that no principle, such as the separation of church and state, is not subject to amendment in the light of new developments. The particular developments which challenge this principle are two. On the one hand the realization that absolute separation leads to the secularization of our culture, and that on the other hand the modern state with its wide taxing powers can not so easily be separated from any vital aspect of community concern as the fathers assumed.

THE CATHOLIC HIERARCHY'S
ANALYSIS OF THE ILLS
OF OUR DAY

In a rather startling statement published November 20, the American cardinals, archbishops, and bishops, through their organization of the administrative board of the Catholic Welfare Conference, addressed themselves to a diagnosis of the ills of our day. They found the enemy to be "atheistic materialism or godless humanism." They did not merely point to the incorporated tyranny which is our political enemy. But they warned that if we are to "escape the fate of China, Yugoslavia and so many others, if we are to survive as a free nation, we must be strong and clear-eyed. It is the blind who fall into the pit." They were insistent that they were not merely talking about the obvious political enemy. "Some see the enemy only as a state or a group of states or as an economic system," they declared. "Spiritual vision gives better intelligence of the fact. The enemy is entrenched in the organs of a foreign state or in one of our own domestic institutions; it is atheistic materialism which threatens to destroy us. This is the enemy."

In order that there be no misunderstanding they repeat, "Materialism is the real enemy whether at home or abroad. In its varieties there is little difference in kind. The difference is largely one of degree. Both are deadly to America."

The hierarchy then proceeds to define this deadly "materialism." It turns out to be the whole gamut of what the rest of us Christians would define as sin. It can be given the connotation of "materialism" so plausibly because the good is identified with "spirit" and the evil with "matter." "The way of the flesh and of matter is the way of death," they declare and, "The way of God and the spirit is the way of life."

Many critics thought they discerned echoes of Platonic dualism in St. Paul's phrases of "carnally minded" and "spiritually minded." But we doubt whether even St. Paul's thought would lend itself to the interpretation which identifies all evil with "matter."

The bishops proceed to identify the various manifestations of evil in our day with this "materialism." They say, "It is not that God is expressly or generally denied. It is rather that so many ignore him and his law in their absorption in the material world which he created. There is not yet a deliberate turning away from God but there is excessive preoccupation with creatures."

This analysis reveals the Augustinian thought which distinguishes between the love of God and the love of the world, and the love of self. But it falls short of the Augustinian definition of sin as the proud self-love or *superbia*. In short, Plato has evidently completely triumphed over the Scriptures in the definition of good and evil. The triumph is so complete that it makes it possible to identify any one who believes in God with virtue, and everyone who does not with evil. Naturally the idea that all men are at variance with God, not excluding Christians, is erased. This makes it possible to divide the world simply between the good Christians and the vile "atheists" who are naturally "materialists."

It is perhaps significant that the Atonement as the content of the Incarnation is reduced to proportions which seem positively heretical from the Scriptural standpoint. It is declared that Christ "set men's feet on the highroad of faith, hope and love; the highroad of happiness through harmony with God, with fellowmen, and with himself. Jesus Christ restored the meaning and purpose of love in human life. He warmed and illumined our life where before it had been cold and dark. He rescued man from the wild wandering and dark despair of the atheistic materialism of that day. In this day of the new paganism we Christians can again triumph in the name of the same cross of Christ." This is really a novel doctrine of the Atonement of the Cross. It is certainly novel to picture the Lord as triumphing over the "atheistic materialism" of his day. We had always believed that he triumphed over the hardheartedness of the fanatically righteous people of his day. But above all he triumphed over the sins of the whole world, including the sins of the people who most certainly believed in God.

In the framework of this conception of good and evil, the sins of our day are excoriated. We are told that "There is no need to instance the growing evils in family life, the growing self-indulgence which leads from birth prevention to divorce, from broken homes to the broken lives of youthful delinquents." The materialism, which is the root of all our difficulties, is said to "reveal itself as secularism in politics, as avarice in business and the professions and as paganism in personal lives and relations of all to many men and women."

The bishops then warn, "unless we push back the domestic invasion of materialism, we shall not be able, as history clearly attests, to withstand the enemy from without."

The most obvious criticism of such sweeping statements is that the bishops have availed themselves of a well-known political technique of identifying every tendency that they do not like with a hated enemy. Jacob Burckhardt, the great historian, once spoke of "the terrible simplifiers." In our opinion this statement is in the category of a terrible simplification.

Ultimately we must object, as Christians, to the statement of the Catholic bishops because it distinguishes between the godly righteous and the godless sinners and obscures the fact that Christ convicts, before he saves, both the godly and the godless for being at variance with God. This, in short, is the old debate between the Reformation and Catholicism. We believe that the Reformation was more true both to Scripture and to the facts of life than this type of Catholic spirituality. It was also right in seeing the whole of the self under judgment rather than the body or even "matter."

But it is also relevant to observe that this kind of division confuses us in "knowing the enemy" in the pluralistic conditions of a quasi-Christian and quasi-secular society. Whether we consider the moral, the cultural, or the political facts, we cannot define the enemy so simply as the bishops propose to do.

Morally it is certainly dubious to identify the sin of "preoccupation with the creature" and the idolatrous devotion to the comforts of the "American way of life" with philosophical materialism. It is particularly ironic because of the fact that the godly have been rather more successful in achieving wealth through technical efficiency than the godless Communists. According to Max Weber, Protestantism is probably more responsible for the development of a commercial and then a technical civilization than Catholicism, which, when left unaided, has preferred an agrarian culture. But there is no evidence that either Puritans or Catholics have been immune to the temptations of riches and comforts in our culture (that is, to lures of practical materialism as distinguished from philosophical materialism) because they believed in God.

We doubt incidentally whether either the godly or the godless can be held responsible for the predicament of a civilization with such high productive standards that it is forced to use tremendous advertising pressure to persuade the consumers to higher and more luxurious consumption. Let the first person who allows himself to be persuaded to turn in a perfectly good used car for a new and shinier one, search his soul and solve this problem.

On another sector of the moral front, it is certainly too simple to derive the frequency of divorce and consequent child delinquency from the practice of birth control. We deplore the gradual decay of family life in an urban society but reflect that the family does tolerably well under the strain of urban conditions, as contrasted with the stabilities of an agrarian world. As for child delinquency, one would guess that too many children in a poverty-stricken home may contribute to the problem.

Culturally the distinction between a "godless humanism and atheistic materialism" and a godly culture is also too

simple. Certainly our culture has a strong strain of naturalistic thought which could be defined as "materialistic."
Whether the naturalism is Freudian or Marxist, it has little
sense of the unique dignity and responsibility of the human
self. But there is also a strong strain of "humanism," usually drawn from classical, rather than Christian sources.
This humanism can hardly be called "godless" though sometimes it is explicitly so. It does not lack a sense of the dignity of the person. Unfortunately it usually lacks what the
bishops' statement also lacked, namely, a sense of the misery of man having the same root as his dignity in the
person's radical freedom. Neither the bishops nor our
humanists have studied Pascal. Both are probably too busy
proving that either faith in God, or disbelief in him, is a
prerequisite of true virtue, that they failed to note the
common human predicament of theists and atheists. This
predicament is that, "There is a law in their members
which wars against the law that is in their mind." When
that fact is discovered the difference between faith and lack
of it may become apparent. For true self-knowledge in the
light of the revelation of the divine justice and mercy may
be "the sorrow that leadeth to repentance." On the other
hand, "The sorrow of the world leads to death." That is to
say, to despair. On this issue the Christian faith can challenge modern culture without embarrassment. But nothing
but embarrassment can result from the policy of commend-
ing Christ by pointing to the righteousness of the believers
and the sins of the ungodly. The goodness of the former
always proves itself to be fragmentary and ambiguous
and the sins of the ungodly are not as consistently black
as the godly debaters would have us believe.

In the realm of politics it is particularly embarrassing to
attribute the freedom of an open society to the Christian
faith and to insinuate that a "godless humanism and materialism" must inevitably lead to tyranny. This is true even
though the Christian is on firm ground when he insists that
without a Biblical faith it is impossible to assert the dignity
of the individual against the encroaching community or to
find the authority upon the basis of which it is possible
to defy the tyrannical community with a resolute: "We

must obey God rather than man." We are also on firm ground when we call attention to the fact that the tyranny of Stalinism was not a fortuitous corruption of Marxist idealism, but a natural consequence of the illusions about human nature in Marxist thought. We might even go further and assert that the thought of the French Enlightenment, revered by many liberals who abhor Communism, was basically totalitarian, as Talman in his *Totalitarian Democracy* has so well established. Its totalitarianism did not stem so much from its materialism as from its naive rationalism and its consequent determination to "redeem" society by forcing men to accept rationally approved standards of justice. In that sense Comte was certainly totalitarian, and so are many contemporary psychologists who dream of a utopia in which men will be "conditioned" to be virtuous. (See Skinner, "Walden Two.")

But these tendencies to totalitarianism in a consistent rationalism which does not appreciate either the dignity of the individual or the peril of his egotism to the community, still does not change the fact that a free society had to establish itself against pious forms of authoritarianism which believed it legitimate to annul freedom so long as such annulment protected God and "God's laws" against the rebellion of men. Perhaps the only Christians who truly believed in freedom were the Levellers and Independents of the England of the seventeenth century. Incidentally Santayana may be right in suggesting that political democracy was originally a unique Anglo-Saxon achievement. That judgment, however, does not do justice to the growth of liberty in the various parts of Western Europe.

In any event, the story of religious authoritarianism and fanaticism is such a sorry chapter in the history of the West that Christians must observe a proper humility and lack of polemical bias when they discuss the various ways in which liberty has been established and imperiled by both the godly and the godless.

We might sum up this critical discussion of the bishops' pronouncement with the observation that any Christian challenge to our culture which does not call both the godly and the godless to repentance must be suspect. For

the Christian faith deals basically with the perpetual variance between all men and God. It therefore senses, with
the prophet Jeremiah, the judgments of God upon "the circumcised and uncircumcised." But this is one of those
instances in which the prophets of the Old Testament saw
the issue rather more clearly than many conventional forms
of Christianity, whether Catholic or Protestant.

PART V: *The Church and the Churches:*
The Ecumenical Movement

A. The Ecumenical Issue in the United States
B. The Problems of a World Church

A. *THE ECUMENICAL ISSUE IN THE UNITED STATES*

THE ECUMENICAL ISSUE IN THE UNITED STATES

Many of the debates of the great world conferences, dealing with the problem of the reunion of the churches on a world scale, seem quite irrelevant to the American scene. The American denominations faithfully send their delegates to these conferences and the delegates listen attentively to the debates on the right order of the church, and are not moved. They do not take the problem of order too seriously, except in so far as many of them are afraid of any order which might imperil the freedom of the congregation.

I

The cause of this irrelevance of ecumenical debates in America is the fact that American churches are historically and predominantly under the influence of the "sect" idea of the church or the "sect" protest against the order, the liturgy, and the theology of the church.• Ecumenical de-

• The distinction of "church" and "sect" used in these pages has been familiar since Ernst Troeltsch first defined the distinction. The very fact that churches become sects in America, and sects churches, because the former are less inclusive in America than in Europe and the latter less exclusive, partly obscures and seems to invalidate the distinction. It is, nevertheless, a useful

bates presuppose the church in the orthodox sense. They take its order, its theology, and, to a considerable degree, its liturgy, seriously. They seek to arrive at the definition of a common order and theology upon which the entire church can unite. But the sect of the sixteenth and seventeenth century came into being in protest against the church and against its liturgy, theology, and order.

The sect protested against the inclusiveness of the church, believing that in it believers were yoked with unbelievers. It believed in a voluntary and exclusive fellowship, entrance into which was not by inheritance but by a clear experience of repentance and conversion. The sect protested against the hierarchical order of the church both because it found the distinctions involved in it a peril to the Christian ideal of equality and because it regarded the authority of the hierarchs as dangerous to Christian liberty. Various sects did not emphasize this equalitarian and libertarian principle equally. Some were more equalitarian and some were more libertarian. But the critical attitude toward the order of the church was general.

The sect tended also to be untheological or antitheological. It emphasized the immediacy of religious experience and regarded rational-theological elaborations and definitions of the Christian faith as a threat to the vitality of that faith. Frequently it preferred lay preachers to a professional ministry or priesthood. For the same reason it was critical of both sacraments and liturgy, fearing that in the one sacramental grace might be claimed by "graceless" men, and that in the other "devotion's every grace except the heart" might be cultivated. It preferred spontaneous prayer, sometimes delivered in the forms of crude immediacy.

These generalizations about sects are somewhat misleading because there were many kinds of sects. Some were socially radical and sought to sharpen the contrast between the world, to which the church had accommodated itself, and the Kingdom of God, which they desired to realize upon the earth. Some were individualistic and pietistic and

distinction for purposes of defining the historical traditions in which two different types of American churches were formed.

emphasized the experience of the saving power of Christ in the individual heart, in contrast to all social and communal, historical and theological expressions of the Christian faith. Nevertheless, generalizations about sectarian protests against the church are justified because there is something common in them despite all diversities. Sectarian Christianity is a form of the Christian faith which is more conscious of the corruptions of the order of the church, of its theology and its liturgy than it is appreciative of them as means of grace. The church on the other hand tends too uncritically to celebrate all these instruments of faith as means of grace without understanding the perils of corruption in all of them.

The problem of ecumenical Christianity in America is the problem of resolving what is true and false in both the church and the sect idea of Christianity, rather than the problem of finding the right order of the church. The reason that this is so is because churches developed from a sect foundation have had the dominant influence in American church history. Of the powerful American denominations the Baptists belong most clearly to the sect tradition, though it must be observed that some of the socially radical implications of the continental Anabaptist movement of the sixteenth century were not transmitted to either the English or the American Baptist heritage. Yet Roger Williams' radical individualism and libertarianism, coupled with his radical "seeker" suspicion of all historical institutional forms of Christianity, have had a potent influence upon American Baptist life.

Congregationalism is not purely "sect," nor was the English Independency from which it is derived. Yet it betrays the typical sect suspicion of bishops and hierarchs, conceives of the local congregation as the significant unit of the Christian fellowship, and historically lays little emphasis upon the inclusive church as a sacramental community.

The Methodist church in Britain was for a long time not quite certain whether it should count itself among the "nonconformists." It thought of itself rather as a leaven within the Anglican communion. It was, nevertheless, brought more and more into the nonconformist camp in Britain. In America it conquered the frontier primarily through typical sectarian instruments, the lay ministry, the prayer meeting with its emphasis upon lay participation, the emphasis upon individual repentance and conversion, the protest against all compromises and the impulse toward "sanctification" and perfection. Coupled with this was a considerable indifference toward theology and sufficient lack of conviction about the right order of the church to enable the Wesleyans to be nonepiscopal in England and episcopal in America.

The Disciples as the only indigenously American group among the larger of our religious denominations, was born with a strong ecumenical impulse, but it gave that impulse a typically sectarian expression. It believed it to be easy to define the "New Testament" character of the church; and thought it possible and desirable to recreate that character. It also exhibited the typically sectarian congregationalism and fear of hierarchical control. The disapproval of some sections of the Disciples church of musical instruments in the services is a typical symbol of the sectarian fear of aesthetic elaborations of worship not specifically authorized in Scripture.

Thus only the Presbyterian, the Lutheran, and the Episcopal churches are left among American church bodies who trace their ancestry indubitably to traditional "church" sources. Among these the Presbyterians have, in common with all Calvinism, certain "sect" tendencies most clearly revealed in American history in the controversy between the "Old Lights" and the "New Lights." Presbyterians have taken theological issues more seriously, however, than the sectarian churches; and their passion for an order of the church which avoided both too much license and too much hierarchical distinction places them predominantly in the category of the church.

Such a cursory and inadequate survey leaves many important issues untouched; but it seeks to establish the fact that numerically and otherwise the church of America stands primarily under the influence of the sectarian protest against the church.

II

The predominance of sectarian conceptions of the church makes most of the ecumenical debates irrelevant, for they deal with the right order, theology, and other instruments of the life of the church but do not deal with the basic issue between the sect and the church. If, for instance, the union of the Presbyterian and Episcopal churches should succeed, it will not, as some hope, establish a pattern for a general reunion of American Protestantism. It will be a union of two denominations which share, whatever their differences, a common conception of the historic church as a community of grace, and the terms of reunion will not deal with the legitimacy of the sectarian protest against the church.

This does not imply that the primary ecumenical task in America is to do justice to the element of truth and validity in the sectarian protest. The primary task is rather to validate the church against the sect and the sect against the church. The task is to find an institutional form broad enough, and a comprehension of the Christian faith rich enough, to give a solid basis for the instruments of grace which the historic church has rightly developed and at the same time to appreciate the validity of the sectarian protest against the corruptions which periodically appear in these means of grace.

Since the sectarian influence is dominant in America it may be well to begin by a more thorough appreciation of the church. The institutional religious situation in America is that the sectarian protest against the church has been so powerful that it has well nigh annihilated the church as a unique institution of grace, resting upon the foundation of the revelation of God in Christ. This tendency is slightly mitigated by the fact that the sect, when it does not have a powerful established or inclusive church to protest against, is inclined to become a church without fully understanding the genius of the church. Thus in America sects tend to become churches because they are more inclusive than the typical historic sect of the sixteenth and seventeenth centuries; and the churches tend to become sects because they are, in the American environment, less inclusive than the traditional churches in their European setting.

This qualification does not, however, obscure the general pattern of American church life, which is, that the sectarian protest again the church is so powerful as to destroy some of the unique virtues of the church. This charge must be elaborated in detail.

In terms of the church as a worshipping fellowship, the sectarian protest against liturgy, which was originally made because liturgical worship may easily degenerate into empty forms, has tended to destroy the liturgical channels and instruments of common worship. The sectarian church believes in free and spontaneous prayer. There is a place for this emphasis because it is not possible to do full justice to all the needs of worship by traditional prayers. But if the emphasis upon spontaneous and free prayer destroys all liturgy, as it has done in the American sectarian church, the free prayer, originally a means of grace, degenerates into banal, sentimental, and chatty conversations with God. The forms of worship (or lack of them) of most of the American churches, including some with an old but forgotten liturgical tradition, are frequently a scandal. The Biblical thought and phrase by which the "worship life" of a congregation is held close to the source of its Biblical faith tends to disappear completely from the pastoral prayers. A very great religious vitality and spontaneity may compensate for the lack of aesthetic form in the original period of sectarian passion. But as the vitality is dissipated the vulgarity of the haphazard phrase becomes more obvious and intrudes itself as an offense to the worshipping congregation. Furthermore, purely free prayers place an intolerable burden upon the minister. No minister, no matter how gifted or filled with grace, is able unaided to do full justice to all the dimensions of the Christian faith in its contact with life. Most ministers of the "free churches" are not even fully conscious of their priestly function in the worship of the congregation, and fail to understand that it is dubious to express personal whimsies and merely spontaneous religious emotions in public prayer. The business of the priest is to lead the congregation in praise and thanksgiving, in contrition and petition, and so to express the great religious aspirations, as informed by the Christian faith, that the congregation will be established and nurtured in its communion with God.

The experience of chaplains in the army in the present war has fully revealed how inadequately most ministers are equipped to conduct the worship of a congregation. Many of the army services have been so inadequate that even religiously untrained soldiers have felt the inadequacy. The Episcopal church, with its liturgical traditions, has a standard of common worship which is the envy of all who have some feeling for the dimension of this problem. Thus we have the paradoxical situation that a sectarian protest against empty forms has tended to destroy all forms, and to destroy with it the real content which the historic form contains. The churches with liturgical forms have preserved certain valuable content with their forms. The Episcopal church may for instance be almost as secular in its preaching as the sectarian church has become. But it can never become, and has not become, as secular in its common life. The historic forms preserve the deeper content, despite the vagaries of the individual preacher. The same may be said for the Lutheran church.

The sectarian protest against the sacraments has never gone the full length of the protest against liturgy. All churches, with the exception of the Quakers, preserve the two traditional Christian sacraments of Baptism and the Lord's Supper. Yet the full Christian witness in them is frequently seriously impaired. Baptism, even in the evangelical churches, is frequently reduced to a ceremony of dedication in which the uniqueness of the Christian community of grace into which the person is admitted in baptism is obscured. The rightful sectarian protest against grace by magic is mingled in the modern sectarian church with a secular indifference toward the life of grace. The sacrament of the Lord's Supper likewise frequently loses its full Scriptural dimensions and, becoming merely a rite of remembrance, ceases to be a means of grace through which the believer is renewed in his faith by repentance and by fellowship with Christ. *It is one of the paradoxical aspects of sectarian Christianity that it ultimately makes more shallow what it first intended to deepen.* Secularism develops in the maturity of sectarianism. This is one reason why the distinction between the church and the world is less marked in America than in other Christian countries, though the original intention of the sect was to sharpen the contrast between the church and the world. All historic Christian means of grace may become either empty or the tools of magical and nonmoral conceptions of religion. This fact justifies the sectarian critical attitude toward them. But they all are genuine means of grace; that is proved by the loss of grace when the means are vitiated or destroyed.

III

The typical sectarian attitude toward theology is analogous to its other criticism against the church. All sects have not been equally hostile to theology. Some have had a simple Scriptural theology, which they usually assumed to be the only possible interpretation of the Scripture. Others have emphasized religious experience in contrast to the rational formulation of faith as developed in theology. In general, the emphasis upon theology has been minimal or the attitude has been hostile. The sect realizes that theology, as well as liturgy and the sacraments, may become empty and vitiated. It usually does not understand how necessary it is to give a reason for the faith that is in us and how the total life of the church depends upon a comprehensive and coherent view of all the implications of the Christian faith. Sectarian theology is particularly inclined to be critical of the theological traditions of the ages and to imagine that an ecumenical theology could be developed if only everyone understood the Scripture as simply as it does.

The consequence of this atttitude in the American sect is that no great theology has developed in this country. All of us have been more or less dependent upon theological developments in Europe. American liberal theology of the past decades was derived more or less from Schleiermacher and Ritschl, and the reaction to it is influenced primarily by the dialectical school of thought. America's greatest theologian, Jonathan Edwards, developed a new and creative relationship between Calvinism and philosophical idealism. In it the evangelicalism which belongs to the sects was vitally related to the solid theological tradition of Calvinism. But Jonathan Edwards has been a long time dead. He labored among us before America was a nation.

Thus the emphasis upon religious immediacy has tended to destroy theology among us. The revival of theological interest in our own day is as necessary a part of a genuine ecumenical movement as any discussions on church polity. Sectarian protests against theology are a necessary part of the life of the church. But a church can not exist without theology. Theology is the skeleton of the faith of the church even as polity is the skeleton of the common life of the church. The flesh on the bones, whether in faith or in life, is nourished by a more immediate transmission of religious vitality. But the full stature requires the support of the skeletal structure.

The question of church polity has a completely different orientation between the sect and the church from that which most debates on church order presuppose. The sect is quasi-anarchistic in its conception of the common life of the church. It is afraid of hierarchical authority and inequality. It emphasizes Christian fellowship and is critical of all instruments of the common life of the church which integrate that fellowship beyond the local congregation. Congregationalism is one of the most natural expressions of sectarian ethos. From the standpoint of sectarianism the detailed issues of the right order of the church are irrelevant because it is not fully aware that the question of order has any great importance. The solemn conclusion of the Anglican communion that the ministry of the non-episcopal churches is "irregular" even though "owned by the Holy Spirit" (to quote the conviction of the late Archbishop of Canterbury, Dr. Temple) has no persuasive power at all. It merely suggests to them that the Anglican communion is engaged in trying to achieve church union upon the basis of its polity and that such spiritual imperialism cannot succeed. Sectarian Christians dutifully attend the ecumenical conferences because they believe that such "fellowship" will gradually produce an ecumenical union or even that it is the very reality of ecumenical union. The Stockholm and Oxford ecumenical conferences, rather than the Lausanne and Edinburgh gatherings, are the real expressions of sectarian ecumenical feeling. Sectarianism would achieve a world-wide union of Christianity on the basis of "life and work" rather than "faith and order."

The real question which must be solved between the church and the sect on the problem of polity is the question of order itself. The sect must come to realize that the congregation is not powerful enough and its resources not great enough to maintain the uniqueness of the Christian witness against the world. It must understand that its very ambition to remain unspotted from the world is negated by the dissipation of the wider integrity of the church. The sect is more afraid of the authority of the bishop than of the influence of the village bigwig upon the faith and morals of the church. It celebrates the ideal of liberty from ecclesiastical authority and does not recognize the value of that authority in maintaining the witness of the church against the world. Thus the sectarian church easily becomes a "community church" which may unite all the religious forces of a community but which has little power to witness to the Christian faith against the sinful forces in a community. One has the uneasy feeling that if the community ever degenerated into the demonic, as the German community did, American sectarian Christianity would hardly possess the spiritual resources to witness against the community. The sect must learn not so much a "right order" as the relation between the instruments of order and the integrity of the church as a supernatural, superracial community of grace. The sect may be pardoned for regarding all insistence on "right order" as somewhat pretentious. The church can hardly bring the sect its own unique contribution if the primary emphasis lies upon right order. Its primary emphasis must be upon the necessity of order as such, as an instrument of grace and as a means of the integrity of the church.

On the other hand, the traditional churches have a too patronizing attitude toward the witness of the sect against the order of the church. Some churches believe that right order is the only guarantee of the preservation of the full substance of the church. Actually there are no such guarantees. If order were the guarantee of the substance of the church, Roman Catholicism would have a better claim to having preserved the full substance of the church than any other communion. The full substance of the Christian faith and of the church as a community of grace is maintained by the continual renewal of the faith through the Scriptures. Yet every interpretation of Scripture may become the vehicle of divisive and fanatic movements which destroy the unity of the church. The full substance of the church is preserved in the sacramental and liturgical observances of the church; but these also may become vitiated. The substance of the church is maintained by religious vitality; but there are forms of religious vitality which defy the Scriptural content of the Christian faith. The substance of the church is maintained by an ecclesiastical order which preserves the fellowship of the church in widest possible terms, which maintains the historic continuity of the Christian witness and which prevents the dissipation of the power of the sacraments through the vagaries of this or that priest or the moods of this or that age. Yet the authority which is necessary for the maintenance of this order can become the vehicle of an unchristian pride, and even the instrument of irreligion and skepticism. (There have been bishops in the very church which regard the episcopacy as the guarantee of the full substance of the church who have preached a type of rationalistic liberalism in which almost every characteristic accent of Biblical religion was absent.)

IV

The real ecumenical problem for American Christianity is how to arrive at a better common denominator between the sectarian and the more traditional and orthodox Protestant conception of the church. In a sense this problem is being solved by progressive stages on the American scene. The fractional character of the various denominations prompts them to a certain degree of humility in assessing their own virtues and in appreciating the excellencies in the traditions of others. The general tendency of churches to become less inclusive and of sects to become less exclusive, makes for a gradual *rapprochement* between the denominations. It is safe to say that American churches will achieve a broad working unity long before the vexing problem of the Established and the Free Churches of Britain is solved.

Yet there is a danger that this unity will be achieved too much in merely practical and administrative policies, and that no sufficient attention will be given to the theological and religious issues which divide sect from church. If those issues are to be solved the church must recognize the necessity of a perpetual criticism of the institutional means of grace, and the sects must recognize that a criticism which destroys these institutions also destroys what the sect desires most fervently: tension with the world and a sense of contrast between the community of grace and all other human communities.

A mere emphasis upon fellowship and upon administrative comity is not enough. On the other hand, the tendency of the Anglican church, at least in its Catholic wing, to introduce the question of right order as a theological issue, intrudes a Catholic conception of the church into this whole problem. The problem of unity between church and sect is capable of solution upon the basis of a Reformation conception of the church. The blindness of the Reformation church in rejecting the witness of its contemporary sectaries must be disavowed. But if that grace of humility is achieved, the high conception of the church and of its liturgy, theology, and sacraments, which characterized the Reformation church, can be maintained.

If, however, the question of church polity, of "right order," is introduced into the whole equation from the standpoint of a Catholic or quasi-Catholic theology, real unity becomes a hopeless quest. In this respect there is a certain conflict between the ecumenical task in the national and in the international sphere. Internationally there can be no ecumenical movement of great significance which does not seek to solve the tension between Protestant and quasi-Catholic views of the church. But on the American scene the primary problem is to bridge the gulf between Protestantism and what might be called "ultra-Protestantism."

It may be observed, however, that even on the international scene we may have to make a choice. Already there are Anglo-Catholics in Britain who assert that they will withdraw from the ecumenical movement if Greek Orthodoxy is not fully brought into the fold. But the problem of Greek Orthodoxy's relation to the ecumenical movement has been complicated by political factors, such as the debate within Orthodoxy itself about the integrity and political independence of the reconstituted Russian Church. If the rest of us should become too afraid of the charge of "Pan-Protestantism" which Anglo-Catholics are beginning to hurl at the ecumenical movement, we might well lose the possibility of a genuine union of the churches within the realm of Protestantism for the sake of following the chimera of a Catholic-Protestant ecumenical movement.

On these issues a special responsibility rests upon the evangelical section of the Episcopal communion in this country and upon Anglicanism in general. No one can doubt the genuine interest of Anglican evangelicalism in the ecumenical task, and of the contribution of Anglicanism in general to the ecumenical program. Nor can it be denied that this church has much to offer to the ecumenical church in both its liturgical traditions and its sacramental piety. But it also introduces a degree of confusion into the whole ecumenical task by the division in its own ranks between those who have an impulse toward closer fellowship with Protestant churches and those who fear that such fellowship may endanger some kind of ultimate (and probably chimerical) reunion with Rome. It may be that the Anglican communion will ultimately be forced to make a decision on the meaning of the Reformation. It must decide whether it regards the Reformation, on the whole, as an aberration or as a creative event in the history of the Christian faith, an event which delivered the church from the heresy of identifying itself with the Kingdom of God and of making a particular and highly authoritarian organization of the church the only possible basis for a world-wide Christian fellowship.

The rest of us must leave that issue with our Anglican brethren. Perhaps even such words of advice as are offered in these pages will seem ungracious. We have meanwhile our own problems, particularly in America. In America a more organic and intimate ecumenical fellowship depends upon a fuller and more conscious exploration of the theological, liturgical, and ecclesiastical issues between the Reformation tradition and the sectarian tradition, as well as the emphasis upon practical, ethical, and immediate forms of fellowship which we have developed. We must, in other words, find a theology, liturgy, and church polity, creative enough to embody both the value of the church's institutions of grace and the perennial, and perennially justified, insistence of sectarian Christianity that the spirit "bloweth where it listeth" and that the grace of God is bound to no institution. Churches have become sects, and sects churches in America without either one or the other fully understanding what they lost in the procedure. They have drawn together in this manner but have not made the peculiar treasure of each sufficiently available to the inclusive church of Christ. We must find a more positive approach which will seek by conscious effort to save the power of all of the institutions of grace; but also to preserve them from corruption by understanding the legitimacy of the perennial criticism to which they must be subjected.

Underneath our present comity there is still too much good-natured (or even ill-natured) contempt for either the "forms" of one type of church or the lack of forms of another type. We ought to face the issue which underlies these judgments more openly and resolve it by a fuller understanding of the needs of the church.

THE REUNION OF THE CHURCH
THROUGH THE RENEWAL
OF THE CHURCHES

I

A very discerning critic in Germany recently called attention to the fact that the now well-known "Stuttgart Declaration," in which the Confessional church of Germany confessed the complicity of the whole German people in the crimes of Nazism, was defective at one point. It confessed the guilt of the nation but did not confess the special guilt of the church in contributing to the moral and political confusion out of which Nazism emerged.

We have had many prayers of "Father forgive us" rising from the congregations of American Protestantism. But one must raise questions about the adequacy of this contrition and ask whether it has really penetrated to the heart of the weakness of American Protestantism. Our contrition is usually centered either upon the sins of the nations or upon the most obvious vice or weakness of Protestantism: our divisiveness. In seeking the "fruits mete for repentance," one may rightly point to the growing ecumenical movement as the proof of the sincerity of our confession of fault. But the ecumenical movement is primarily a movement for the increasing unity of Protestantism across national barriers. It has not greatly changed the relation between the various denominations in this religiously heterogeneous nation. We do, of course, have forms of comity on a somewhat higher order than some other nations, partly because we are driven to them by the very degree of our religious pluralism and partly because the absence of any religious establishment puts all denominations upon an equal basis, eliminating the vainglory of an established church in its relation to other churches.

We do have certain standards of decency and tolerance in the relation of the denominations to each other. But the genuine ecumenical task of appropriating each other's treasures for a fuller testimony of the many-faceted truth in Christ has hardly begun. We confess our disunity while we proudly hold on to our particular treasure or tradition as containing the truth more fully than the traditions of other churches. The pride of nations, which we condemn, hardly approaches the pride of denominations in intensity because it lacks the specific religious pretension which gives human pride its final dimension. Even when we seek a wider unity than we now possess, we frequently betray our lack of understanding for the basic issues by giving the wrong reasons for desiring such unity. We desire it either because we want to be less impotent and futile in our competition with the more highly integrated Catholic faith, or because we imagine that a united church will give our message more power and prestige. Actually the authority of the gospel is not derived from the power, prestige, or authority of the church. On the contrary the authority of the church is derived from the gospel. The gospel must be validated by proving itself "sharper than a two-edged sword" in speaking to the condition of man, in moving him to repentance and in revealing the glory and the redemptive mercy of God to him in the experience of repentance and faith. The disunity of the church is of course a serious handicap to the triumph of the gospel; because it proves that the church, which mediates the gospel, has, itself, not been fully moved to repentance and faith by its own message. But in a sense that is always true. It is not the goodness of the historic vehicle: the church, nor yet the virtue of the preacher, which moves men to repentance and faith. It is, in fact, one of the serious weaknesses of our proclamation of the gospel in a moralistic age that we so frequently call attention to the virtues of our saints and martyrs, our missionaries and heroes, the far-flung empire of our missionary hospitals and schools to prove the validity of our message. The cynics can easily puncture these pretensions; for they can match every ecclesiastical achievement with some vice of the church, some flagrant involvement in social evil, some cowardly evasion of obvious duty. When the gospel is heard at all, it is heard by those who have discerned the voice of Christ beyond and above the confused counsels of us poor preachers and recognized a majesty of power and love considerably more glorious than any ecclesiastical majesty or power.

II

The unity of the churches does not as such renew the church. Yet a renewal of the church may lead to wider unity of the churches because it will rigorously separate the "traditions of men" from the truth of the gospel. We lack an ecumenical movement in this depth in our American church life. Consider, for example, either the theological or the liturgical issues and the questions of order which divide the Protestant churches. On every one of these issues a deeper unity waits upon a more thoroughgoing recognition of the problematic character of the truth or the value which each of us cherishes. Theologically the point of division among us is still between "fundamentalism" and "modernism," between orthodoxy and liberalism. In this debate, which is no less a source of division because it transcends the ordinary denominational lines, the orthodox pose as defenders of the true faith against modernistic betrayals of the truth of the gospel. The liberals on the other hand are the defenders of enlightenment against obscurantism. We are so busy, as St. Paul observes, in establishing our own righteousness that we are not brought under the judgment of the righteousness of God. Orthodoxy "requires a sign" and liberalism "seeks after wisdom." Thus they miss "the wisdom of God and the power of God" between them. To preach the gospel as a series of "signs" means to assure men of salvation through belief in a history of miraculous events. Such "belief" does not touch the human heart at its center. It does not move proud men to repentance or help powerful nations to stand in the fear of God. That is why so much orthodoxy is so graceless, so full of hatred, so easily compounded with reactionary social positions and is such a ready tool of our political animus against foreign "isms." The end result of such orthodoxy is magic. It offers salvation to men whose hearts remain graceless.

The liberal or "modernistic" opposition to this orthodoxy, on the other hand, has been seeking wisdom with the Greeks. It has tried to validate the gospel by proving that it is nothing more than a pious rendering of the creeds which all modern men believe. Usually it shares with modern men the belief that evil comes primarily from ignorance and that there is a final redemption in "enlightenment." It does not know what to do with the Pauline observation that "the world by its wisdom knew not God," or with the prophetic warning, "Let not the wise man glory in his wisdom." Sometimes it believes with modern man in the redemption of man through historical progress. Therefore, it is just as confused as our secular age when it seeks to interpret the facts of our contemporary history. For these facts prove that the progress of man toward increasing freedom and power over nature may mean global and total wars and the peril of atomic destruction. These facts prove, in other words, that there is no salvation in history, but rather that history accentuates every basic predicament of sinful man.

Or perhaps our modernism believes simply in human goodness and in the necessity of exhorting men to be good or of proving to them that the highest good is the love of one's neighbor. It has not heard the cry of despair from the human heart about its impotence to do the good which it knows. The liberal church offers salvation through endless cascades of moral exhortation. Men, on the whole, know that they ought to do good rather than evil; and they have a shrewd suspicion that usually the good may be defined in terms of generosity toward the brother rather than concern for the self. But they are not fully conscious (though they may be darkly conscious) of the fact that they violate moral commandment by their own impulses of pride and lust for power, and that their anxieties about self make it impossible for them to consider the neighbor.

Furthermore, the liberal church, preaching in a catastrophic age in which the communal life of man is torn by a thousand hatreds, in which the newly won freedom of India is almost drowned in the blood of fratricidal strife, in which conflicting rights of Jews and Arabs reveal how terribly complex problems of justice are, and in which the vicious circle of mutual fear between two great centers of power in the community of nations threatens to tear the world apart, blandly advises men and nations to love one another, if they would escape disaster. There is in this preaching no understanding either of the complex problems of the justice which is required to preserve a tolerable peace among nations, races, and groups which do not love each other, nor yet of the agony of rebirth required if the individual would turn from self-love to love.

Thus in a recent sermon of this type all men were simply divided into three groups: the "peace makers," the "warmakers," and the "peace fakers." The first class included a few pacifists; the second class a few generals, diplomats, and men of power; and all the rest of us, caught in a tragic situation in which one world is dying and another is powerless to be born, were simply catalogued as "peace fakers." That is an indication of the futility of the liberal moralism which turns a gospel of repentance and faith into an intolerable moral commandment, which no one can keep.

Thus the real ecumenical task between orthodoxy and modernism has hardly been touched. Schemes of church organization do not touch it nor do confessions from both sides about the sins of society touch it, when they merely assume that nations do evil because they have failed to follow the creed of the part of the church which makes the confession.

The divisions between the churches on liturgy and church polity may be as serious as these theological issues, but they are nevertheless important. The liturgical churches know that the religious community must be nourished, not merely by sermon and exhortation, but by a life of common prayer, in which the full breadth and extent of the Christian life and thought is expressed. The nonliturgical churches represent an age-old sectarian revolt against the gracelessness of formalism in religion. The liturgical churches refuse to believe that, though liturgy and order are means of grace, they may also become enemies of grace when made ends in themselves. The nonliturgical churches on the other hand are only dimly conscious of the fact that one does not acquire more grace by destroying these corruptible means of grace. In as far as they are conscious of liturgical deficiencies they may seek to add a little "aesthetic" color to otherwise uninspiring "opening exercises." The liturgical problem is one of the most serious issues for us because American Protestantism stems primarily from sectarian protests against all the established forms of the church, theological, liturgical, and governmental. We are only beginning to realize that a protest against the corruption of a form of faith, which destroys the form, tends to expose religion to formlessness. It easily degenerates into a pious feeling without well-articulated theological convictions, to habits of prayer in which banality and sentimentality run rampant and into organizational anarchy which robs the church of the power to maintain any standards, whether of faith or morals. The churches which have preserved traditions of order are of little ecumenical help in this situation because they are usually touched by idolatrous conceptions of both the church and its order, regarding them not as means of grace but as necessities of salvation. They think they can beguile those who are children of the Reformation and who have a proper fear of the church's self-worship with a patience not unmixed with a condescending patronage. We think, on the other hand, that among the many idolatries against which the Christian must bear witness is the idolatry which places the church in the position of Christ, and makes the right order of the church a *sine qua non* of salvation.

We do not gain the authority to speak to the nations by achieving the prestige of organizational unity. The authority to speak to the nations is in a gospel which discloses a majesty and a mercy beyond all historic majesties and all human justice. Where that gospel is preached with power it will heal both the nations and the church. But it will first wound the pride and the self-esteem of the churches as much as the vainglory of the nations.

HAS THE CHURCH ANY AUTHORITY?

The *Reader's Digest* recently stirred the apprehensions and fears of many timid Christians by giving wide publicity to a chapter of John T. Flynn's book *The Road Ahead*, in which every organization and personality, not devoted to the pure principles of laissez-faire is castigated as either in league with Communism or as the innocent dupes of totalitarianism. Naturally the Federal Council of Churches and many of its leaders were subjected to Flynn's lash. His previous claims to fame consisted primarily of books about the Roosevelt era, in which the venom of the author against the wartime President colored every judgment.

The book itself has no particular significance, except as an expression of a rather hysterical creed, prevalent in some parts of America. According to this creed any use of the sovereign power of a state for human welfare is the first step down the slippery slope which leads to Communism. What is rather disturbing is that so many Christians, pastors and laymen, should take it seriously. The Federal Council refuted its misstatements in a special pamphlet for which it secured the support of some of the leading Christian laymen of America. It might be mentioned, in passing, that in a recent Federal Council conference on the church and economic life, 400 outstanding business and labor leaders gave thoughtful consideration to the problems of "freedom and order" in our economic life and freely, and almost unanimously reached conclusions in complete harmony with the general social philosophy which underlies the political attitudes, not only of the Federal Council of Churches but of the World Council of Churches.

This general position might be defined as governed by a concern for both freedom and justice, and as allowing for a great variety of pragmatic approaches to the vexing problems of modern economic life. But it does not assume, either that the free play of all economic forces will make justice automatically, or that the solution of every problem of justice lies in bringing economic life more and more tightly under political control. The Detroit Conference expressed this general framework of principles as follows:

> We seek a dynamic free society in which there is opportunity to agree and disagree on many important goals for society and the means of achieving them; and a society in which people find their highest freedom in the use of their liberties to increase the freedom of others. We seek an ordered society in which individuals and groups will use their liberties to increase the freedom of others. We seek an ordered society in which individuals and groups will use those social controls which will stabilize the economy at levels of employment providing work opportunities for all.

This statement was not made by the conference in terms of any slavish conformity to previous ecumenical documents. It is, nevertheless, significant that the conference, in which many more laymen participated than in ordinary ecumenical gatherings, freely arrived at the conclusions within the framework of a general consensus in the Christian church which modern Protestantism has formulated in the three great conferences of Stockholm, Oxford, and Amsterdam in 1925, 1937, and 1948. This consensus of Protestant thought is the more remarkable in that it closely approaches the main emphases in the social teachings of the Catholic encyclicals since the *Rerum Novarum*. Whatever may be the differences in Catholic and Protestant social policy, and however much the theories may vary because of the stricter interpretation of natural law in Catholic thought, the similarities are more striking than the differences. Both reject Communism. Catholic theory once rejected socialism unequivocally while Protestantism tended to do so in practice but not in theory. But now the encyclical of Pope Pius XII has declared: "It may well come about that the tenets of a mitigated socialism will no longer differ from those who seek to reform society according to Christian principles. For it is rightly contended that certain forms of property carry within them an opportunity for domination too great to be left in private individuals."

This does not mean that either Catholic or Protestant theory is committed to socialism. It certainly does mean that it rejects the theory that every form of socialism is but a half-way house to Communism, and that every form of social control upon economic process is inherently wrong.

The consensus in Christian thought is not merely the consequence of the presence in the Christian churches of people of varying political and economic convictions, whose thought must somehow or other be harmonized. There are specifically Biblical viewpoints about man and history which help to establish this consensus. It is, for instance, not possible to justify the pure laissez-faire doctrine from the Christian standpoint, because Christianity knows that any "pre-established harmony of nature" is not applicable to human history. It knows human history to be filled with boundless possibilities of good and evil not known in the bounded harmonies and discords of nature. Christian thought, except for a few sectarian anarchists, has always taken the function of government seriously because it is convinced that, because of the sinfulness of man, the order of the human community is never purely "natural" but partly contrived. It is bound to refute any socialist theory with equal force which assumes that the root of human evil lies primarily in the institutions of property, and expects the abolition of property to usher in a utopia of perfect good-will.

Christian thought is equally rigorous with both the ideologues who persuade men to fear economic power but not political power, and those who teach that political power is dangerous but not economic power. It knows that any form of power is dangerous, and that any form of power can be both the occasion of sin and an instrument for organizing the affairs of the community. If both Catholic and Protestant theory tend to justify a subordination of economic to political power, that is because political power can, at its best, express the will of a total community while economic power is by its nature private and partial.

American Protestant political and economic theory has gone through immature phases in which "free enterprise" was too uncritically accepted, and in which subsequently the "social gospel" introduced some utopian illusions into the thought of the church. The remarkable fact about developments in recent decades is that these contradictory errors have been overcome, and that lay opinion has participated in these revisions.

When, therefore, Mr. Flynn attacks the Federal Council of Churches for its social positions, he is not attacking the individual vagaries of individual religious leaders. He is attacking a well-established consensus of Christian social thought, extending far beyond America. He is doing so from presuppositions which are thoroughly heretical from the Christian standpoint. This Christian consensus cannot accept either of the warring secular philosophies of redemption.

According to this consensus there is no simple harmony of all social and economic forces on either this side, or on the other side of a social revolution. It is, therefore, bound to be critical of the social complacency which assumes that problems of justice in a technical society can best be solved by interfering as little as possible with the free play of economic forces. It is naturally even more critical of the Communist creed of world redemption because there are demonic forces in that creed which threaten to engulf the world in disaster.

On the whole, Christian laymen and pastors have a proper regard for the moral and spiritual authority of the church, though the church cannot bind the conscience of individuals in economic and political decisions. But the Flynn book has revealed one of the great weaknesses of Protestantism. There are members of Protestant churches, both lay and clerical, who treat the consensus in the church with complete disrespect upon the prompting of a second-rate and hysterical critic. They seem to have no understanding that when the church regards all social and political institutions as standing under divine judgment this conviction is no vagary, but a consequence of having its mind renewed by the mind of Christ. If Christians find fault with consequent social opinions because these opinions do not justify a given social creed of a given social class of America, this merely means that there are Christians who do not take either the gospel or the church seriously at all. It means that there are men in the church who resent having their "idealism" challenged, particularly if the light of the gospel should reveal that all human ideals are curious compounds of self-interest and ideals.

It means that the religion which is being preached and practiced in some of our churches is not the Christian religion at all, but merely a religious sanctification of our own ideals and interests. On all such idealism St. Paul has spoken a definite word: "For I bear them record that they have a zeal for God, but not according to knowledge. For they, being ignorant of God's righteousness, and going about to establish their own righteousness, have not submitted themselves unto the righteousness of God." This ought to be clear: Wherever the Divine word does not illumine the ambiguity of our human virtues, including our social ideals, wherever men are sure of themselves, of their virtues and their good intentions, wherever they simply identify their will with God's will there is no church at all, however pious the practices.

Protestantism is inclined to vaunt itself because of its liberty as distinguished from Rome's authoritarianism. We fear that Roman Catholicism deifies the church. But, as a friendly critic in the Roman church recently suggested, does not Protestantism deify the individual conscience to an extent which gives men a sense of security about the "dictates" of their conscience and no sense of repentance about the mixture of interest and self-seeking in the ideals of conscience? The Roman church defines the community of grace rather sharply against the world and may give some sinners in the church a spurious sense of ease. But at least they know themselves to be forgiven sinners; and they have some respect for the church as bearing the "oracles of God." The Protestant church has no well-defined community for grace, its members shading off in indeterminate shades of heresy until we reach a type of church member who rages and rants if any word of the church is sufficiently penetrating to disturb his ease. Some of the reactions to the Flynn criticisms of the church might well prompt us as Protestants to be less concerned with the characteristic weaknesses of Rome, and a little more anxious about the vast morasses of sentimentality and human pride in which parts of the Protestant church are sinking.

THE CHURCH SPEAKS
TO THE NATION

At the beginning of November the Commission on International Justice and Goodwill of the National Council of Churches held a conference in Cleveland. The deliberations of that conference resulted in a message to the churches and to the nation which reveals how much the Christian gospel is the source of wisdom for the collective life of man as well as a source of grace for the individual.

This has not always been apparent in American Christianity. The individualistic traditions of early American evangelicalism and the excessive moralism in the liberal Christian tradition made the Christian witness on international problems frequently irrelevant. Evidently these weaknesses have been overcome, to judge by the Cleveland message.

The primary virtue of the Cleveland message is that it shows clearly that our responsibility as a nation to the international community derives from the sense of responsibility which Christians feel they owe to God. "As a nation and as individuals," it declares, "our responsibilities to God rise above all other claims and responsibilities." But this ultimate responsibility clarifies rather than annuls the responsibilities which we have as citizens of a very powerful nation. The message declares: "As American Christians, citizens of a nation of great wealth and power, we feel the need to affirm our common bond with Christians of other nations. Yet at the same time we must speak as Christians who are also citizens of the United States. It would be presumptuous and irresponsible if we tried to speak as if we were not bound by our particular responsibilities as Americans." Here is Christian universalism which does not cancel out particular responsibilities.

The second mark of maturity in the message is its disavowal of previous interpretations which have equated the Christian faith with a kind of moral panacea, which would solve all the world's problems if it were only accepted. The message declares:

> The Christian faith does not provide us with a blueprint or easy answers for the tragic problems of the world's disorder. We must guard ourselves and others against the illusion that there is any simple or permanent solution to the problems of the world's order.

The third virtue of the message is that it speaks soberly against both the disciples of "appeasement" and the proponents of the idea of an inevitable war. "Since it is our Christian faith," the message declares, "that God can bring about changes which are beyond human powers, we refuse to believe that a reconciliation (with Russia) is finally impossible." But the message makes it plain that there is no possibility of such a reconciliation now. Instead, it insists with soberness that "the minimal condition for coexistence is the recognition by both sides that peace is better than armed conflict, especially when war means mutual annihilation."

One has the feeling, when reading the document, that if

America is maturing under the weight of its responsibilities, one factor in its increased wisdom is the counsel of a maturing church.

THE NATIONAL COUNCIL DELEGATION TO THE RUSSIAN CHURCH

Nothing but good can be said about the visit of the National Council of Churches delegation to Russia. It is true that some of the leaders of the churches in exile, particularly from the Baltic states, protested against the visit and warned that it might lead to illusions in the West. But the statesmanlike procedure of the delegation and particularly of its chairman, Dr. Eugene Carson Blake, dispelled these fears. The delegation met with the Russian religious leaders but they were not taken in by any of their political naïveté. The Russian leaders proved themselves rather simple followers of the Communist "peace line." They had no views of their own about international relations, and Dr. Blake made it clear that we could not expect an independent line from them. The traditions of the Russian Orthodox church, declares the report of the delegation, persuade the church to think of the function of the church as "that of saving souls and preparing them for heaven and therefore it shows little concern for the intellectual and social life of the people. . . . Educational, economic and political life are the functions of the state. Worship from birth to death is the task of the church."

Naturally, with such a circumscribed function, the church has little influence on the total life of the nation or indeed upon individuals. The delegation gave it as its opinion that, even though freedom of worship is now fully accorded, the materialistic education of the youth is bound to further limit the authority of the church. In short, the Russian church is not a full-bodied church and certainly not in any obvious way the "body of Christ." It is the product of long ages of otherworldly interpretations of the Christian faith.

Dr. Blake was therefore quite right in emphasizing that we could not expect the church to influence the state or to exert an independent moral influence on international problems upon the people. Incidentally, it might be possible to say without cynicism that probably one reason for the increased freedom of the church is the complacency of the state with regard to the influence of the church or its will to exert it.

Why then was it valuable to make the visit? There are several reasons. One is to give the Christians of Russia some contact with Christians in democratic lands and impress upon them both the freedom with which they deal with international issues and to contribute a little to the emancipation of the Russian mind from the preconceptions in which all citizens of totalitarian states are imprisoned. But beyond these immediate objectives, it is important to explore every avenue of contact by which Russia might gradually be brought into the community of nations after long isolation. The Kremlin leaders have encouraged these contacts for the purpose of increasing the technical efficiency of the Russian production, particularly in agriculture. But there is no reason why the West should not try to open any gate which has not been absolutely locked. Certainly the gate of common Christian conviction is one of these, even though one cannot speak of too much "common" conviction; for long before the Communist revolution, "Eastern Christendom" became divided from the West, and some of the spiritual realities which the delegation found were due not to the Communist, but to the previous schism, long centuries ago.

We cannot afford any illusions in regard to the intransigeance of the Communist political foe. But we also must not leave any avenue unexplored by which bridges might be built across the deep chasm which divides us. If we think not in terms of years but of decades, we may hope that ultimately the Russian isolation will be dispelled or overcome.

Certainly the Christian church has a bounden duty to be one of the bridge builders, even if it must compete with agricultural technicians in the task of bridge building. While the chasm between the Russian church and the churches of the West is very wide, it is not quite as wide as the political chasm between Communism and democracy. The delegation was therefore quite right in regarding this visit as but the first in a series of many contacts to express the hope that "the Churches of Jesus Christ may be used for the reconciling and salvation of the nations."

B. THE PROBLEMS OF A WORLD CHURCH

THE OXFORD CONFERENCE
ON CHURCH AND STATE

One does not expect too much of an ecumenical conference. Too many viewpoints must be harmonized in the official reports to permit the church to speak unambiguously on the great problems of the day. Yet the five reports of the Oxford conference, dealing with the five problems of church and state, church and community, church and the social order, church and the community of nations, and church and education achieved a remarkably high level of genuine Christian testimony.

The report on church and community was so unequivocal in its insistence that "in Christ there is neither Jew nor Greek, neither bond nor free" that one of the South African delegates expressed the apprehension that it "would prove very embarrassing to the church in South Africa," a fear shared by some of the southern delegates of our own nation. The report rigorously opposed racial bigotry and pride and insisted on the transracial character of the church as a community of grace.

The report on the church and the social order made a vigorous and clear analysis of the destructive forces at work in the present economic order and insisted that the irreligion of modern radicalism was in a large measure due to the failure of the church to understand the problem of social justice in the modern age and to bear clear testimony in favor of the cause of justice in the various crises of our era. This interpretation of the modern situation was opposed by those sections of the conference which regard the irreligion of Communism as a manifestation of "anti-Christ" in conflict with the Christ of the church. This "Catholic heresy" of regarding the historic church as the unqualified representative of Christ on earth so that the enemies of the church become the enemies of God was resisted by the conference in various ways, though it was held by some of its members. In that emphasis the conference was "Protestant" in principle though non-Roman Catholic in its total membership.

The report on the church and the world of nations was rather unsatisfactory in that it listed three possible positions which Christians might take toward the problem of war with little discrimination. They might regard obedience to the state under all circumstances as the duty of the Christian (the extreme Lutheran position); they might feel obligated to support the state only in "just" wars, that is wars of defense or wars in support of the principle of collective security; or they might refuse participation in all wars. The first position was only mildly condemned as embodying the danger of giving the state an authority which belongs only to God. The report called upon Christians to respect each other's conscientious scruples, whatever position in regard to war they might severally take. It was quite correct in calling attention to the fact that it is impossible to arrive at a single position on war (the pacifistic one for instance) and to declare all other positions unchristian. But the demand for mutual respect for each other's conscientious convictions hardly does justice to the real situation in war time. At such a time the Christians who support a war are tempted to succumb to the hysteria of war and to become corrupted by the immense spiritual pride and self-righteousness of the nations. This peril was not sufficiently considered. On the other hand the danger that the church disown its pacifists in time of war was not warded off with sufficient charity.

Though, as is generally known, this journal does not accept pacifism as the only possible attitude of Christians toward the problem of war, it is nevertheless obvious that pacifism in the modern church has something of the same functions as asceticism in the medieval church; and this in spite of the fact that pacifists are not usually as clear-headed about the implications of their abstention from social responsibilities as were the ascetics. Nevertheless, the church would be the poorer and its counsels in greater danger of corruption by popular hysteria if it lacked the pacifist testimony. War is such a terrible catastrophe in modern life that anyone who participates in it ought to do so only with a very uneasy conscience; and his conscience ought to be kept uneasy by the influence of those who find it impossible to reconcile war with Christ. In that sense pacifists are not fools to be tolerated by the church but witnesses which must be heard.

The Oxford reports are on the whole carefully thought out documents in which the issues are defined with fine precision, even though everyone will not agree with the conclusions. They ought to contribute greatly to the clarification of the Christian mind on modern social issues.

THE WORLD COUNCIL
OF CHURCHES

Other journals will deal with the religious significance of the first assembly of the World Council of Churches. We must confine ourselves to the statement of the assembly which diagnosed the "disorder" of modern society and the relation of the churches to it. The portion of the statement which received the greatest amount of publicity declared: "The Christian Church rejects the ideologies of both Communism and laissez-faire Capitalism, and should seek to draw men away from the false assumption that these extremes are the only alternatives. . . . It is the responsibility of Christians to seek new creative solutions (for the organization of modern society) which never allow either justice or freedom to destroy the other."

This statement gives an accurate picture of the social convictions of the first assembly of the free churches of the world. Those convictions were sufficiently radical to refute all the critics of the church who regard religious institutions as naturally conservative, and to baffle conservative members of the church, particularly in America. The idea of making an equilateral condemnation of capitalism and Communism is enough to fell quite a few conservatives in America with a stroke of apoplexy. Yet it represented the considered convictions of most of the delegates who worked upon this particular report. Some of the delegates, particularly from Asia, would probably have preferred a stronger condemnation of capitalism than of Communism. The Christians of Europe have certainly moved toward the left in politics during the past century; but they are on the whole very antagonistic to Communism and are baffled by the romantic attitude of Asiatics toward the Communist cause. But even the Europeans would not have accepted a criticism of Communism which did not bring capitalism under equal condemnation.

This equilateral indictment is unfair at one point. The "ideology" of capitalism is the belief that justice will be achieved automatically from the free play of all competitive economic forces. This is a mistaken belief which has resulted in much injustice in modern society. But it could hardly be said that it generates the demonic fury which characterizes modern Communism. If one were to be absolutely fair, one would have to point out that the mistaken ideology of capitalism is not wholly incompatible with the preservation of a free society, while the Communist dogma results inevitably in the destruction of freedom. But the delegates at Amsterdam were in no mood for such niceties of discrimination. Many would, in any event, be concerned to say an appreciative word for Communism as springing from a passion for justice, however mistaken, and a critical word against capitalism, as responsible for the social maladjustments of the modern world.

The sympathy for Communism among modern Asiatic

and African Christians, manifest at Amsterdam and at many previous ecumenical gatherings is one of the outstanding social facts of our time. There are few Christian Communists even in Asia. But evidently thousands of Christians in Asia are sympathetic to Communism. There are many reasons for this. The Asiatics know little and care less about what Communism does in Europe. In Asia they think of it in terms of Russia's championship of the cause of the colonial peoples against the "imperialist" powers; of the practice of interracial fellowship in Communist youth groups; of Communism's challenge to China's corrupt government; and in general of the hope which it holds out to the miserable and poverty-stricken people of the Orient. Asia has not, in other words, awakened to the deepest tragedy of our age, which is that the alternative to capitalism turned out to be worse than the disease which it was meant to cure. Even Christian Asiatics are not too inclined to heed the warnings about Communism from Europeans, and more particularly not from Americans. Whatever the virtues of America may be, it is much too rich and powerful to make much of a moral appeal to people in Africa and Asia. Moreover, resentment against racial discrimination is such a large part of the propulsive power of the Communist creed in Asia, that America, with its segregated churches, is not in a good moral position to give the warnings which Asiatics need.

One has the uneasy feeling, therefore, that Communism will spread in Asia long after it is checked in Europe. In Europe it is certainly checked ideologically, though there is still the possibility of its victory over that continent by political and military pressure. One added factor for the growth of Communist sentiment in Asia is the absence of those middle parties of democratic socialism which play so large a role in the politics of Europe.

In India, for instance, there is increasing danger that the Congress party will become more and more a tool of the reactionary mill owners, despite the socialistic convictions of Nehru. The protest against this rising reaction is being expressed primarily by the growing Communist movement in India. The Socialist party is small and ineffectual. Nehru is too preoccupied with the total problems of India to give it leadership. In Europe the middle ground is always in danger of being immersed by the floods of passion from the right and left. In Asia there is a danger that the middle ground, which the World Council of Churches so strongly prefers, may not even establish a foothold. It exists neither in China nor in India.

We have dealt with only one aspect of the report of the World Council on the disorder of the modern world. The general tenor of the total report is such that one might imagine that the churches of the world had adopted the basic creed of our Fellowship (of Socialist Christians). The cynics may suggest that this is not exactly a coincidence, since the secretary of the section which wrote the report, Professor Bennett, is a member of the Fellowship. But however great his contribution to the report, the inference would be wrong. Dozens of people contributed to the report; and it undoubtedly crystallized the social and political convictions of the free churches of the world. Those churches have "moved left" particularly in Europe and Asia. They have done so not merely because (as a Socialist member of the Assembly at Amsterdam declared) the whole world has become as insecure as once only proletarians were. It has moved left also because religious convictions have increasingly made the church aware of the social and ethical problems of our modern world.

PROTESTANTISM IN A DISORDERED WORLD

The readers of this journal would not be particularly interested in a discussion of the religious significance of the first assembly of the World Council of Churches, recently held in Amsterdam. I will, therefore, confine my report to an analysis of the assembly's social and political attitudes and merely record my conviction that it is too early to estimate its importance in religious history. Subsequent developments will have to prove whether or not it really marked a turning-point in the life of non-Roman Christianity, the point where the free churches consciously turned their back upon the divisiveness and anarchy of freedom and sought a wider unity and greater order within the framework of a non-authoritarian Christianity. Meanwhile it must be observed that democratic religion is always in greater peril of anarchy and disorder than democratic politics. The road toward religious order and unity is therefore a hard one.

Socially and politically the assembly was significant because it recorded convictions which confute those critics of the churches who identify religion with reaction. It is true that the assembly as a whole did not have to subscribe to the diagnoses of the various commissions which examined the "disorder of the world" and the relation of the churches to that disorder. It merely "received" and "commended" the reports. It could however, have rejected any of them, and it frequently exercised the right of amendment. The reports, as accepted, therefore represented roughly the common mind of the most representative group of churchmen ever gathered together from all parts of the world.

The statement which aroused the greatest degree of interest was the equal condemnation of both capitalism and Communism. "The church," declared the committee, "should reject the ideologies which underly both laissez faire capitalism and Communism . . . Each has made promises which it could not redeem. Communism . . . promises that freedom will follow automatically upon the completion of the revolution. Capitalism . . . promises that justice will follow as a by-product of free enterprise. That too is an ideology which has been proved false."

Positively, the report called upon Christian churches to help explore the middle ground and "to seek for creative solutions which do not allow either justice or freedom to destroy the other." This middle ground will be generally recognized as the realm of democratic socialism. But it would be wrong to make the identification too complete, for many Christian conservatives or at least Christian non-Socialists at the assembly accepted the report because they rightly felt that the church did not and could not commit its members to the doctrine of a particular party, and that in any event there were many "creative" approaches to politics which were not strictly Socialist, though they would hardly be creative if they did not, in the words of the report, "subordinate economic activities to social ends."

On the question of the socialization of property the report declared: "The church cannot resolve the debate between those who believe that the primary solution is to socialize the means of production and those who fear that such a course will merely lead to new and inordinate combinations of economic and political power, culminating finally in the omnicompetent state." But it can remind the advocates of socialization that the institution of property "is not the root of the corruption of human nature" and that its abolition cannot therefore achieve the utopian ends usually expected. And it can remind "the defenders of existing property relations that ownership is not an unconditioned right, and it must therefore be preserved, curtailed, and distributed in accordance with the requirements of justice." The requirements of justice are that we, on the one hand, "vindicate the supremacy of persons over purely technical considerations and subordinate all economic process and cherished rights to the community as a whole," and that "on the other hand we seek to preserve the possibility of a satisfying life for 'little men in a big society.'"

The secular reader probably will note that the whole approach to political justice is informed by the Christian conviction that human nature is "corrupted," and that there is therefore no guaranty that the elimination of specific social evils through new social institutions may not create fresh evils. "Men are often disillusioned," the report declares, "by finding that changes of particular systems do not bring unqualified good but fresh evils. New temptations to greed and power arise even in systems more just than those which they have replaced, because sin is ever present in the human heart." This Christian conviction will probably not be as quickly rejected as it once was, since our generation has had opportunity to see the utopian illusions of both liberals and Marxists refuted by actual history. But at any rate there it is, as an inevitable part of a characteristically Christian analysis of social evils. The present writer regards it as a source of wisdom.

Communism was condemned because of (1) its "promise of what amounts to the complete redemption of man in history"; (2) "its belief that a particular class is free . . . from the sins and ambiguities which Christians believe to be characteristic of all human existence"; (3) "its materialistic and deterministic teachings . . . (which) are incompatible with the Christian belief in man as a person, made in the image of God and responsible to him"; and (4) the policies of a Communist dictatorship in "controlling every aspect of life."

But Christians were asked to "recognize with contrition that many churches are involved in forms of economic injustice and racial discrimination which have created conditions favorable to the growth of communism, and that the atheism and antireligious teaching of communism are in part a reaction to the checkered record of a professedly Christian society." However the secular reader may view the relationship of Christianity to modern society, he must admit that this kind of analysis is free of the notes of self-righteous judgment upon "atheism" which have characterized the pronouncements of many churches, and particularly those of the Roman church.

The question is, where did these strong convictions come from? There will be conservative churchmen in America who will ascribe them to a cabal of "leftists" in the inner circle of the assembly. As one who might possibly be included in such a category I should like to testify that most of the judgments in the reports were made much more rigorous than they were originally by the pressure of European and Asiatic delegates. I would not myself, for instance, attempt an equilateral condemnation of capitalism and Communism, partly because I believe that the

latter has a demonic fury which capitalism as a creed lacks
and partly because I believe that the "ideology" of capitalism in its original form no longer exists except in the minds
of a few—or perhaps many—American Republicans. It is
not a live creed in the rest of the world. The resolution's
equal condemnation sprang from the feeling of a radical
Continent and an even more radical Asia.

Protestant Christianity in continental Europe was once
quietistic and either indifferent to politics or frankly a sup-
porter of the old order. The Amsterdam conference proved
how seriously the events of the past decades and the experience of the churches in resisting Nazism have altered the
social outlook of the churches and increased their sense
of social responsibility. As one delegate, the Christian
mayor of a German city and a Socialist, put it,

> Recent history has reduced all bourgeois existence in
> Europe to the insecurity which once characterized prole-
> tarian life alone. Whatever spiritual insights are derived
> from that social insecurity are therefore no longer ex-
> clusively proletarian. If Christianity insists that the social
> environment does not finally determine the meaning of
> our existence, it can make that point only if it recognizes
> the immediate and pressing importance of all questions
> relating to the organization of a tolerable justice.

The radicalism of Europe at the conference was strongly
anti-Communist. The lone voice in favor of Russia was that
of the Prague theological professor, Hromadka. It might
be mentioned in passing that the most powerful theological influence on the Continent, that of Karl Barth, is
obliquely pro-Communist but not actively so. The radicalism of Africa and Asia on the other hand is friendly to
Communism. The poverty of the Orient, the resentment of
the colored peoples of the world at the white man's arrogance, the aspirations of colonial peoples, rightly or
wrongly imagining that Russia is their champion against
the "imperialistic" powers—all these factors contribute to
the formation of something new in the history of Christianity. This something new is not exactly Christian communism but a form of Christianity tremendously sym-

pathetic to Communism. I should add, from the standpoint of Western prejudices, that it is also tremendously naïve about the actual workings of the Communist political machine and rather ignorant about recent political history in Europe. The general hatred of Britain as an imperial power and the envy and moral loathing aroused in the East by America's technical power and economic wealth contribute to this whole orientation. After attending three ecumenical Christian conferences in the past year I have come to the conclusion that even if there were no other evidence available the attitude of Christians in Africa and Asia would prove that the greatest triumphs of Communism will be achieved in the non-European world.

THE WORLD COUNCIL AT AMSTERDAM

An ecumenical conference is at once a thrilling and a disheartening experience. It is thrilling because there are so many evidences of a genuine unity of faith and life beyond the national and denominational differences which divide Christendom. One has the feeling that the church does really worship one Lord who rules its mind beyond differences of administrations and diversities of gifts. One realizes too that there is not only a given unity but also a growing unity. Misunderstandings are actually being overcome in days of fruitful discussion and common prayer. New definitions resolve old perplexities. New insights make for a genuine exchange of the various gifts of grace in the various traditions of Christendom.

The conference just ended at Amsterdam was particularly heartening because it brought a long history of growing understanding to both a culmination and a new beginning. Here the churches committed themselves to each other officially in such a way that it marks a real

milestone to their history. They have done something ir-
revocably. They cannot be quite the same again. They
have decided that they will maintain this permanent instrument of unity in which they may encounter each other
in the spirit of charity rather than competition, through
which they will engage in many common tasks and in
mutual support of each other; and by the aid of which
they will seek to appropriate each other's treasures of
faith and of grace. The conference was heartening too because of the strong note on the renewal of the church as
the real objective. It was recognized how frequently the
causes of disunity are also the roots of the church's irrelevance to the problems of men today. The emphasis was
not upon unity merely that a united church might gain the
authority which a divided church lacked. It was fortunately
recognized again and again that the truth of the gospel had
its own authority which was not derived from the church
but which was frequently prevented from reaching the
hearts of needy people because of the various sins of the
church, its flight from the world into irrelevance, its alliance with powerful classes and groups in society, its mix-
ing the notes of national self-esteem with the truth of the
gospel, its failure to preach a prophetic word of judgment
to the proud and the complacent, and its neglect of the
poor and needy. The emphasis was upon a renewed
church, more instant to show forth the love and mercy of
Christ to those whom the tumults of modern history have
reduced to despair; more courageous in exalting the majesty of a crucified and risen Savior against all principalities
and powers; and more ready to make the church a true
community of grace in which racial, national, and class
distinctions are overcome. It was felt that the reunion of
the churches must be a part of a total process of its
renewal.

One heard the witness of the so-called younger churches,
the representatives of Asia and Africa and one realized
that the great missionary movement, begun over a century
ago, was beginning to bear fruit in the universalization of
the church in history as well as in idea. The younger
churches brought new insights into the discussion which

prevented many a possible one-sided emphasis. Furthermore the discussions between the older churches on polity and order, on theology, and the life of the church, revealed how much of what divides the church represents facets of truth which belong in a total unity. When, for instance, the communion service was held according to the rite of the Dutch Reformed church on Sunday morning with most of the delegates participating, many representatives of the liturgical churches felt that the special form of the service, involving the seating of the communicants around a common table and the passing of the communion cup from one communicant to another, was a more vivid reminder of the historic last supper and a more telling sacramental exposition of the words "this do in remembrance of me" than any alternative service. These notes of appreciation were generally associated with criticisms of the words of introduction to the communion which expressed a rather hard legalism, a strict separation of the goats who could not participate in the communion from the sheep who could. If the definition of the sinners had not been so archaic and had described the relevant sins of our own day one would have had the feeling that no one really had the right to participate, since no one is worthy to do so. One was tempted to forget that the sacrament is for repentant sinners and that there must be a note of gratitude and rejoicing in it for the mercy of God.

This is merely one illustration of the real ecumenical problem and promise; the endless possibilities offered to the churches to learn of one another rather than to hold jealously to their own particular emphasis, practices, or traditions.

The assembly was distressing as well as heartening because it is so apparent that most churches actually do assume that they have the only right order, theology, or way of life. Statements of agreement were sometimes so general and vague that they said practically nothing at all. In these vague statements neither significant agreement nor significant disagreement is clarified. The amount of sheer empty verbiage which flows in an ecumenical gathering is so great that it seems like a mighty stream of murky water which threatens to engulf the necessarily tiny streams of grace and truth.

The Anglo-Saxon world, unwilling to sacrifice the freedom of historical criticism of the Bible as a real and lasting achievement of the liberal movement, was baffled by the growing literalism of the Continent. Thus Karl Barth fought for the rights of women in the church against ecclesiastical traditionalists who were certain that a priest must be a man because Jesus was a man or even because God is masculine. But the thoughtful women in the church were not so well pleased when Barth took back in the name of Biblical literalism what he had won against tradition. He warned the women to be more careful not to violate any of the Biblical, mainly Pauline, injunctions about the place of women in the church. He granted that some of these were "time-bound" and were therefore not the word of the Lord. But he never made clear just by what measure you determine what is time-bound in Scripture and what is not.

Perhaps the most discouraging aspect of an ecumenical gathering is the complacency with which pious representatives of the churches approach the problems of the relativity of historic viewpoints. Considering that the Christian faith has in its essence a profound understanding of the fact that man is man and not God and that he does not easily achieve a timeless truth, being himself involved in all the conditions and contingencies of time, one should imagine that Christians would have a little more appreciation of the contingent and conditioned character of particular theological, liturgical, and ecclesiastical traditions. The fact that Christ himself transcends these historical contingencies is recognized because it is realized that it is the power of His mercy which draws Christians together above and beyond their differences. But almost every theological or ecclesiastical tradition insists upon adding something which belongs to the historically contingent to this final truth and regarding it as absolute. It does this with a curious air of complacency which makes one understand the belief of the secular age that the one way to get rid of fanaticism is to get rid of religion. There were touching and gracious examples at Amsterdam of the mood of humility and charity, of the readiness to learn as well as to teach. But there were also many examples of the opposite mood, which were obvious enough even though they were expressed with the greatest urbanity and never in terms of a shrill polemic. One realized from all this that the ecumenical process had only begun and that it had a long and hard road ahead; and that indeed the church would have to be shaken and disturbed by the hand of God much more than it has been before there could be a more genuine disposition of each not to look at his own things but also at the things of the other.

In contrast to the sharp differences of conviction on almost every question of theology and polity there was a remarkable consensus on social issues. The churches cannot agree in defining what the true church is, but they have a fairly common mind on what it should do in the present world. The old contrast between American activism and Continental quietism has disappeared completely. The European churches awakened to their social responsibilities in the last tragic decade. In doing so they have become considerably more radical than most American churches. With this radical (generally socialist) political conviction they combine an eschatological note, an insistence on the final triumph of Christ over sin, evil, and death, no matter what may happen in the next year or decade or century. This note of New Testament faith was found very baffling by many Americans who thought it connoted irresponsibility toward the pressing problems of the world. Indeed, it was expressed in words which seemed to suggest the possibility of human beings achieving a kind of timeless serenity, which had no concerns with this world. Yet the same man who baffled us with such words insisted that the church was much too sentimental in dealing with problems of political justice. It found some of the Anglo-Saxon devotion to such matters as the Human Rights Declaration of the United Nations quite irrelevant in the light of the more pressing decisions confronting the world. Despite the presence of many church leaders from behind the Iron Curtain, only one, the well-known Professor Hromadka of

Prague, espoused the Russian cause. Every one else was apprehensive about a possible war but every one also seemed quite certain that the best way to avoid it was not to yield to Russian pressure.

There is no sympathy for Communism among Christians in Europe. But there is a great deal of hope in it in Asia. It was interesting to hear bishops from India and China argue that Communism must not be too rigorously condemned since the millions of Asia were attracted to it by genuine needs arising out of their poverty, their resentment against Western imperialism, and the white man's arrogance. One has the uneasy feeling that, as certain as the march of Communism is stopped in Europe, it is on the march in Asia.

This note from Asia served to divide the conference on Communism but to increase the consensus on a generally radical approach to social and economic issues. More conservative Americans did not challenge this general consensus on political issues partly, it seemed, because they were convinced as Christians, rather than as political partisans, that the indictment of the old order in the West was necessary and justified from a Christian standpoint.

Beyond these particular political convictions the discussions at Amsterdam did give the impression that the churches were more certainly in a process of renewal than in a process of reunion. Few saw the irrelevance of many churches to the immediate and the ultimate issues of life very clearly and they constantly insisted that the church must help men to solve the immediate issues of social justice and community and to preach the gospel of the Crucified and Risen Lord more boldly and faithfully that men may not despair in a day of social anxiety, insecurity, and frustration.

THE WORLD COUNCIL AND THE PEACE ISSUE

The statement on the Korean crisis by the World Council of Churches is significant primarily because of its unequivocal position. The body which passed it has a world-wide membership; and there was naturally a great deal of searching of heart about its possible effect upon the members of the Council in lands behind the Iron Curtain. These churches were, for the first time, not represented at all; but they were present in spirit and everyone was anxious that nothing be done to make their lot more difficult.

Yet these scruples did not prevent the Council from speaking without equivocation on the world situation. The two most important emphases in the document are: (1) the commendation of the action of the United Nations, as an instrument of world order in resisting the aggression in Korea; and (2) the insistence that this conflict need not be the beginning of another world war if both the military pressures of totalitarianism are resisted and the injustices and disorders, which Communism exploits, are corrected.

There were only two pacifist abstentions from the statement, one from a representative of an historic "peace church." It is significant how Christians from all over the world had the common conviction that the way to avoid a general conflict was to resist totalitarianism in its various "thrusts," whether by military power as in the case of Korea, or by political intrigue, as in other instances. There was a general feeling that military circles, and perhaps all the rest of us, have been too concerned with the possibility of a world war and had not considered sufficiently the possibility which is now unfolding, namely engagements in many parts of the world, both military and political. It must be admitted that many European and Asiatic delegates, while grateful for the prompt action of the United States and the United Nations in the case of Korea, were not at all sanguine about the ability of our country to deal as adequately with the endless political and moral issues which this kind of conflict implies as with the technical problems of a world military conflict.

While the pacifist position is one of three possible Christian attitudes, defined by the Amsterdam assembly of the World Council, it is significant that this position had little support in the World Council, certainly far less than it has in American church life. The Council did include a strong condemnation of atomic and bacteriological weapons at a time when some of our hysterical congressmen were calling for the use of atom bombs in Korea. It is clear that both the United Nations and the United States high command understand the awful loss of moral prestige which would result from the use of these weapons. It is now fairly certain that they will not be used.

The realism of the World Council statement stands in significant contrast with the efforts now being made by American pacifists in the name of a newly organized committee, entitled, "Committee for Mediation Now." This committee asks that the churches shall place all their support behind Nehru's efforts at mediation. We are told that he

in a large measure inherits the leadership of Gandhi and is therefore probably best qualified to . . . inaugurate and conduct the delicate negotiations . . . He would be much heartened in his efforts if there were indications of support from the United States and other parts of the world.

The statement of the committee declares:

We must strive to bring the bloodshed to an end and find a peaceful alternative. It would be tragic if a few weeks or months from now, in the midst of a full-fledged world conflagration, we were burdened with the suspicion that there was something we might have done but failed to do.

Yet Nehru's greatness as a statesman, cannot change the purposes of the Kremlin. They are willing to negotiate on terms which would practically deliver Asia into the hands of Communism. Here is the old dilemma. Pacifism as a measure of practical statesmanship means appeasement of a resolute foe, who hopes to expand his power without a general conflict. Pacifism in the realm of practical politics assumes that a little conflict is necessarily the beginning of a big one. The chances are that the best way of avoiding the big one is not to yield on the little one. Nothing, in a sense, has changed in the past ten years. Peace, as a religious absolute, can be held by sensitive spirits, who cannot abide the horrible ambiguities and risks of so tragic an age. Peace as a political absolute is confusing. If we strive for political peace too desperately we deliver the world into the hands of those who have no scruples.

It is rather unfortunate that the debate in Christian circles must always be upon this issue. It prevents us from engaging the conscience of the nation upon a more important point. That point is our inadequacy as a nation to help establish what the World Council statement calls "an expanding justice," particularly in the vast complexities of Asia, with its desperate poverty and its unfulfilled ambitions of national independence and unity. We ought to be grateful that the prospect of a world-wide conflict is less, rather than more, ominous through recent developments. But the change of emphasis has brought up issues which tax our conscience less, but engage it more, than our previous fears. The question is not how to appease Communism but, in the words of the World Council, to achieve enough justice to "render the world morally impregnable to totalitarian infiltration."

THE PROBLEMS OF A
WORLD CHURCH

These lines are being written in the midst of a ten-day discussion of a World Council of Churches committee which
has been given the task of preparing material for the next
assembly of the World Council. The experiences of our
committee are a revelation in microcosm of the problems
of the world church in macrocosm. The basic problem is to
state the full truth of the Christian gospel in such a way
that it will be relevant to all historic situations. Consider
some of the divergencies of viewpoint and experience at
such a meeting as ours, as symbolic of the world situation.

There is one group of Christians, living close to the Iron
Curtain, which wants the Christian message stated in such
a way that it will bring comfort and hope to Christians
behind the Iron Curtain, some of whom are undergoing
great suffering and few of whom could possibly exercise
any significant political choices. On the other hand a message to Christians in America deals with people who suffer
little but who bear great responsibility, America having become the center of a world-wide system of democratic
order. Americans are not tempted to despair, as are people
in those parts of the world in which there is little prospect
of freedom or justice. But Americans may well be tempted
to pride on the one hand or to complacency on the other.

But these two extremes do not exhaust the divergencies
in the world-wide church. The peoples of Asia do not have
the securities which we enjoy; but they do have the new
possibilities and perils of their various new freedoms. They
want to know how the Christian faith may be related to
the creation of a viable economic and political order and
what the Christian resources are for preventing the spread
of Communism. This does not mean that they take a merely

utilitarian attitude toward the Christian faith. But naturally they are bound to relate their ultimate confidence to their immediate confidence and anxieties.

There is another type of situation, different from America, Asia, or the prisoners behind the Iron Curtain. Many people of Europe, perhaps particularly in France, are in a condition of hopelessness. They think that all alternatives offered today are not necessarily equally bad but that none of them are good enough to give any real hope to modern man. France is, as far as it is not Communist, deeply affected by the mood of "existentialists," who find no significant meaning in life.

There is a part of the Gospel which is meaningful particularly to those who have no earthly hope but need to be assured of the love of God from which "neither death nor life will be able to separate us." There is a part of the gospel which is meaningful particularly to nations, classes, and peoples who are secure and successful. It could be expressed in the text, "Be not therefore high-minded but fear." There is a part of the gospel which is directed to those who are not in an impossible situation, but think they are, such as some of the people of Europe. They need to be reminded of their responsibilities. The parable of the talents is meant for them, particularly the warning to the servant who hid his talent in the ground.

The peoples of Asia, who need so much to establish basic security and to escape from the grinding poverty of an inefficient economy, must learn how to relate their justified striving for more justice and plenty to the more ultimate judgment and mercies of the Kingdom of God. One would like to quote the text to them, "Seek first His kingdom and His righteousness," except that this text cannot be pressed upon people who desperately need "all the things that will be added" by comfortable people who have these things.

In these many situations there are not different gospels. But different facets of the gospel are variously relevant. The task of the church is to define the different facets but also to insist on the unity of the one message in Christ. Finally that message is of course found in his Cross and Resurrection from which those who are comfortable and secure must learn that "if ye will not die with him, neither will ye live with him"; while all the weak and despised and lowly and oppressed must learn the meaning of Paul's assurance in his second letter to the Corinthians: "We are treated . . . as dying, and behold we live."

HOPE NEEDS FAITH AND LOVE

As one who participated in formulating the first, but not the second, report of the Advisory Committee on the theme of the General Assembly, I am glad to participate in general approval of the second report and to associate myself with the equally general opinion that it is very superior to the first report. One might draw some interesting conclusions about the methods of arriving at an ecumenical consensus in accounting for this superiority. A noted European theologian is reported to have accounted for the superiority partly by asserting that the American delegation to the second meeting was superior. A more plausible reason for the excellence of the second report was that it profited by the wide discussion and criticism to which the first report was subjected, thus proving the value of ecumenical discussions in the most comprehensive possible terms. But I have drawn an additional conclusion from the indubitable facts. The first report was inferior because some of us were so anxious to reach an ecumenical accord that we did not represent those viewpoints which were bound to express themselves in the church and to influence the second report rigorously enough. If this be true, it proves that if it is important to avoid the notorious *rabies theologorum* in theological discussion, it is also important to avoid what the general secretary of the World Council, Dr. Visser'T Hooft once defined as "theological pacifism." The point is that the first report affirmed what is undoubtedly the Scriptural faith in regard to the Christian hope. But every part of Scriptural faith has a long history of interpretation, and also of possible misinterpretation. The first report stated the convictions of that part of the church which has made the eschatological emphasis of the New Testament its spiritual possession; it may have guarded it against misinterpretation and related it to other parts of Scriptural truth in so thorough a manner as to find further explanations and reservations unnecessary. But those of us who represented portions of the church which had to deal with sectarian distortions of Biblical eschatology or who wanted to be sure of guarding the truth embodied in the Biblical affirmation of the ever-present Christ as distinguished from the hope of his second coming did not present the concern of our churches vigorously enough. The second report is more comprehensive because it embodies the viewpoints, reservations, and interpretations of that part of the church which has not lived with the eschatological emphasis so long and is not persuaded that the whole Gospel can be expressed in the New Testament eschatology.

The excellence of the second report in my opinion is due to the following reasons:

1) The second report gives a comprehensive account of the Biblical eschatology and shows that the whole New Testament thought is involved in the balance of the two affirmations that Christ has come and that He will return. It may be observed in passing that the criticisms which have been leveled even at the second report are due to fears that the emphasis on the coming Christ is in danger of upsetting this balance.

2) The second report guards against the apocalyptic misinterpretations of New Testament eschatology and warns against fruitless millenarian speculation on "the day and the hour."

3) The second report tries to prove the relevance of the Christian hope by appreciating on the one hand, and criticizing on the other, the various hopes and forms of creativity in which our secular culture is involved and in which Christians too must be involved in so far as they recognize their responsibility for the peace and justice of the world. This section of the report has been criticized on the ground

that it did not make sufficient distinction between "democratic utopianism" and "Stalinist utopianism." I noted that the Hungarians criticized it because it did not sufficiently criticize "chauvinism" along with Stalinism. As one who believes it to be very important for Christians to make discriminate judgments about political movements and who would believe it to be inexcusable to find Communist tyranny and modern democracy, however imperfect, as equally under judgment from the standpoint of the Kingdom of God, I nevertheless believe that the report is right in finding fault with all these movements from the standpoint of New Testament eschatology. For whatever their merits they, like all human efforts, are in danger of claiming a final and ultimate sanctity for their values and of obscuring the creaturely limitations of the men who are engaged in these various forms of creativity. On this point Christian eschatology reveals itself as very important. It must remind men, including Christians, constantly how great the difference is between the Lord of history and the little creatures who are called to be co-workers together with him. This is the more important because we have many modern reminders of the fact that the worst evils are brought into history by those "idealists" who think they can bring history to some final conclusion. Whether it is Hegel or Marx or the late N. Berdyaev, speculating about the validity of Russian Messianism, these pretentions are either pathetic or dangerous.

While the second report stands up very well under the various criticisms leveled against it, and while I do not believe that it can be significantly improved short of giving up the original idea of the theme for the General Assembly, the criticisms which have been made of the report in the Central Committee at Lucknow and by various study groups are nevertheless significant.

Let us review them. Mr. M. M. Thomas said that it was not enough to destroy utopian hopes but that the church must give guidance for present Christian action and responsibility. Dr. Fry thought the document was deficient in emphasis on the Holy Spirit, and Dr. Mackay thought emphasis on the vocation of Christ should be added to the hope of Christ. Some critics found the report too pessimistic, for any emphasis on Christ as our "only hope" would seem by implication at least to dismiss all other forms of hope for at least partial realizations of Christ's will in history. Finally there was the criticism by one of the committees at Lucknow, that all of the report's antimillenarian emphasis would not in fact save it from being interpreted in millenarian terms. I would draw a single conclusion from these evidences of continued uneasiness in the church about what is actually an excellent report, and that conclusion is fairly well expressed by one of the study groups, which criticized the report. It declared that any isolated discussion of hope would run the peril of violating the Pauline dictum, "Now there abideth faith, hope and love. But the greatest of these is love." The question is whether the generally-accepted principle of theological exposition is true that a wise exposition of any facet of the Christian truth will finally do justice to every other facet, or whether this trinity of "faith, hope and love" is one that cannot safely be dissolved or looked at merely from one of its three facets, if only for a moment.

In answering these questions we must observe that the emphasis of all the critics upon Christ as a revelation in a present dimension of the God whom we encounter, upon the Holy Spirit, upon present obedience as contrasted with future hopes, all include what might be defined as faith as distinguished from hope. The recognition of our encounter with God in Christ challenges every form of the interpretation of life which imparts meaning to human existence by finding some coherence of nature or of reason or of history as the final clue to the meaning. These alternatives prove themselves wrong in the end because they do not reveal the true God ("the world by its wisdom knew not God") and because they fail to do justice to the heights of both good and evil which men are capable of in history. The encounter between the soul and God in which the despair caused by sin and death is overcome by the mercy, mediated in Christ, is first of all a personal experience, and no questions are raised about the whole drama of history and what kind of outcome it will have. It is an encounter in which the soul cannot grasp the mercy of Christ unless and until it ceases trying to conquer sin and death by its own power and acknowledges its dependence upon the mercy of Christ. If one is asked to bear witness to the truth of this faith one may try negatively to prove that all other forms of faith accentuate the problem of sin and death by persuading men to run into sin in their effort to avoid death, that is, they accentuate the human predicament by offering a solution for man's weakness in terms of some false show of strength. But this is a theological witness. The only effective witness of faith is love, or more specifically "the fruits of the spirit are love, joy and peace." That is the true witness of a faith which has found the Lord of history within and above the tragedies and frustrations, the disappointments of false fulfillments and the fear of the decline of health and wealth which follows inevitably upon its provisional increase, is an unconcern about the self and its ambitions, so well expressed in the Pauline confession: "Whether we live we live unto the Lord, whether we die we die unto the Lord: whether we live therefore or die we are the Lord's."

The assertion of our hope in Christ's coming again will answer the question about the present difference between the will of the Lord of history to which our faith and love bear witness and the confused realities of human history. Our hope completes the structure of the Christian faith, but to those outside of the faith our affirmations will seem to be merely speculative. The affirmation that the "coming Christ is our only hope" will seem unduly pessimistic in addition, for it casts a doubt upon the various forms of hope to which men cling and which are legitimate on their own level, until we have discovered the limits of all historic fulfillments in that experience of faith which has measured the final inconstancy of even the most constant values of life and civilization. For that matter we have no guarantee that the expression of the Christian hope is safe in any particular instance against the sin of encouraging irresponsibility toward some legitimate forms of fulfillment, whether in man's individual or collective life. By what formula can I guarantee the pastoral wisdom which will rejoice with a young man or woman in their budding maturity but also remind them that the final end of maturity is death? Or encourage a wise statesmanship to build a precarious peace in a catastrophic age while reminding it that every peace of the world must be precarious?

In the first meeting of the Advisory Committee we heard a great deal about the fact that those who lived in islands of security in an insecure world were less interested in Christian eschatology than the Christians behind the "Iron Curtain." I have therefore studied with special interest the various descriptions of Christian life under totalitarian régimes and I have not found a single instance of the eschatological hope as an element in the Christian witness. The emphasis lies upon integrity and courage which reflects the Scriptural injunction, "We must obey God rather than men," and upon love of the neighbor which surmounts the fears and resulting cowardice in a world created by tyranny in order to bear witness to the love which casteth out fear. No doubt the total faith of the Christians who have this capacity to witness would include the New Testament hope that the whole confused drama of human history will come to a close by the victory of Christ over all principalities and powers. There is no doubt also that without this hope the Christian faith is in danger of pietistic distortions in which the faith and hope of the individual for forgiveness and fulfillment is isolated from the destiny of the whole of mankind. That is why the Christian hope as affirmed in the New Testament is so integral a part of the whole Gospel. But it seems to me that nothing can change the fact that the love of Christ is a more effective witness of the faith and the hope which is in us than the hope which is the fruit of the faith which love declares. While it is necessary to insist on the hope as a part of the Gospel news, one may expect a good deal of uneasiness in the church about any implication that the affirmation of our hope is an effective way of witnessing to the reality and relevance of our faith before a generation composed largely of skeptics and unbelievers.

Perhaps the question about the suitability of an eschatological theme for an ecumenical meeting is reduced to the question about the primary end and purpose of such a meeting. Is it to "establish the brethren" and create the broadest and most satisfactory Biblical basis for an ecumenical consensus? In that case the eschatological emphasis is necessary, for it represents a neglected portion of the Biblical inheritance; it corrects two errors which are prevalent in the church, an individualism which does not take problems of the whole drama of man's total history seriously but seeks to find fulfillment for each soul independently, and an optimism which usually infiltrates into the church from the secular movements of a bourgeois era and which expects the course of history itself to be redemptive. It is important to refute both of the errors.

Or is it the purpose of an ecumenical meeting to bear witness of our faith to the world? This can hardly be its primary purpose, but no one will deny that what is said at the Assembly will be overheard in the world and will be meant to be overheard. In so far as it will be overheard one must admit that the eschatological theme is not the most effective theme from an apologetic standpoint, whatever may be its theological importance. To admit this is to admit that a wide chasm yawns between the Biblical truth and the ethos of the modern man. Perhaps it is mistaken to look for bridges across that chasm, but such bridges are actually suggested in the Bible. The best witness to the Lordship of the crucified Savior is to live under the reign of his love and to show forth his *Agape*. A General Assembly is not, of course, the most adequate vehicle for this kind of witness, but there seems to be some uneasiness in the church lest the Assembly should fail to bear testimony to the importance of this witness.

CHRIST THE HOPE OF THE WORLD: WHAT HAS HISTORY TO SAY?

I

It is significant for the chasm which separates America from the Continent that so eminent a Christian historian as Professor Latourette should interpret the theme of the Second General Assembly of the World Council of Churches, to be held in Evanston this summer, as implying that Jesus Christ is the "hope of the world" in the sense that the Christian faith offers the world some hope of a gradual triumph, in actual human history, of the "values" embodied in Christ.

For the Continental theologians, who were chiefly responsible for formulating the theme, chose it, I am persuaded, because they thought it most strategic to challenge precisely the form of historical optimism which Professor Latourette elaborates in his article. They regard such a hope as a form of secularism, and they replace it with a Biblical account of Christ's second coming—which in America will be regarded as a purely illusory projection of hope to the "end of history," which cultured Christians had left to literalistic sects to claim as their article of faith. The average intelligent Protestant Christian will interpret the phrase "Jesus Christ the only hope of the world" in exactly the same way as Professor Latourette has interpreted it.

I think this whole misunderstanding proves that the definition of Christian hope is not the best way of consolidating an ecumenical consensus or of challenging the remnants of "secularism" which the Continent suspects in the Christian thought of the "Anglo-Saxon" world. The "secular" element in Christian thought, particularly in America, is of course the identification of Christian hope with the idea of progress.

Professor Latourette assumes it to be his function to interpret Christian hope in this way. But he is also an honest historian and he therefore has great difficulty in fulfilling his assignment. Thus he calls attention to the spread of Christianity from the Western world to the entire globe; but he is forced to concede that this phenomenon is balanced by the secularization of Western Christendom and that a part of this secularization includes the emergence of the demonic secular religion of Communism. He also faithfully records that the dynamic of Western civilization is the fruit of Christianity's affirmation of man's historic existence, but that this dynamic has both evil and good fruits. This latter admission contains the refutation of any simple identification of Christian hope with the idea of historical progress. It is very plain that human history is open to endless possibilities of both good and evil, because human freedom is radical and real. There is therefore the possibility that any historic development of human freedom will result in both destructiveness and increased creativity.

In the report of the World Council Advisory Commission on the central theme, this character of human history is described in the following words:

> The long history of the world which He created and sustains from day to day and for the sake of which He sent His Son, is not rendered meaningless by the coming of His Kingdom. Nor on the other hand is His Kingdom simply the final outcome of the world's history. There is no straight line from the labors of men to His Kingdom. He rejects that history of which man fancies himself to be the center, creator and lord. He accepts that history of which the beginning, middle and end He Himself fixes.

In short, the theme of the General Assembly elaborates a New Testament hope according to which the culmination of history is not within history itself but at its end. History is recognized as being problematic to the end. It solves no human problems but rather accentuates every human problem.

Therefore from the standpoint from which the Christian hope has been defined by the Advisory Commission, some of the evidence adduced by Professor Latourette is rather irrelevant: that Christian influence entered the formation of the League of Nations, that it was powerful in the organization of the Red Cross, that the Salvation Army responded to the needs of the poor who were driven to revolt by Marxist dogmas, that it was responsible for the abolition of slavery and for the organization of the Y.M.C.A.'s. Some of these assertions are highly problematic, incidentally. Wilson may have been a Christian, but the dream of a world community which brought forth the League of Nations is a Renaissance, rather than a specifically Christian, achievement. However great may be achievements of the Salvation Army, they do not seriously challenge or abate the evils of world-wide Communism. In most of the achievements which the historian enumerates, secular idealism cooperated with more distinctively Christian idealism in bringing them about. This is true of the abolition movement and of the growth of political democracy. One therefore feels it a little pretentious to assert that "it is through lives made radiant through Christ that these movements begin."

One must be even more hesitant to affirm with Professor Latourette that "judged from the scope of the entire human scene and the course of history to our day, Christ and his Church are making themselves more and more felt and have never been more potent than in our time." Perhaps it is the phrase "Christ and his Church" which makes the assertion so dubious. We are convinced that the Sovereign Lord of history has been supremely revealed in Christ. We can detect proofs of this Lord's sovereignty in the whole course of history, particularly when we see Him making the wrath of man to praise Him; and when we see movements not specifically Christian and far beyond the confines of the church, serving providentially to do God's will. But this vision of a divine Lord is obscured when we say

"Christ and his Church" and particularly when we make the claim that the two, "Christ and his Church," are becoming increasingly potent in our day. The claim that the church is becoming increasingly potent in our day is certainly open to doubt. But it is even more dubious to link "Christ and his Church" in this way. For thus we make the glory of Christ dependent upon the weak human instrument of the church.

Let us take just one example from current history: the struggle with Communism, and previously with Fascism. In each of these struggles some Protestant and Catholic Christians bore heroic witness to their faith, but the total Christian witness was ambiguous. The Catholic church, which resisted Nazism in the end, first made compromises with it because it saw it as a foe of Communism. It resisted Communism more unequivocally. But it was also involved in the decadent feudalism, of Eastern Europe for instance, the injustices of which furnished the resentments upon which Communism fed. Protestant Christianity had its own heroes of resistance to both Fascism and Communism. But it contributed by its indifference to political and economic justice to the rise of both; and it was, and is, tainted by Communist sympathies.

The self-destruction of these two demonic movements is, therefore, a manifestation of the sovereignty of God over history which is greater than anything suggested by the phrase "Christ and his Church." For the church is deeply involved in the sins of the world; and never more so than when it pretends to divine sanctity, as in the case of Catholicism. One suspects, in fact, that the phrase "Christ and his Church" hides the heresy which the Advisory Commission wanted to warn against by distinguishing between the divine sovereignty and the history conceived in terms of human virtues and human powers. The point is that the divine sovereignty expresses itself not chiefly by the aid of human virtues and powers but despite human weaknesses; and it uses all kinds of instruments for its purpose, including the virtues of non-Christians and the self-defeat of the sins of men.

II

This does not mean that the conscious effort to do God's will is irrelevant or that the church, as that community where the mystery of the divine sovereignty is disclosed, does not play a significant part in God's designs. Most of the illustrations which Latourette uses are in fact excellent examples of the working of Christ's spirit in the affairs of men. They only become absurd when it is implied that the triumph of Christ depends upon them. For not only are the historical fruits of Christian men and the church continually ambiguous, but the effects in history of those who do not consciously follow God's will are very important. The design which the Bible discerns in God's sovereignty over history is in every case more majestic than can be seen if we try to isolate Christian virtues and attribute certain types of moral progress to them.

Most of the examples which Professor Latourette gives of men and women who incarnated the spirit of Christ, and particularly his emphasis upon humble men and women whose lives cannot be obviously fitted into some grand pattern of history but who are nevertheless significant in the eyes of faith, call attention to the fact that the witness of faith, and of love as a fruit of faith, is more important than the witness of hope.

The situation seems to be that the Christian faith affirms that the drama of each individual life and of the whole human enterprise is played on a larger stage than the one-dimensional nature-history which the historians chart. It is declared to be under a higher sovereignty than the system of nature and of reason which scientists and philosophers discern. The only real but important proof of such an affirmation is that the human self transcends all the sovereignties which are known, and that life does not make any sense if it is measured in the dimension of the "wisdom of the world." We are either driven to despair by its meaninglessness or to various types of madness by trying to make sense out of it from our own standpoint. The mad-

ness is the consequence of our grasping for power or prestige or wisdom beyond the obvious limits of creatures. The
alternative is to discern by faith the higher dimension and
to be assured that "neither life nor death nor any other
creature is able to separate us from the love of God which
is in Christ Jesus our Lord."

A concomitant of the faith that Christ is a clue to the
mystery of the divine sovereign of human life and history
is that human life transcends our earthly existence. There
is no witness for such a faith and such a hope except the
nonchalance of perfect faith and love, which is able to say
"whether we live we live unto the Lord, whether we die
we die unto the Lord, whether we live therefore or die we
are the Lord's." This nonchalance is a perfect witness
to the faith only if it results in an actual mitigation of the
lust for power and prestige by which the faithless people
try to make sense out of life.

But such a faith leaves the question unanswered how the
whole human enterprise will come to a conclusion. The
New Testament eschatology assumes that human history
will be fragmentary and contradictory to the end, that the
worst form of evil, the "anti-Christ," will appear at the end
of history; and that the final victory of Christ will therefore come not in history but at the end of history. This
assumes that the moral ambiguities of history and its con-
tradictions will not be mitigated. They may even be heightened. The New Testament eschatology assumes that they
will be heightened. "In the last days" many evils will appear. Men will be "proud, boasters, lovers of themselves."
This eschatology seemed highly speculative; and since the
Renaissance it has also seemed irrelevant because another
way was found to give history meaning. The meaning was
furnished by the development of all good things in history.
The Christian faith did not relinquish its faith in personal
immortality, but it substituted the modern idea of progress
for this eschatology of the New Testament.

The choice of the World Council theme is an effort to
recall the church to the hope as expressed in the New
Testament. In a sense this is an appropriate era in which
to make the attempt. For the substitute faith which seemed

so plausible in the nineteenth century is rather fantastic now in an age of probable atomic wars and of global conflicts instead of the hoped-for global peace. Professor Latourette, as a good historian, allows the evidence for this nature of history to appear in his analysis, though he clings to the old faith by his insistence that "Christ and his Church" are becoming progressively more influential. We are living in an age in which the modern substitute for Christian eschatology, which was once so plausible, has become more fantastic than the Christian hope of the parousia of Christ.

III

I would maintain nevertheless that the selection of eschatology was faulty statesmanship, if it was the concern of the church to bear witness to its faith before the world. The New Testament eschatology is at once too naïve for a sophisticated world and too sophisticated for the simple-minded modern man, who has become so accustomed to try to make sense out of life by measuring history in terms of some scheme of rational intelligibility. It is just as foolish to bear witness to our faith by insisting on what will seem to the world a fantastic hope as to bear witness to our faith by our personal hope of "the resurrection." These two hopes are indeed an integral part of the faith. But we might not in the hour of death be perfectly certain of our destiny after death and we might, despite these doubts, have given a genuine witness to our faith, if we had borne pain and sorrow with patience and had been released from self-concern so that our hearts went out to our brethren.

While the present seems a very strategic era in which to restore a part of the New Testament faith which had become discredited and obscured, we need only to analyze the needs of our generation to recognize that it is not particularly redemptive to approach a disillusioned generation with a proud "I told you so" and a fanciful picture of the end of history, or at least a picture which will seem fanciful to our generation, whether Christian or secular. What would be more to the point is to bear witness to our faith in terms of attitudes of watchfulness and soberness rather than alternate moods of "sleep and drunkenness" which St. Paul describes as the moods of "the night," that is, as the consequences of the lack of faith in the Lord of history who has been revealed to us in Christ.

Our generation has these moods of sleep and drunkenness, of complacency and hysteria, not only alternately but simultaneously; for we are curiously hysterical about Communism but complacent about the possibilities of an atomic war. The poor Civil Defense Administrator has difficulty in getting any one to man the civil defense, and he rightly surmises that the dangers of atomic destruction are so monstrous that the imagination either refuses to comprehend them or is incapable of doing so. Yet these dangers are no more than the most vivid expressions of the peril of death which we have always faced, and which our generation by some legerdemain has sought to banish from the imagination.

To "watch and be sober" means that, armed by our faith, we will not be surprised by any evil which appears in history; and in our surprise we will not seek escape into either complacency or hysteria. Such a genuine Christian nonchalance might actually help our civilization to survive; since its dangers are actually increased by complacency on the one hand and by hysteria on the other.

But the final paradox of faith is that the Christian faith and hope will be most creative if we are not too preoccupied with its current relevance and pragmatic efficiency. In that sense the contemporary preoccupation of our culture with history has made it less effective in historical action than it ought to be. This is an ironic refutation of the secular humanism which believed that if only it disavowed the transhistorical interests of the Christian faith and centered the attention of man upon historical goals, it could establish a heaven upon earth. This heaven on earth turned out in the case of orthodox Marxism to be a Communist hell. In the case of liberal utopianism it has degenerated into the far less dangerous but equally pathetic hopes for a "scientific" management of human affairs, which would in time eliminate human "aggressiveness" and establish some kind of human consensus through the "common faith" of all right-minded and "enlightened" people.

These modern faiths were fantastic enough and they have suffered tragic refutation. But they must be answered by a faith which does not place its main emphasis upon a hope which will seem equally fantastic, but upon a life of soberness and watchfulness, of faith and of love—which will appeal to a world in the night of despair as having some gleams of light in it, derived from the "Light that shineth in darkness."

OUR DEPENDENCE IS ON GOD •

We represent fragmented portions of a universal church, a covenant community, gathered out of the many races and climes, to bear witness to the faith that we have seen the "glory of God in the face of Jesus Christ." We declare this faith against the wisdom of the world, which does not acknowledge the mystery of the Creator and the Judge whom we meet at the final limits of our conscience and consciousness, and which therefore thinks our faith foolish; that the mystery has been clarified, and the loving purposes of God have been revealed to us in the life, death, and resurrection of our Lord; that we have, through him, a sure knowledge of the truth, and a mediator of the divine grace, entering our life as pardon and as power.

We acknowledge this God who has been revealed in Christ, both as the Lord of our life, whose goodness and severity are equally necessary for our redemption; and as the Lord and sovereign of this strange drama of our human history, of all our collective destinies. The scoffers find our faith strange. But we live in a day in which every effort to

• An address written for delivery at the Evanston Assembly of the World Council of Churches.

give this drama a simpler meaning and a simpler ending than the Biblical faith gives it, proves itself to be the source of both confusion and evil. That is why it is so necessary to emphasize that in the final instance our dependence is on God and not man, not on human virtue, not on human power to bring this fragmentary human life to a conclusion, to purge it of its evils and to complete its incompleteness.

I

Our insistence that it is God's power and grace, and not any human virtue or power, which can give meaning to our existence and redemption from our sins, must not be misunderstood (as it is frequently misunderstood) as encouraging irresponsibility. The same Lord who is the pledge of God's grace to us is also our example. He bids us "to work while it is day, for the night cometh when no one can work." He assures us that we are co-workers together with him. And the Scripture warns us that we have not resisted unto blood fighting against sin. Man in the Christian view is undoubtedly a creator, and he undoubtedly participates in the strange drama, in which he is also a creature, the mystery of which he cannot fully discern and the destinies of which he cannot fully bring under his control.

We must be responsible to the limits of the power with which God has endowed us. If we affirm, nevertheless, that our dependence is on God rather than men, we merely look at the whole drama of life in the wisdom borrowed from the cross. There we see that the divine goodness was in conflict, not chiefly with obvious human evil but with human goodness. It was Roman justice, the best justice of its day, and Hebraic religion, the highest religion of its day, which were implicated in the crucifixion. And all through the Christian ages we have additional testimony of this truth revealed in the cross. The tragedies in human history, the cruelties, the fanaticisms have not been caused by the criminals, who were incidentally crucified with Christ; but by the good people who crucified him, by idealists who did not understand the strange mixture of self-interest and ideals which is compounded in all human motives, by reformers who fail to understand the necessity of personal reformation, by priests who do not know that "judgment begins in the house of God," by prophets who do not know the word of the Lord but speak "out of the imagination of their own hearts," by the wise who do not know the limits of their wisdom, and by the righteous who do not know that in "God's sight no man living is justified."

It is in the light of this overwhelming testimony in history to this truth, first discerned by the prophets and then conclusively proved in Christ's revelation, that we insist that the church's duty is to point to God, our creator, judge, and redeemer, as the source of our peace, rather than to any human virtue or power.

Recently I had a visit from a distinguished abbot of a Japanese Buddhist monastery. He was an amiable man, free of all malice. But he revealed a most natural confusion about the very meaning of the Christian faith. The Christian West, he declared, unlike the mystic East, believed in God and trusted in God to right all wrongs, thus absolving men of responsibility. The result was a quietistic complacency and injustice, which prompted the Communist rebellion against our civilization. I spent some time trying to set him straight on the virtues and vices of the historical dynamism of the Christian world; how the prayer "Thy kingdom come on earth as it is in heaven," taught us by the Lord himself, expressed the life- and history-affirming faith of Christianity; how the injustices which had produced rebellion against our civilization were not due to inactivity but to another type of complacency, the complacency which identified the status quo of a feudal or capitalistic civilization with God's Kingdom; how sectarian Christianity created a ferment of revolt against these injustices, but mixed with its justified sense of injustice an unjustified reliance on the virtues of the righteous, in most instances of the poor; how the original symbol of the fall of Adam, as the cause of a universal corruption of sin, was subtly changed by 17th century sectarians into the subsequent story of Cain and Abel, so that a sharp—too sharp—

distinction could be made between the righteous and the unrighteous; and how modern Communism, which he erroneously regarded as a justified protest against Christian faith, was in effect but the last fruit of a Christian heresy, which was intent on taking the Kingdom of God by violence and remained unaware that its utopian prophets, turned priest-kings of an atheistic theocracy, changed the righteousness of the poor into the cruelty of the powerful because it did not understand the ambiguity of all human virtue and the foolishness of all human wisdom.

I did not tell the Buddhist abbot—for I could not expect him to understand—these curious ironies of Western history, that we did have to contend with a tyranny, Nazism, which was based on law-defiance or moral cynicism. It gave many righteous people the illusion that the chief problem of human history came from law-defiance. But just as we had vanquished this tyranny another one arose, derived not from moral cynicism, but from a fierce idealism, which knew nothing of the ambiguity of human virtues. It resulted in cruelties as grievous as those of the cynics. We have not yet learned the lesson which the similarity of the fruits from such contradictory causes should have taught us.

II

It is tempting for us as Christians to regard the evils of Communism as but the final fruits of modern secular idealism and as a final refutation of the hopes of a secular age that, if modern men could only be beguiled from their faith in God and in the consummations of another world and could give their undivided attention to the betterment of their lot in this world, all ancient evils would be rectified. The refutation of this faith and these hopes, not only by the undoubted evils of Communism but by the very predicament of possible global atomic wars, is very instructive for the understanding of the whole character of the drama of human history and for the peril of human pretensions of power and virtue. Surely the most dangerous actors in this drama are the men who do not acknowledge the limits of man's power, wisdom, and virtue, who usurp the divine majesty and feel themselves unneedful of the divine pardon.

But we must not make too much of this part of the modern refutations of secular pretensions. If we do we will falsify the gospel and make the Christian cause appear to be a contest between God-fearing believers and unrighteous unbelievers. That interpretation would be contrary to both Scripture and experience. It would not heed the word of the prophets that God's judgment is upon the "circumcised as well as upon the uncircumcised" and the word of the New Testament: "There is none righteous, no not one . . . for all have sinned and fallen short of the glory of God." Nor would such an interpretation do justice to the facts of our history, to the fact of the religiously sanctified forms of injustice at which modern secularism revolted, and the various forms of religious fanaticism and persecution of which we have been guilty. All these evidences prove that it is not only those who deny God but those who profess him but claim him too simply as an ally of their purposes and as an aid for their ambitions, who bring evil into the world.

These facts of history and these Scriptural injunctions must warn us that it is the business of the Christian church to bear witness not to the righteousness of Christians but to the righteousness of God, which judges all men, and to the grace of Christ which saves all who truly repent of their sins. It is true, of course, that an unrighteous Christian may be a scandal to the cause of Christ. There must be "fruits meet for repentance" in our lives individually and collectively as testimony of the grace and truth in Christ. But all of us must have noticed the very revealing embarrassment which occurs when we point to our individual or collective virtue as a witness to the gospel. Augustine, a long while since, pointed to this embarrassment. If we call attention to the saints in the church, he declared, the world will remind us of the hypocrites in it.

III

If we apply the lesson of the reliability of God and the unreliability of men, even in their wisest and most virtuous moments, to the problem which brings us together as a divided church, seeking to purge ourselves of the human pretensions which have divided us and obscured the truth in our gospel, we shall appreciate how much the movement which has purged us of our divisions and has restored the full substance of the gospel against our cherished heresies and parochialisms has been the movement of God's grace against our sins.

We must begin by the rehearsal of the historic movements which destroyed the unity of the church for the sake of restoring the purity of the gospel, so that we do not make the mistake of assuming that the majesty and unity of the church as the body of Christ is necessary to his glory. The unity of the Roman church is indeed impressive, and in some respects enviable, in comparison with our unhappy divisions. But the Roman church maintained this unity and a part of the substance of the gospel truth at the price of building two great heresies into the Christian message. The one heresy was to exalt the church as the "extension of the Incarnation," as essentially divine, as the mediator of God's judgment, rather than as the locus in human history where the judgments of God can be heard, whether on the righteous or the unrighteous. This heresy was to obscure the chasm between the human and the divine, which the prophets of Israel understood so well; to pretend that there were priests who were privy to God's counsels, were in control of God's redemptive powers and purposes and in possession of the "keys to heaven."

The other heresy was either consequent or ancillary. It changed the gospel of forgiveness to contrite souls into a great scheme for assuring men of their salvation if they would climb a "ladder of merit," chiefly by castigating the passions of the body. This ladder of merit, these ascetic disciplines, did not however guarantee that the self in the pretensions of its self-esteem would be shattered by the "severity" of the divine judgment, that a new self would arise from the crucifixion of the old self.

It is not necessary to recount how these heresies not only changed the message of redemption in Christ but also constructed a very imposing institution and a very vexatious and pretentious priesthood, pretending to have dominion over all the nations in the name of Christ. Justice and freedom could not be established on earth, even as the gospel could not be truly preached, until these pretensions were challenged.

But the fact that it has not been possible to purge the gospel of these Roman heresies without exposing it to the corruption of new heresies and of dragging the church behind the chariot wheels of every nation is as instructive to the Christian as the first chapter of this contest between the righteousness of God and the righteousness of men. The Roman church has a right to interpret our condition, divided by the intrusion of every historically relative insight and condition into the Christian message, as analogous to the Biblical parable of the "house swept and garnished," of the man exorcised of one devil of heresy who was visited by "seven devils more evil than the first." It is not only that every national and parochial viewpoint colored the Christian message among us, but that our necessary commerce with the culture of the world produced, particularly in the nineteenth century, every form of quasi-heresy in which Kantian or Hegelian, Freudian or Marxist forms of thought usurped the wisdom of Christ and the foolishness of the cross with some form of worldly wisdom.

The most thrilling part of the ecumenical enterprise has been not so much the increasing unity which we have experienced, but the increasing purity of the gospel message by the elimination not only of nationalistic and other parochial heresies, but of all those forms of worldly wisdom which colored and obscured the plain truth of the gospel, with its exaltation of the righteousness of God against all human righteousness. The ecumenical movement does not try to establish one unified church with the power to convict this or that church of heresy. Rather it establishes a place of encounter in which we can instruct each other by bringing our cherished treasures of grace and where, by allowing the criticism of our fellow Christians to aid us in separating the "precious from the vile," we may all draw closer together by all coming closer to the truth in Christ. Thus it is God's judgment and grace and not any virtue of our own which works mightily among us to heal the broken body of Christ and make us one.

IV

We face two temptations as we try to profit from the experience of extricating the Christian gospel from its various heresies, so that we might have unity in the acceptance of the substance of the gospel. The one temptation is to renounce all commerce with the wisdom of the world, with the various disciplines of culture, all of which contain the danger of deflecting us from the truth of the gospel. If we succumb to this temptation we will be like the man who hid his treasure in the ground. We will not learn to appreciate the truth of these disciplines which are valid on their own level, and we will not be able to validate the truth of the gospel on the level where its truth is apparent and the truth of the wisdom of the world turns into error. That is the level of the self's freedom and responsibility, the self's sin and need of redemption: of God's freedom as creator and redeemer; of the self's encounter with God and of its redemption through divine grace and the self's response of repentance and trust.

Nor will we be able to exploit common experience in our generation to extricate ourselves from the heresies in which we have become involved. Let us take as an example the experience of that section of the ecumenical movement which has studied the problem of "The Church and a Responsible Society." It has made as great progress in reaching a Christian consensus as any part of the ecumenical movement. It has, in effect, overcome the chasm between a Christian conservatism on the one hand, based on an undue pessimism, and on the other hand a Christian perfectionism which approached perilously close to the utopian illusions of a secular culture. This creative consequence has brought us all closer to a viable Christian social and political ethic, free of illusions about human nature but also with a strong sense of responsibility for establishing a maximum of freedom and justice within the limits set by human sinfulness. This whole development has brought us closer to the Biblical analysis of the human situation, which we should never have forgotten. But it was achieved partly by analyzing and profiting from the errors in which partial Christian political theories and secular schemes of salvation were involved.

The whole of middle-class culture rested on the erroneous conviction that history was like nature, and that natural harmonies would prevail in human society if only "left alone." The rebellion against the injustices of an industrial society was also based on the erroneous conviction that society was like nature and could easily be "managed" and "planned" for the ends of social justice. Both errors could have been refuted out of hand by a Christian interpretation of history and of man's ambiguous status of creator and creature in it. But meanwhile both errors left a free and flexible economy. The other error, robbed of its virulence, became the basis of all programs of justice in a free society. Thus we have arrived at a viable Christian political ethic, both by reclaiming the Christian insights into the character of the person and his history, of his dignity and his misery, which is to say, of his creative freedom and of the corruption of that freedom in his selfishness; and also by profiting from the tension between the Christian faith and a secular culture.

We have also learned the modesty of not pretending that the Christian faith can offer a perplexed and fearful generation a simple way out of the predicament of a prospective or possible, though not probable, atomic conflict, except the counsel that powerful nations should be patient and wise in the use of their power, should refrain from vain threats of the use of these destructive weapons, and should not rely on a military power too exclusively, but know that their final security must depend on their unity, their moral and political health and the increase of justice in their alliance.

V

The other temptation for us is to make too much of, or to make too uncritical application of, the rediscovered Biblical fact that all men are sinners and that every historic struggle is therefore a struggle between sinful men. The temptation is to imagine that the cry of "a plague on both their houses" is a Christian solution of every problem; that neutralism is an answer to every political perplexity. This error consists in an effort to rise above the responsibilities which we have as men for the order, the justice, and the preservation of our civilizations and painfully nourished systems of justice, seeking to play the part of God, in whose sight no one indeed is justified. But we are men and not God; and we must distinguish between the moral level of our decisions, where we must carefully weigh whether the ostensible foe may not be a friend with whom we must come to terms and whether the ostensible friend and ally may not be a foe who must be resisted resolutely if our prized liberties are to be preserved; and the religious level, on which we have some knowledge of the fact that both we and the most dangerous foe are equally sinners in God's sight and are equally in need of his forgiveness.

National heroes are, on the whole, not as interesting to other nations as to the patriots. I will therefore apologize for mentioning the example of the greatest hero of America, who solved this problem more satisfactorily than any statesman or any theologian of my knowledge. Lincoln was opposed to slavery. "It may seem strange, that men should ask the assistance of a just God in wringing their bread from the sweat of other men's brows," he declared. But this moral judgment did not prevent him in the heat of a terrible conflict from rising to the religious level from which he could survey the pathetic spectacle of each side claiming God as its ally against the other. "Both sides read the same Bible," he declared, "and pray to the same God. The prayers of both cannot be answered. The prayers of neither will be answered just as they intended."

This sense of an overarching providence and grace can rob our conflicts of their virulence because it purges us of our arrogance. Thus we decide and discriminate and even fight for our causes in history. We cannot escape these responsibilities. But every effort to end history, to bring it to a conclusion by a victory over our foe or by the triumph of our scheme of wisdom, only brings the final evil into history by the claim of a final righteousness. Therefore we are saved, not by what we can do, but by the hope that the Lord of history will bring this mysterious drama to a conclusion, that the suffering Christ will in the end be the triumphant Lord.

To this hope we have dedicated the labors of this conference. It is, like all hopes, strictly derivative from our faith. As a hope it may seem highly speculative. But the faith on which it is based is not speculative. That faith is grounded in the daily experience of the forgiven sinner, in the experiences of redemptive grace which shine as a light into our darkness.

GREEK ORTHODOXY AND THE ECUMENICAL MOVEMENT

The opposition of the Greek Orthodox leaders to the projected merger of the World Council and the International Missionary Council, voiced in the session of the World Council's Central Committee this summer, is a reminder to all devotees of the World Council that it is not a pan-Protestant movement. The Council contains both Protestant and non-Roman Catholic churches. The Catholic churches comprise both the Anglicans of Catholic persuasion and the Greek Orthodox churches.

The Greek Orthodox churches object to the Missionary Council because it conducts missions on Greek Orthodox soil. Many of us would not like the Missionary Council to abandon its efforts in these fields, even if the price is the failure to achieve complete amalgamation with the World Council. This position will, of course, be questioned by those who think Protestants should not do mission work in any Christian nation. But few of us would be prepared to disavow all missionary activity in the Latin American nations, for instance, in many of which Roman Catholicism is not a vital spiritual force and is sometimes a very reactionary social force, in league with an anachronistic feudalism.

But quite apart from the question whether any version of the Christian faith should, in the name of ecumenicity, refrain from doing mission work in any traditionally Christian field, the objections of the Orthodox brethren remind us that the World Council has not solved, and cannot solve, the problem of the contradictory conceptions of the church held by the Protestants and the Catholic portions of its membership.

Broadly speaking, the difference is that Protestantism regards the church itself as standing under the judgment of God and of being holy only as it mediates the judgment and mercy of God. Roman Catholicism regards the church as "the extension of the Incarnation," as sharing the sanctity of Christ; and Greek Orthodoxy, although claiming no sanctity for the hierarchy, does claim sanctity for the unbroken tradition of the church.

This difference is wide and deep. Many theological issues today run through the different churches rather than between them. Many of the issues will yield to friendly debate; but this issue will not yield, for each side would yield something of what it regards as its essence if it yielded on this issue. For that reason the World Council will never become, as some hope and others fear, a superchurch. It will have commissions on "Life and Work" and on "Faith and Order," but the Commission on Faith and Order will never achieve a perfect consensus.

This need not trouble us too much. It is enough that the World Council should be a ground on which the churches meet each other in friendly encounter, and an instrument for doing common work of the type which differences in theology do not make impossible and which common convictions about our Christian witness in the world make imperative.

SOURCES AND ACKNOWLEDGMENTS

I. The Weakness of Common Worship in American Protestantism

"A Christmas Service in Retrospect," *The Christian Century*, January 4, 1933.

"Sects and Churches," *The Christian Century*, July 3, 1935.

"Sunday Morning Debate," *The Christian Century*, April 22, 1936.

"Worship and the Social Conscience," *Radical Religion*, Winter 1937.

"A Problem of Evangelical Christianity," *Christianity and Crisis*, May 13, 1946.

"The Religious Pluralism of America," *Christianity and Crisis*, December 22, 1947.

"The Weakness of Common Worship in American Protestantism," *Christianity and Crisis*, May 28, 1951.

"Religiosity and the Christian Faith," *Christianity and Crisis*, January 24, 1955.

II. Can the Church Give a "Moral Lead"?

"The Weakness of the Modern Church," *Christian Herald*, May 1931.

"Moralists and Politics," *The Christian Century*, July 6, 1932.

"Church and State in America," *Christianity and Crisis*, December 15, 1941.

"Which Question Comes First for the Church?" *Christianity and Crisis*, November 12, 1945.

"Can the Church Give a 'Moral Lead'?" *Christianity and Crisis*, August 2, 1948.

"The Church and Equal Rights for Women," *Christianity and Crisis*, October 31, 1949.

"Utilitarian Christianity and the World Crisis," *Christianity and Crisis*, May 29, 1950.

"Social Christianity," *Christianity and Society*, Winter 1950-1.

"The Protestant Clergy and U.S. Politics," *The Reporter*, February 19, 1952.

"Prayer and Politics," *Christianity and Crisis*, October 27, 1952.

"Communism and the Clergy," *The Christian Century*, August 19, 1953.

"Literalism, Individualism, and Billy Graham," *The Christian Century*, May 23, 1956.

"The Security and Hazard of the Christian Ministry," *Union Seminary Quarterly Review*, November 1957.

III. Barthianism and the Kingdom

"Barth—Apostle of the Absolute," *The Christian Century*, December 13, 1928.

"Barthianism and the Kingdom," *The Christian Century*, July 15, 1931.

"Barthianism and Political Reaction," *The Christian Century*, June 6, 1934.

"Marx, Barth, and Israel's Prophets," *The Christian Century*, January 30, 1935.

"Karl Barth and Democracy," *Radical Religion*, Winter 1938.

"Karl Barth on Politics," *Radical Religion*, Spring 1939.

"We Are Men and Not God," *The Christian Century*, October 27, 1948.

"An Answer to Karl Barth," *The Christian Century*, February 23, 1949.

"Why Is Barth Silent on Hungary?" *The Christian Century*, January 23, 1957.

"Barth on Hungary: An Exchange," *The Christian Century*, April 10, 1957.

IV. The Catholic Heresy

"Arrogance in the Name of Christ," *The Christian Century*, September 2, 1936.

"Pius XI and His Successor," *The Nation*, January 30, 1937.

"The Catholic Heresy," *The Christian Century*, December 8, 1937.

"The Pope's Christmas Message," *Christianity and Society*. Winter 1942.

"Three Elements in Papal Leadership," *Christianity and Society*, Summer 1944.

"The Pope on Property," *Christianity and Society*, Fall 1944.

"Our Relations to Catholicism," *Christianity and Crisis*, September 15, 1947.

"The Godly and the Godless," *Christianity and Crisis*, December 13, 1948.

"Catholics and Divorce," *Christianity and Crisis*, January 10, 1949.

"Catholics and Motives of Action," *Christianity and Crisis*, March 7, 1949.

"The Rising Catholic-Protestant Tension," *Christianity and Crisis*, August 8, 1949.

"The Pope's Domesticated God," *The Christian Century*, January 18, 1950.

"The Increasing Isolation of the Catholic Church," *Christianity and Crisis*, September 18, 1950.

"Catholics and Politics: Some Misconceptions," *The Reporter*, January 22, 1952.

"Protestants, Catholics, and Secularists on the School Issue," *Christianity and Crisis*, February 2, 1953.

"The Catholic Hierarchy's Analysis of the Ills of Our Day," *Christianity and Crisis*, December 27, 1954.

V. The Church and the Churches: The Ecumenical
    Movement

A. The Ecumenical Issue in the United States

"The Ecumenical Issue in the United States," *Theology
    Today*, January 1946.
"The Reunion of the Church through the Renewal of the
    Churches," *Christianity and Crisis*, November 24, 1947.
"Has the Church Any Authority?" *Christianity and Crisis*,
    April 3, 1950.
"The Church Speaks to the Nation," *The Messenger*,
    December 15, 1953.
"The National Council Delegation to the Russian Church,"
    Christianity and Crisis, April 30, 1956.

B. The Problems of a World Church

"The Oxford Conference on Church and State," *Radical
    Religion*, Autumn 1937.
"The World Council of Churches," *Christianity and Society*, Autumn 1948.
"Protestantism in a Disordered World," *The Nation*, September 18, 1948.
"The World Council at Amsterdam," *Christianity and
    Crisis*, September 20, 1948.
"The World Council and the Peace Issue," *Christianity and
    Crisis*, August 7, 1950.
"The Problems of a World Church," *The Messenger*,
    August 21, 1951.
"Hope Needs Faith and Love," *The Ecumenical Review*,
    July 1953.
"Christ the Hope of the World: What Has History to Say?"
    Religion in Life, Summer 1954.
"Our Dependence Is on God," *The Christian Century*,
    September 1, 1954.
"Greek Orthodoxy and the Ecumenical Movement," *The
    Messenger*, October 8, 1957.

LIVING AGE BOOKS

published by MERIDIAN BOOKS, INC.
12 East 22 Street, New York 10, New York

Titles listed here are not necessarily available in the British Empire

MERIDIAN BOOKS

12 East 22 Street, New York 10, New York